USS
COLUMBUS

TURNER PUBLISHING COMPANY
PADUCAH, KENTUCKY

T0145834

TURNER PUBLISHING COMPANY
Publishers of America's History
412 Broadway•P.O. Box 3101
Paducah, Kentucky 42002-3101
(270) 443-0121
www.turnerpublishing.com

Editor: Randy Baumgardner
Designer: Peter Zuniga

Library of Congress Catalog No.
2003102162
ISBN: 978-1-68162-200-2
LIMITED EDITION

Previous page: The men of the USS Columbus

USS Columbus (CA74) 1950; Venice, Italy.

3

TABLE OF CONTENTS

USS Columbus C-74

LETTER FROM THE PRESIDENT

   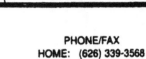

U.S.S. Columbus
Veterans Association

AL LEWIS, PRESIDENT
726 E. COVINA BLVD.
COVINA, CA 91722-2955

CA-74   SSN-762   CG-12

PHONE/FAX
HOME: (626) 339-3568
WORK: (626) 966-8341
FAX: (626) 966-5481

THE USS COLUMBUS SHIPS

To my shipmates:

This book will preserve forever the memories of the men that sailed aboard the USS Columbus ships.

Following are many untold stories about the ships and the brave young men that dedicated their lives in the defense of their country.

It is said that you can take the man out of the navy but you can't take the navy out of each and every man that served aboard the Columbus. She was built a little late to take an active part in defeating the axis, but she took her station and made sure that peace was sustained.

Malcolm Young has spent fifty years writing this outstanding tribute to the men that sailed aboard the Columbus. This book will cover the thoughts and emotions of the men that made up the crew of the Columbus.

Our love for our ship is only surpassed by our love for our country. Fighting to keep our country free is our first duty. We love our families but without freedom it would be difficult to maintain the quality of life that all of us Sailors and Marines fought for and many died.

Our prayers go out to all the brave shipmates that served aboard the Columbus and are with us in spirit only. Our ship, the Columbus, united us; it made us buddies; it made us one; it made us shipmates forever.

Our "USS Columbus Veterans Association" is to perpetuate the memory of the USS Columbus ships and crew over the many years it has patrolled the world to keep the peace. The CA-74, the CG-12 and the SSN-762.

Reminisce, remember, and enjoy the history of our ship that once was our home at sea and will live in our hearts and souls forever.

Yes! "Shipmates are Forever."

Al Lewis, President
USS Columbus Veterans Association

Acknowledgements

The USS Columbus Veterans Association was founded in 1988 by Gene Hickam. Bill Olinger was the first President and John Harvey Thomas was the "glue" that held things together, serving as Secretary, Treasurer, Membership Chairman and Reunion Planner. John continued in this effort until his death in 1993.

We would like to acknowledge the first 40 members of this Association, as we have continued to build upon their shoulders.

Carl Altz
Dan Ashton
Charles Bowman
Richard Bremer
Dale Brown
Alexander Bubniak
Myron Cashel
James Curran
John Dayberry
Charles Dixon
Frank Gonzales
George Harvey Hendrickson
Ralph Hendrickson
Gene Hickam
Don Homer
Robert Ilas
Donald Johnson
Edward Kauphusman
Billy Kirby
Robert Kronen
Herbert Krout
Ray Krout
John Morgan
Robert Moss
Stan Mullins
William Olinger
Paul Pedersen
Albert "Bud" Porter
Earl Riddle
Alex Rudewicz
Nick Ruef
Anton Sedivy
Carl Sekol
Alex Senibaldi
Charles Shepard
William Smith
John Harvey Thomas
Emery Wacaser
Nelson Walton
Glen Wolf

DEDICATION

MALCOLM YOUNG

AUTHOR/RESEARCHER

BORN, MARCH 12, 1927

ENLISTED IN THE U.S. NAVY, MAY 5, 1945

TRANSFERRED TO THE USS COLUMBUS, AUGUST 1945

Malcolm spent many years researching and writing this book. His daughter lived in Washington, D.C., and when he went to visit her and her family, he would visit the Navy Shipyard Archives and Library to review the reports that the captain's had submitted to the Navy Department. From these reports he was able to gather enough information for this book.

As veterans and shipmates of the Columbus, we would like to thank Malcolm for his hard work in compiling this history. His determination and dedication to this work is an outstanding achievement.

His wife, Mary, also helped him in this effort, which she described as a "labor of love." Working on the book for over 30 years goes far beyond the call of duty. Mary passed away in 1996. It would have been wonderful if she were with us to share the joy we feel in reading this book.

Malcolm was a tool and die maker in the Navy, and spent his time as a boiler tender. After discharge, he attended the University of Wisconsin (Whitewater), and earned a Masters Degree. He taught school for 40 years, including business, typing, bookkeeping, shorthand, and other subjects related to business operations.

Raising four children, going to school and then teaching school, he somehow found time to write our history. From all of your shipmates, we thank you.

PUBLISHER'S MESSAGE

It has been a pleasure working with the fine men of the USS *Columbus* Veterans Association. From her beginnings in 1944 as CA-74, through her conversion from a heavy cruiser to guided missile cruiser CG-12, and in her current role patrolling the seas as SSN-762, the name Columbus has continued to serve our Nation in defending waters across the globe. Although the CA-74 and CG-12 are long gone, their spirit is alive in the men who served aboard them. May this book serve as a lasting record of their service.

I would like to give special thanks to Al and Renee Lewis, whose efforts made this book possible. Working on behalf of the Association, their leadership, guidance and support were much appreciated by our staff, and we could not have completed this project without their help. In addition, I must thank Malcolm Young for his diligence in documenting the *Columbus'* rich history—a task that took him decades to achieve.

Finally, I must thank the hundreds of Columbus veterans whose records of service are preserved within these pages. Your biographies, stories and photographs will serve as a source of inspiration for years to come.

Todd Bottorff

President

Dave Turner

Founder

USS Columbus
HISTORY

Portsmouth, England. November 8, 1949 (L-R): GMC Gizant (CMAA), CS Division (Background), 6th Division (Being Inspected), H.M. King George VI, Lt. (jg) Dordeen (to rear), Ambassador Douglas(to rear), Captain E.R. McLean (C.O.), Admiral Conolly (Cincnielm), Admiral Frazer, R.N. (First Lord of Admirality).

PREFACE

Much of the information in these articles was obtained from government reports submitted to the Navy by the captains of the CA-74 and CG-12 as required by Navy Department regulations. These reports were declassified and placed in the ships' history section of the Washington, D.C. Navy Shipyard Archives and Library, Washington, D.C. by the Navy Department. The personnel at this facility were very helpful in finding the data necessary to make this history possible. Other information was located in the National Archives, Washington, D.C. and the Smithsonian Archives, Suitland, Maryland. Pictures and articles were provided by former crew members of CA-74 and CG-12, and were gratefully accepted.

U.S.S. (COLUMBOS. 74) 10

INTRODUCTION

The launching of Hull No. 1506 on 30 November 1944, was the beginning of a long and illustrious career for a ship that was looked upon by her crew with admiration and affection. The USS *Columbus* (CA-74) came to life on 9 June 1945, when Mrs. E.G. Meyers, the sponsor, smashed the traditional bottle of champagne on its hull and gave the ship its name, USS *Columbus*.

The USS *Columbus'* career was one of distinction, sailing to many ports in the world, not as a deadly instrument of war, but as a keeper of the peace. If need be, she would become a powerful weapon to face any aggressive force and to make her might felt.

As Captain Allen Hobbs stated at the commissioning:

"No one can foresee where destiny will lead us. But the day will come when we will meet the enemy. With God's help on that day we will face the supreme trial of battle with courage and with determination to uphold the fighting tradition of our Navy."

As a member of the original crew, I have tried to put together a comprehensive history of a true "Lady." Collecting material from numerous sources makes it possible that some parts of the history of this "Lady" may be omitted. I have tried to be as complete with my research as possible, and if something has been left out I am truly sorry.

Malcolm C. Young
Historian
USS *Columbus* Veterans Association

2, 1946 AT SHAI, CHINA

Courtesy of Elmer A. Cook

SPECIAL THANKS

Organizing and researching a project of this magnitude takes assistance from many people and sources. Those who supplied me with valuable information and encouragement need to be mentioned. Many thanks go to the late John Harvey Thomas for his continual supply of information and his interest in this project. Thanks also go to Al Hope, John Wise, the late Captain Boyd, and all those other shipmates too numerous to mention who supplied me with much needed information.

I wish to thank, also, the correspondents from Columbus, Ohio, who were on board during the shakedown cruise in the Caribbean. G.A. Smallreed was with the *"Dispatch"* and John C. McConaughy was a staff writer for the *"State Journal."* Both of them contributed many articles for the shakedown edition of the *"Discoverer."*

I wish to thank all of the staff members at the Washington Navy Yard, Washington, D.C. Ships Histories Archives and Library, for their assistance in locating materials and the interest that they have shown in this project.

And a final "thanks" to my family, who had to suffer through many of my "sea stories" and who lent a sympathetic ear, especially my wife, Syd, when things were not going according to plan or who shared in my exuberance when new materials were found. Preparing this history was a labor of love – the USS *Columbus* (CA-74/CG-12).

Admirals Barge returning to Columbus Adm. Lynde D. McCormick , supreme Allied Commander Atlantic. 20 Sept 1952. Courtesy of Ronald P. Dolinsky

THE SHIP'S BELL

IT IS CLOSELY IDENTIFIED WITH THE WHOLE CAREER OF THE VESSEL

LT John M. Ellicott, USN, in 1897 wrote on "What is Told by the Bell," in which he stated:

Nothing in a ship becomes so closely identified with her throughout her whole career as the ship's bell. Officers and crew come and go; masts, decks, engines and boilers become old, and are replaced by new ones; but from the day that she first glides into the water the same ship's bell remains always a part of her, marking her progress all over the world, and finally going down with her to a lonely grave at the bottom of the sea, or surviving her as a cherished souvenir of her existence and achievements. On a man-of-war the bell is usually inscribed with her name and the date of her launching; and as it is probable that it may some day become a memento of a glorious history, the bell is often the subject of special carre (care) in casting or selection. Sometimes the hundreds of workmen who have built the great ship contribute each a silver coin to be melted and molded into a bell, which shall be the token of their love for the object of their creation and the interest in her future career. Often the people of the city or state after which a man-of-war is named may present to her a magnificent bell appropriately ornamented and inscribed with works of goodwill and good wishes. Such a bell is usually presented with ceremony after the ship goes into commission.

Ships' bells, in general, are made of bronze, like other bells. The addition of silver in their composition gives them a peculiarly clear and musical tone. They are placed in such a position on the upper deck that they may be heard from one end of the ship to the other; and usually near the mainmast or at the break of the forecastle. One peculiarity exists in a ship's bell which is necessary on account of her motion at sea. The tongue is hung so that it can swing in only one direction. If it were not so, the bell would be continually ringing as the ship rolled and pitched. The direction in which the tongue can swing is another important point. If it were athwartships, the bell would ring at every heavy roll of the ship; and if it were fore and aft the bell would ring at every deep pitch; so the direction in which the tongue can swing is nearly half-way around between these two.

A TALE OF THREE VESSELS

CA-74

The USS *Columbus* (CA-74) was launched 30 November 1944 by the Bethlehem Steel Co., Quincy, Massachusetts; sponsored by Mrs. E.G. Meyers; and commissioned on 9 June 1945. It rained intermittently during the whole day until 15 minutes before the commissioning, the clouds parted and the sun shone down upon the gathered crowd on the fantail. The Navy Band, Receiving Station, Boston, presented a musical program. The ceremony opened with the reading of the order of the Navy Department to commission the ship, by Rear Admiral Felix X. Gygax, US Navy, Commandant First Naval District. All hands faced forward and saluted, and all guns slowly rose, as the National Ensign, the Jack and Commissioning Pennant were hoisted. After the Invocation by the Chaplain, Admiral Gygax turned the ship over to Captain Allen Hobbs, USN. The Captain read his orders from the Bureau of Naval Personnel, ordering him to command the USS *Columbus*. He then turned to Admiral Gygax and said, "Admiral, I accept the ship with plea-

Commissioning ceremony for the SSN 762, 23 July 1993. Courtesy of L.P. Greene.

sure." His first official command was to the Executive Officer, Commander E.O. Davis, USN, to order the watch to be set.

The Honorable Maurice J. Tobin, Governor of the Commonwealth of Massachusetts, stated that the naming of this cruiser for Ohio's Capitol was truly a great honor. Mayor James A. Rhodes of Columbus, Ohio, spoke on behalf of all the people of Columbus, a number of whom were present. The Mayor said, "This is another milestone in the history of our great state and city. We know the men of this fight-

ing ship are just as proud of this ship as we are of the US Navy."

With Captain Allen Hobbs in command, this ship completed fitting out at the South Boston Navy Yard and on 6 September 1945 she headed for the Caribbean for her shakedown cruise.

Statistics

Cost	$30,000,000.00
Length	675 Feet
Beam	70 Feet
Armament	9 8-inch guns
	12 5-inch guns
	Scores of 20 and 40mm
Nicknames	The *Discoverer* and *Colombo*

CG-12

In 1959, the USS *Columbus* (CA-74) reported to the Puget Sound Naval Shipyard in Bremerton, Washington for deactivation and conversion. In December 1962, the heavy cruiser emerged as the Guided Missile Cruiser, USS *Columbus* (CG-12). Her first captain was Gideon M. Boyd.

Armament consisted of the TALOS and TARTAR long and short-ranged missiles for anti-aircraft defense: ASROC (Anti-submarine Rocket), torpedoes and ASW Helicopters. Later, five-inch guns were added for use against small surface targets. For rapid transfer of missiles from supply ships at sea, the FAST (Fleet Automatic Shuttle Transfer) was added.

The superstructure of the new cruiser was entirely aluminum; the interior was air-conditioned, and living conditions were tremendously improved over the earlier gun-mounting cruisers of the fleet.

The Mission of the CG-12: To be capable of independent or combined operations against air, surface or subsurface threats.

1. Provide area defense for a task force with guided missiles.
2. Destruction of ships and shore targets by use of existing missile systems.
3. Operate and support helicopters.
4. Control aircraft.
5. Operate aggressively against and destroy submarines.
6. Provide facilities and accommodations for Task Group Commander and his staff.

SSN-762

USS *Columbus* is a submarine of the Los Angeles 688 Improved Class, one of the most advanced undersea vessels in the world. While undersea warfare (USW) is its primary mission, the inherent characteristics of the submarine - stealth, endurance and agility - is used in roles and missions to meet the challenges of a changing global geopolitical climate. USS *Columbus* has the ability to get on station quickly, stay for an extended period of time, and carry out her mission. These missions include deployment of special forces, minelaying, precision land attack, or anti-submarine or surface warfare while remaining undetected.

These 360 foot, 6,900-ton ships are well equipped to accomplish these tasks. Faster than their predecessors and possessing highly accurate sensors, weapon control systems, and central computer complexes, they are armed with sophisticated ADCAP and MARK 48 anti-submarine/ship torpedoes and Tomahawk cruise missiles. The *Columbus* is the fifty first 688 and the twelfth improved version of

Commisioning 1945

this class which includes a vertical launch system for Tomahawk cruise missiles and an improved hull design for under-ice operations.

Columbus completed a Post Shipyard Availability in June 1994 in Groton, CT after initial construction and shakedown operations. In September 1994, the ship conducted an interfleet transfer to Pearl Harbor, Hawaii and joined the U.S. Pacific Fleet Submarine Force. *Columbus* deployed to the Western Pacific in late 1995 through early 1996 and conducted a variety of operations as a unit of the U.S. Seventh Fleet.

USS *Columbus* (CA-74)

8 June 1945 to 9 December 1945

The USS *Columbus* a heavy cruiser of the Baltimore class, was ordered on 9 September 1940. She was built by the Bethlehem Shipbuilding Company in Quincy, Massachusetts, where she was delivered four months ahead of the estimated date of completion. Named in honor of the capital city of Ohio, and the third ship of the Navy to bear the name, the *Columbus* was launched on 29 November 1944, after being christened by Mrs. Edward G. Meyers of Columbus, Ohio, mother of two sons killed in action.

On 8 June 1945, the *Columbus* arrived in Boston Navy Yard, Boston, Massachusetts, and on the same day, in a ceremony attended by many distinguished guests, including Governor Maurice Tobin of the Commonwealth of Massachusetts and Mayor James

A. Rhodes of Columbus, Ohio, Rear Admiral Felix X. Gyqax, U.S. Navy, Commandant of the First Naval District, formally commissioned the *Columbus* into the line of the Navy and turned over command to Captain Allen Hobbs, U.S. Navy, of Washington D.C. Captain Hobbs then directed the Executive Officer, Commander Elmer O. Davis, U.S. Navy, to set the watch.

On 7 September 1945, with a complement of 100 officers and 1500 men, the *Columbus* departed Boston for her shakedown cruise which was conducted out of the Naval Operating Base, Guantanamo Bay, Cuba. After six weeks of intensive training, which was concluded by a military inspection, the *Columbus* returned to New York to take part in the Navy Day ceremonies from 25 to 30 October 1945.

After a post shakedown availability in Boston, she returned to Guantanamo Bay, Cuba for a ten day refresher training period, during which time she fired shore bombardment exercise at Culebra, Virgin Islands. Upon the completion of this training, on 7 December 1945, the *Columbus* sailed for the Panama Canal with orders to report to the Commander-in-Chief, U.S. Pacific Fleet for duty and ultimate assignment to the Seventh Fleet at Shanghai, China.

On 10 December 1945, *Columbus* entered Lemon Bay and started transit of the Panama Canal. At 1457 completed transit of the Canal and moored at Balboa, Panama Canal Zone, Panama on the Pacific side. On 13 December the *Columbus* departed for Pearl Harbor, T.H. Arrived Pearl Harbor on 25 December 1945 and proceeded to Pearl City, Oahu, T.H. where the *Columbus* moored. Liberty commenced as soon as the ship was secured. On 28 December 1945 *Columbus* got underway for Okinawa and encountered its first rough seas. Crossed the 180 Meridian on 31 December 1945 and the date changed to 2 January 1946. New Years Day was lost.

1 JUNE 1945 - ORIGINAL OFFICERS

Captain Allen Hobbs, USN, of 3631 Upton St. N.W. Washington D.C. will assume command of the *Columbus*.

Commander Elmer O. Davis, USN, of Ferry Farms, Annapolis, Maryland will be Executive Officer.

Commander John S. Lehman, USN, of 395 South Mentor Avenue, Pasadena, California, Navigator.

Commander Hinton A. Owens, USN, of Washington Rd., Augusta, Georgia, Gunnery Officer.

Commander Clarence A. Abele Jr., USNR, of 854 "A" Avenue, Coronado, California, first lieutenant and damage control officer.

Commander Oscar E. Poole, USNR, 512 S. Park Avenue, Springfield, Illinois, Engineering Officer.

Lieutenant Commander Alexander S. Angel, USN, 9317 Kennedy Avenue, Cleveland, Ohio, medical officer.

Lieutenant Commander Charles W. Kolek, USNR, St. Procopires Abbey, Lisle, Illinois, chaplain.

Lieutenant Commander Harold W. Leahy, USNR, 88 Meadow Drive, Rochester, New York, Communications Officer.

Lieutenant Commander Walter R. Seaburg, USN, 200 Norwood Avenue, Allenhurst, New Jersey, Supply Officer.

CAPTAIN'S MESSAGE TO HIS CREW

The commissioning of a ship is a solemn and momentous occasion for her crew. We, the officers and men of the *Columbus*, are dedicating ourselves anew to the service of our country. For the first time the entire complement of the ship is assembled. Not many weeks ago we were scattered far and wide. Some of us have recently returned from combat duty in the fleet, others have come from special training schools and other types of duty, and many are very new to the naval service and the *Columbus* is their first ship. Regardless of whence we come we are now one group—one team—whose task is to prepare ourselves in the shortest possible time to take the *Columbus* into active combat area.

This task of preparation is a difficult one. It will require intense application on the part of all hands. It will mean long hours of drill and schooling. Only in this way can we learn to utilize to the maximum degree the fighting strength which has been built into this magnificent ship. All the latest and best equipment in ordnance, engineering, damage control, navigation and communications is here. We must use it again and again until every function of the ship and her equipment is as familiar to us as the palms of our hands. When we achieve that

state of training we will have full confidence in our ship and full confidence in ourselves.

No one can foresee where destiny will lead us. But the day will come when we will meet the enemy. With God's help on that day we will face the supreme trial of battle with courage and with determination to uphold the fighting tradition of our navy.

CAPTAIN'S MESSAGE TO THE SPONSOR

When Mrs. Edward G. Meyers smashed a bottle of champagne on the stem and said "I christen thee *Columbus*," as the hull slid down the ways, she carried out a ritual which seafaring men have known for years is necessary to make a ship worth going to sea on. But she did more than launch a ship; she gave a soul to an inanimate hull which we who are to serve aboard her will come to love, cherish, and honor during the years she passes in the service of the nation that created her. It is our earnest desire that these years be many and pleasant both for the ship and her worthy sponsor.

And so, Mrs. Meyers, on this our commissioning day, we, the officers and men of the USS *Columbus* salute you.

1946

En route to Buckner Bay, Okinawa in accordance with Commander Cruisers, Pacific Fleet and ordered to relieve the USS *Wilkes Barre*. Arrived Buckner Bay on 9 January 1946 and reported to the Commander of the Seventh Fleet for duty; further reported to the Commander Task Force 71 for duty in accordance with Commander of the Seventh Fleet dispatch of December 1945.

Underway from Buckner Bay, Okinawa 11 January 1946 with the USS *Tomich* in company as escort, en route to Tsingtao, China as commanded by Commander of the Seventh Fleet.

Arrived Tsingtao, China 13 January 1945 and relieved the USS *Wilkes Barre* at 1000 How time. It was very cold with the wind coming down from the north. Some of the engineering crew slept in the firerooms to take advantage of the heat from the boilers.

Liberty was granted. This was the first time many of the crew had been to a foreign country and it was a new experience. It was an eye-opener for many of the crew.

On 17 January the flag of RADM T.G.W. Settle, U.S. Navy, Commander Task Force 71 and Commander Cruiser Division Three, was broke. On 22 January the flag of RADM T.G.W. Settle, U.S. Navy, was hauled down.

On 24 January the flag of RADM A.M. Bledsoe, U.S. Navy, Commander Cruiser Division ONE, was broke.

At anchor, Tsingtau Outer Harbor, China until 31 January.

Through 31 January 1946, a total of 20 officers and 555 enlisted men were transferred to demobilization centers for discharge.

On 2 February 1946 the *Columbus* held a searchlight display in honor of the Chinese New Year. 7 February saw the *Columbus* underway for Shanghai, China anchoring at Woosung, China on 9 February and on 10 February underway up the Whangpoo River, up the Yangtse River, anchoring at 0807 in Shanghai off of Pootung Point. Liberty was granted for the starboard side. This was the crew's first encounter with a very different lifestyle. There were a number of things that many of the crew will remember, such as, the Russian Village, the Pony Track, the Park Hotel (Red Cross Headquarters), the enlisted men's club on Bubbling Well Road, firecrackers, Russian boots, bartering on the streets, the waterfront buildings (the Bank of China bells), the smells, the filth, the people, and the river. On 13 February Generalissimo Chiang Kai-Shek and his wife viewed the anchored fleet and was honored by the crew lining the rails. 15 February saw Admiral Bledsoe detached and on 16 February RADM Bennett reported on board as ComCruDivOne as relief for RADM Bledsoe.

1453 on February 1946 the *Columbus* resounded to the command, "Up Anchor" and sailed for Woosung, China at the mouth of the Whangpoo River, arriving there at 1722 and dropping anchor. 24 February found the *Columbus* underway for Yokosuka, Japan, arriving there on 27 February, dropped anchor in the bay. Our first look at the great Mountain Fujiyama. Liberty parties went ashore visiting Yokosuka, Yokahoma, and Tokyo, plus many smaller communities in the area. There was still considerable damage visible from the bombings by allied planes, but the process of rebuilding was evident everywhere. Tokyo railroad station had no roof, but the trains ran as usual. Some of the crew had the opportunity to take a tour of the two cities that were hit by the atomic bombs. This will be a lasting impression on the minds of those who went.

Captain W.E. Moore relieved Captain A. Hobbs as Commanding Officer of the USS *Columbus* on 13 March 1946. Underway for Sasebo, Japan on 27 March 1946 and moored at Sasebo on 29 March. On 1 April at 0902 along with other members of the fleet conducted the Operation "Road's End, Deep Six." At 1320 *Columbus* arrived at the DEEP SIX site. Commenced sinking 24 Japanese submarines by demolition and gun fire. The I-58, the sub that sunk the USS *Indianapolis,* and the I-402, an airplane carrying sub that is believed to have dropped incendiaries on the forests of the state of Washington, were among the ships that were sunk.

2 April found the *Columbus* underway for San Pedro, California. It took the ship 15 days to reach San Pedro on 17 April 1946. Moored at a dock in Long Beach until dry-dock facilities were available. Entered dry-dock for repair and maintenance. Leave was given to regular Navy personnel and the Navy Reserve personnel were frozen until all of the personnel had completed their leaves. While in dry-dock *Columbus* under went hull cleaning, engineering repairs, and above all, peacetime gray paint.

September 1946 found the *Columbus* operating out of Long Beach, California conducting weekly radar tracking of radio controlled missiles launched from Point Mugu, California.

November 1946 the ship participated in joint Army-Navy exercise called "Operation Duck" held on the Southern Coast of California and San Clemente Island.

1 December 1946 participated in the Fifth Fleet Maneuvers.

14 December *Columbus* returned to Long Beach where it celebrated both the Christmas and New Year's holidays.

1947

On 15 January 1947, the *Columbus* set sail for her second visit to the Orient. Arriving in Pearl Harbor on 21 January, Captain Milton E. Miles, USN, relieved Captain Moore, USN, as Commanding Officer of the *Columbus*, Captain Moore having been skipper since 13 March 1946.

Leaving Pearl Harbor on 23 January, the *Columbus* made a brief stop at Saipan before proceeding to Shanghai, China. Arriving on 7 February, she became the flagship of RADM W.A. Kitts III, USN, Commander of Cruiser Division 3.

Leaving Shanghai, the *Columbus* proceeded to Tsingtao where in company with her sister ship, USS *St. Paul,* three arduous weeks

Operation Deep Six, in which 24 Japanese submarines were sunk by demolition, April 1946. Courtesy of Bud Kathan.

were spent in more underway training. Upon completion of these exercises and the transfer of the flag, the ship got underway for Yokosuka, Japan on 23 May and commenced its first leg on a homeward journey. Arriving in Yokosuka on 26 May, six days were spent by all hands just being tourists.

On 1 June 1947, the ship once more got underway and set sail for San Francisco, California, to arrive there on 12 June.

The *Columbus* proceeded to Mare Island for minor repairs and remained there until 16 July. She then set out for Long Beach, California, to operate with Cruiser Division Thirteen and there, participated in competitive gunnery exercises at San Clemente Island.

On 20 August 1947, RADM Roscoe F. Good, USN, hoisted his flag in the *Columbus* as Commander Cruiser Division One. He left the ship early in 1948 after the *Columbus* spent Christmas at Long Beach and the remainder of the winter at the Puget Sound Naval Shipyard at Bremerton, Washington. At the completion of her trials, the heavy cruiser sailed to join a new naval family, the Atlantic Fleet as a component of Cruiser Division Two.

ber sailed, again, for Europe and her assignment as flagship for RADM Richard L. Conolly, Commander-in-Chief, Eastern Atlantic and Mediterranean Sea. In the months that followed, the cruiser added many new names to her list of places visited, her crew spending liberties in Norway, Denmark, Germany, Holland, Belgium, France and Portugal before returning to Plymouth, England.

During these cruises, *Columbus* was host to many distinguished persons, among whom were King Paul and Queen Fredericka of Greece, Prince Bernhardt of Holland, and the late King George VI of Great Britain.

After celebrating Thanksgiving Day at Plymouth, England, the same city from which the Pilgrim Fathers set out for the "New World," centuries before, *Columbus* sailed "stateside" and arrived in New York on 9 December.

During January and February *Columbus* completed sea trials and set sail for the Panama Canal to join CruDiv Two in the Atlantic Ocean.

1948

1949

In April 1948, *Columbus* returned through the Panama Canal en route to Norfolk, Virginia. That Summer, NROTC students and Midshipmen from the Naval Academy at Annapolis boarded her for the Midshipmen Cruise to southern European waters. She returned in the Fall of that year and on 15 September.

In compliance with reference (b), the *Columbus* made an operational visit to Casablanca, arriving at 0800, 9 January and departed at 1700, 12 January 1949.

The *Columbus* fired national salute of 21 guns after rounding the entrance buoy when south of the eastern end of the breakwater.

Seaplane on the catapult, May 1947. Courtesy of Ralph Lehde.

Thomasian, Case, Chapic, and Fine at a Buddhist Temple in Shanghai, February 1946. Courtesy of Robert Case.

O'Neil, Romans, girl, Richardson, Carter, Ely, Tracey, Carlilse, Schramm, Schnieder, and Koshes in Tobruk, February 1944. Courtesy of Robert Schramm.

An orphanage for unwanted girl babies, Shanghai, February 1946. Courtesy of Robert Case.

Capt. F. Warder with John and Doris Leh, Ship's Dance, 1950. Courtesy of William Polcsa.

The Cerifion (Moroccan) Ensign was flown at the main during the national salute. The salute was returned by the shore battery at Sour Djidiel.

Liberty was granted on port and starboard basis expiring at 2400 for enlisted and 0100 for CPOs. Shore Patrol report is being submitted, there were no occurrences in Casablanca that would bring discredit to the United States Naval Service.

Two tugs and a pilot assisted in mooring; the ship furnished lines to the tugs. The pilot boarded off the entrance buoy. The *Columbus* moored port side to Jetee Delure in berth Roger. The shallowest draft recorded by lead line at low tide was seven fathoms. There is no crane service available at this berth. The approach to the harbor is well marked.

Two dial telephones were placed aboard, however, it was not possible to connect to the ships switchboard due to the difference in line voltages. One phone was to the French Naval Exchange and the other to the Casablanca Exchange. A French sailor was detailed by the liaison officer at each telephone during the day, this assistance was very helpful.

Water was received from a connection on Jetee Delure at a cost of six cents per ton. A garbage lighter was placed alongside daily for several hours. Seasonal fresh fruit and vegetables were in plentiful supply, but rather high in price, quality was good to excellent. Lettuce, cabbage, celery, apples, bananas, and grapefruit were purchased.

CinCNELM was received by General Juin at residence at Rabat and was entertained by the American Consul General and RADM Jozon, French Navy. CinCNELM entertained at dinner aboard the *Columbus.*

Ship's officers were entertained by Hajd Ben Jedia (American Protege) with a Diffa at his residence. The Commanding Officer entertained the American Consul General at luncheon on the *Columbus.*

The American colony and invited guests of the French Armed Forces were allowed to visit the ship.

Lt. J.M. Quitard, French Navy boarded with the pilot and acted as liaison officer during the visit. He was most helpful and co-operative.

During cruises to Norway, Denmark, Germany, Holland, Belgium, France and Portugal, *Columbus* hosted a number of distinguished guests, King Paul and Queen Fredericka of Greece, Prince Bernhardt of Holland, and King George VI of Great Britain.

On 20 November 1949, the ship made a brief visit to Bremerhaven, Germany, where General Hardy, CinC Europe, inspected the ship and crew. The ship returned to Plymouth, England in time to celebrate Thanksgiving Day from the same city from which the Pilgrim Fathers set out for America centuries before. The *Columbus* set sail for the U.S. once again, arriving in New York on 9 December 1949 after 15 months overseas.

1950

PLYMOUTH, ENGLAND

On 12 June 1950, with a long blast of the bugle, the *Columbus* started on her way down the channel at Boston and headed for the open sea. Threading her way past the many islands of Boston Harbor, once the scene of piratical operations, the city was soon just a thin line on the horizon, and a memory in the minds and hearts of the crew.

Then on the 22 June, after an uneventful nine day passage across the Atlantic, the *Columbus* entered the harbor of Plymouth, England, and wound her way up the Hamoaze to Buoy No. 9.

It is well to note here that the *Columbus* is (or was) the only major American Man-of-War (cruiser class and above) with an oversea home port. And now before continuing, how about a few words on this home port of ours.

Originally a small fishing village, Plymouth has grown until it is now one of the two major naval bases in Britain (Portsmouth is the other). Plymouth has played a role in the history of not only England, but America as well. Sir Francis Drake began his voyage around the world, and Sir Humphrey Gilbert sailed on his colonizing expeditions to America from Plymouth. Drake's famous battle against the mighty Spanish Armada, which sought to invade England and make it a Spanish colony, was fought off Plymouth. And it was from Plymouth that the Pilgrim Fathers set sail for the New World, and freedom from religious persecution. It seems rather paradoxical that a good three centuries should find the *Columbus* arriving at Plymouth, England, just as the Pilgrims had come to Plymouth, Massachusetts. The village slowly expanded, and in 1928 became a chartered city. Hit heavily in World War II, it is gradually being restored to its former position of honor.

On the south side of town, facing the harbor, is the picturesque Hoe, with its promenades and various monuments dedicated to the British Armed forces. The Hoe is also the site of the city's aquarium, and a fort dating back to the 18th century. The broad green lawns are the favorite for strollers in the brief summer season, and there is a large open-air bandstand, miniature golf course, and bowling greens for other amusements. Leaving the Hoe and heading towards the city, we come to the NAAFI Club, similar to the USO, and open to the Armed Forces of all nations. From the NAAFI Club it is but a short walk to Union Street, the center of the town's night life, where a majority of the pubs are located. The south end of Union Street runs into the shopping district at Drake Circus, and just beyond that, Muntley Plains. Skipping back to the north end of town we come to the Royal Navy Dockyards, headquarters of the British Fleet.

England is a country rich in history and color, and this brief history could not begin to include all the spots to see. However, there is one other city that should be mentioned - center of a once-great empire, capital of the country, and one of history's most important cities - London. One cannot begin to describe the places to see, but here are a few: London Bridge, the Tower of London, Downing Street, Baker Street, Regent Street, Trafalgar Square, Leicester Square, and Piccadilly Circus, center of London's night life (which should be seen to be enjoyed), Buckingham Palace, the Parliament Building, and last but not least, the world-famous waxworks of Madame Toussard. Throw in a number of museums, libraries, and universities, and there is enough to keep the sightseer busy for days, provided he gets past Piccadilly Circus.

On 10 July, CinCNELM, Admiral R.L. Conolly embarked, and we got underway for Brest, France. After a fogbound passage across the English Channel, the *Columbus* entered the harbor at Brest on the morning of the 11th, and exchanged salutes with the French battleship *Richelieu,* which was salvaged after being torpedoed in the harbor during World War II.

FRANCE

Brest began as a Roman Fortress in the middle ages, and gradually developed into one of the major naval bases of the 16th century. In World War I, Brest became the disembarkation port for all American troops. Later, in the second World War, the Nazis established a submarine base in Brest. Unfortunately in destroying the sub base, the Allies also removed a major portion of the city. Brest has been a fishing port for centuries, and is now one of the major bases of the French Navy.

There was little to see or do in Brest, and it would have been poor liberty except for some fine games by the basketball team. Then, too, a party was given by the French Navy which was enjoyed by all that attended - no doubt helped along by liberal portions of fine French wine and champagne.

On our next voyage to France the Sixth Fleet arrived at the famous Cote D'Azur or French Rivera on 22 August and split up - the *Columbus* anchoring at Cannes. Although the folks at home were beginning to plan for Autumn, *Columbus* men were enjoying the sandy beaches of this famous resort city, and having swim call on the ship every afternoon. Camera fans held field day on the film supply, and souvenir hunters returned daily with fresh loads of perfume, dolls, and a dozen-and-one other things to send home.

There are a number of places nearby worthy of mentioning. First, is the very elite resort at Antibes where the very rich of the world have built beautiful villas. Second, is the small town of Grasse in the mountains north of Cannes, whose perfume factories ship their fragrant bundles all over the world. Originally noted for its glove factories, the perfume industry slowly began edging its way into the prominence in the 16th century, when Catherine de Medicis, an Italian noblewoman, was queen of France. She could not stand the smell of the leather-tanning process, so established a small laboratory to manufacture perfume, which was used to counteract the stench of the tanning. It was from this modest beginning that one of the largest perfume centers in the world was created.

A small place, but quite well known, is Monte Carlo, part of the tiny principality of Monaco, which was found in 50 B.C. by the Romans. The chief industry of Monte Carlo is, of course, gambling, and it supports the bulk of the population. Visitors and gamblers from all over the world visit the Casino every year, to enjoy the motor and yacht races, swimming, sailing, parties, and opera. The Casino employs about 3,000 people, of which 500 are croupiers in the gambling hall. They are highly skilled and attend a school for six months to learn the trade.

Nice is just a ten minute bus ride from Villefranche. It is situated in the "Baie des Anges," and is a highly frequented summer and winter resort known all over the world. Nice is the largest city on the Riviera, and what a city! With its bathing beach all along one side of the famous avenue "Promenage des Anglais," its gardens and flowers everywhere, it is no wonder that its quarter million inhabitants consider themselves so lucky, and that it rates high on the list of good liberty ports. There is much to do and see in Nice, and the night life is the finest on the Riviera.

Our arrival at Villefranche marked the first time we had hit port alone since entering the Med. The name Villefranche means "free town," and it has been a port of call for the American Navy for 100 years.

On 26-27 September we held a ship's dance at Jimmy's Place, just a few steps from the liberty landing. About 150 girls from the Nice YWCA came as hostesses, and with the ship's cooks supplying the chow, and a local nine piece band, the affair was very successful. Since then many private parties have been given there, plus another *Columbus* party given in July 1951.

On our visits to Villefranche, many tours were conducted to the perfume factory at Grasse. There also are five day tours to Paris and Geneva, Switzerland, which made our stay in Villefranche more enjoyable.

ANTWERP, BELGIUM

After our first visit to France we found ourselves in Antwerp, Belgium, after a tortuous trip up the Schelde River; for although it is one of the major European ports, it lies more than 50 miles from the sea.

Large crowds gathered to see the *Columbus* throughout the daylight hours and remained well into the night. It was probably due to the fact that the *Columbus* was the first major American warship to visit the port in years.

Because of her great value as a major port, the history of Antwerp has been a bloody one. In the middle of the 16th century it fell to the Spanish, who plundered the town and massacred 7,000 citizens. During the French rebellion in the 19th century, the city was besieged for two years before it finally surrendered. The city fell to the Germans in both World Wars after fierce, but futile resistance. Antwerp was severely damaged in the last war, but the majority of the damage has been repaired.

During our stay in Antwerp, tours were conducted in the capital of Brussels, and war-famous city of Bastogne, now know as "Nuts." It got its name from General McAuliffe's famous reply to the German surrender terms. In Antwerp itself, there were a number of places to see. Add a few bars, a friendly populace, shake well, and you have a wonderful liberty port.

ROTTERDAM, HOLLAND

Rotterdam is another major port, and like Antwerp, has had a bloody history. It was battered by the French in the 15th century, the Spanish in the 16th, and again by the French in the latter half of the 18th century. In May 1940, the Nazis subjected Rotterdam to the most tremendous bombing then known, and the tiny country fell in a few days. Rotterdam was used by the Germans as a transit point for supplies, and the port was all but destroyed in the following Allied aerial attacks. Now it is rebuilt, and larger than before the war.

While in Rotterdam, tours were conducted daily to the capital city of Amsterdam and the nearby tiny fishing village of Vollendam, which still clings to the dress and traditions of the ancient Dutch. The fair, "Rotterdam Ahoy" was visited by a majority of the crew, and again the friendly people made the visit a wonderful experience and put Rotterdam on the list of good liberty ports. There was one thing that many people noticed, which after subsequent trips about the Mediterranean, greatly added to the opinion of the Dutch. That is, of course, their cleanliness. Every morning the Dutch housewife was out scrubbing the sidewalk, the steps, and the windows. Just goes to show you that the Navy isn't the only place with a passion for getting rid of dirt.

CinCNELM returned to his headquarters in London on 22 July, and the next day we left Rotterdam for Plymouth, England. The morning of the 24th found the *Columbus* again tied at Buoy No. 9.

Days passed and each one saw the flames of war creep farther over Korea. Then on Saturday, the 29th of July, just as the liberty party was to leave for the weekend, the word was passed that the ship would get underway at 2000 Monday night - destination unknown, and how the rumors flew!

Monday night, 31 July, we were underway again. Shortly after clearing Plymouth Harbor, the commanding officer, Captain E.R. McLean Jr., informed the crew that the ship was heading for the Mediterranean to join the Sixth Fleet and that our next stop would be Gibraltar.

We arrived at Gibraltar on the 3rd of August, and immediately began loading on stores and ammunition from the Beltrami. There was no liberty granted and loading continued on into the night.

Although it has an area of roughly two square miles, it enjoys a prestige greatly out of proportion only to its size, for it commands one of the two entrances to the Mediterranean. It has been a British Crown Colony since 1713. The Spanish attempted to capture it in 1779, but after a four year siege, which ended in the sinking of the major portion of the Spanish Fleet, left it to the British.

It was while in Gibraltar that Captain McLean congratulated the crew on their winning of the Battle Efficiency Pennant, on the basis of the excellent showing made on operations at Guantanamo Bay, Cuba, in April and May 1950.

FAMAGUSTA, CYPRUS

In August 1950 we pulled into Famagusta Bay, Cyprus with other units of the Sixth Fleet. Liberty was granted that night, and although there was little to see in Famagusta itself, it was a pleasure to get off the ship and stretch, and sample the local vintage. The nearby ruins at Salamis and some local color gave camera fans some practice, but prices were high, the town was small, and Famagusta rated only "fair" as a liberty port.

CinCNELM flew down from London the next day, and the *Columbus* helicopter was sent to the airfield to pick him up. In landing on the return trip, it struck the port boom, broke in two and sank in 14 fathoms of water. There was no loss of life, and thanks to the quick action of SN Z.C. Kleczkowski, who immediately dived over the side to render assistance, there was no serious injury. That afternoon CinCNELM made the official presentation of the Battle Efficiency Award to the commanding officer, and the "E" flag was broken out at the main. Diving operations for the helicopter were finally completed shortly before midnight, and the ship got underway for Beirut, Lebanon.

BEIRUT, LEBANON

We arrived at the capital city of Beirut with other units of the Sixth Fleet. Beirut was a city of contrast with its ancient donkey carts and modern American automobiles, the tourist, and the desert tribesman; modern buildings and tiny native shops; Christian churches and Mohammedan mosques. The city had little to offer except its local color, but tours were conducted to the cities of Damascus and Baalbek.

Damascus, which lies just across the Lebanese border, was a leading city even before the birth of Christ. Although noted for its fine swords and knives, it is a trade center for many other articles brought from through out Syria.

Baalbek, considered by the ancients to be one of the Seven Wonders of the World, is a remarkable spot. Thereon stands a Roman temple, the construction of which amazes scientists even today. The stones of the temple are almost the largest ever quarried; and yet, using only the simple machines of that day and manpower, they raised these gigantic blocks carved from a single piece of rock, and placed them on stone columns more than 60 feet high. Considering that the temple is 1,000 feet long, its construction is as amazing as it would have been if the Panama Canal had been dug with picks and shovels.

BIZERTE, TUNISIA

On our first trip to Bizerte in September 1950, Captain E.R. McLean Jr., was relieved by Captain J.H. Wellings. In the morning various emergency drills were conducted, which gave Captain Wellings his first chance to watch the crew in action. At 1300 the crew fell in at divisional parade and at 1315 Captain McLean and Captain Wellings inspected. Immediately following inspection, all hands fell in on the fantail for the official change of command ceremonies. Captain McLean then left the ship to report to Commander Destroyer Forces, U.S. Atlantic Fleet for duty.

The city of Bizerte had little to offer the liberty party, except a few bars and limited souvenir buying, but recreation parties took up the slack and it wasn't too bad. Tours to Tunis, the capital city, and the ancient city of Carthage, one of the leading cities of the Old World, were conducted daily.

Bizerte began as a Roman colony, which was captured by the Arabs in the 7th century. The French took control in 1881, when all of Tunisia became a French Protectorate. When the Allied armies swept across North Africa in 1943, it was used by the Germans and Italians as a major supply depot. With the fall of North Africa, the Allies took control of Bizerte, and used it as a jumping-off place for the Sicilian invasion.

We left Bizerte on the 13th, joined the fleet, and headed for Oran, Algeria. A few hours after sunrise on the 15th found the fleet tied up at the breakwater at Mars-el-Kebir, the French naval base.

ORAN, ALGERIA

Oran was settled by the Arabs in the 10th century and was captured, pillaged, and rebuilt by the various conquerors that followed. Its ever-changing leadership ruined Oran's prosperity, and Mers-el-Kebir became a pirate stronghold. Spain conquered Mersel-Kebir in 1505, and Oran in 1509, and massacred a third of the population. The inquisition was introduced, fortifications restored, and Oran became a Spanish penal settlement. After the devastating earthquake of 1790, the Arabs again took control, but after Algiers had fallen to the French, the Arabs surrendered Oran, and the French took formal possession in 1831.

Liberty in Oran wasn't bad, and the "horse-traders," who by now had learned the fine art of bargaining, picked up quantities of leather goods and rugs. Tours were conducted to Sidi-bel-Abbes, base of the French Foreign Legion. The men were shown "selected" parts of the base, including a small museum depicting campaigns in which Legionnaires have fought. After seeing the base the men got a chance to go through the local casbah, or native district.

ARANCI BAY CAGLIARI, SARDINIA

We join the *Columbus* at her anchorage in Cagliari, Sardinia, where she arrived 29 September 1950, on a "strictly business" mission. On the 30th, the Commander-in-Chief of the French and Italian Navies, CinCMED, ComSixFlt, and their staffs embarked, and the next day (1 October) we were underway again. We stopped by Valletta early on the morning of the 2nd, long enough to transfer the flag personnel to various destroyers, where they had grandstand seats for the afternoon's shore bombardment and antiaircraft exercises.

We returned to Valletta, and the various Commanders-in-Chiefs met for a critique of the previous day's exercises. Noon found the *Columbus* underway again with the fleets to observe the French torpedo exercises. The *Columbus* returned later that afternoon and disembarked the various Flag units, CinCNELM returned to London the following day.

MALTA

In Malta short tours of the city were conducted through the courtesy of the Royal Navy. The majority of Vallette's beauty was destroyed in World War II. Valletta was the principal objective of the unparalleled bombing raids on Malta by both Italian and German aircraft, which commenced on 11 June 1940, and continued for three years on a scale unequalled elsewhere in the world. There is a story of how at one period there were only three antiaircraft guns in commission at one time, and after each raid the guns were loaded on trucks and moved to a different section of the city to keep the enemy from locating and destroying them.

The tour began at a tiny memorial park set on top of a high bluff overlooking the harbor, and from there went to the ancient city, which is nothing more than medieval castle complete with moat. The Maltese are highly religious, the Knights of Malta being world famous. There are a number of beautiful churches in Valletta, perhaps the most famous being St. Paul's Cathedral with its mosaics and catacombs underneath.

Liberty here is generally what you made it. All hands however enjoyed the drives through the city in beautiful horse-drawn carriages. The people were very friendly, and much could be enjoyed though liberty was short.

ATHENS, GREECE

Athens is rich in history, much too long to be included here, but there are a few points worth mentioning. It was originally built on the plateau off the sacred rock of the Acropolis, and was inhabited 16 centuries before the birth of Christ. In the 6th century B.C. a lower town was formed at the bases of the Acropolis. Alexander the Great brought prosperity to the city, but finally in the 2nd century B.C., it fell under Roman domination. A few centuries later it formed the Byzantine Empire, and during this period the spirit of Christianity began to replace the worship of the pagan gods. Athens followed the fate of the Byzantine Empire, and in 1456 became part of the Turkish Ottoman Empire. It was controlled by the Turks until 1833 when they withdrew, and Athens was chosen to be the capital of the newly established Greek kingdom.

In a way Greece was unique, for people there were as much interested in buying as they were in selling. A few opportunists took advantage of this to dispose of battered pea coats at prices averaging around $15. But a few days later they found themselves faced with the prospect of doling out $40 for a new one - the new price list had come in.

When one visits Athens, especially on tour, the dominant feature is the hill of the Acropolis (literally "upper city") crowned with the world-famous Parthenon, and a number of other renowned examples of Greek architecture. In 1687, during the war between the Turks and the Venetians, a shell exploded some gunpowder stored there and blew it to ruin after it had stood intact for over two thousand years. In Athens itself there are a number of museums housing various works of art and sculpture found in the excavation of the ruins.

Athens and Piraeus stand side by side, and while visiting one, the other always looked tempting. On visits to Greece liberty was always enjoyed.

PIRAEUS

On 1 November 1950, Admiral R.B. Carney assumed command as the commander-in-chief, U.S. Naval Forces, Eastern Atlantic and Mediterranean, relieving Admiral R.L. Connoly who reported to the Chief of Naval Operations for duty.

On the 3rd, the *Columbus* stood into Piraeus, Greece, and there disembarked the Marine detachment who flew to Stockholm, Sweden, to form a guard of honor at the funeral of the late King Gustav.

Piraeus, although it is the second city of Greece, and the port of entrance for Athens, had little to offer except for a few bars, which managed to do a fairly good business, selling coke, of course.

Our last visit, which was in June 1951, proved to be a great success. A Seamans' Club was opened in Athens, and with all the American girls, free food and beautiful music, the entire Sixth Fleet had an unforgettable time.

IZMIR, TURKEY

In November 1950, we arrived at Izmir, Turkey with the Albany. The following morning we fell in at quarters for inspection for Rear Admiral J.L. Holloway, Commander Cruiser Forces Atlantic Fleet, and his party. After personnel inspection, Admiral Holloway and his party inspected the upper decks. In their opinion, the *Columbus* and its crew was one of the smartest ships in the fleet.

As for Izmir itself, there was little to see or do. There was a certain amount of "local color," but little else, despite the historical background of the area. There was little recreation, few bars or clubs, and prices were sky-high.

Izmir (also known as Smyrna) is said to be the birthplace of the famous blind poet, Homer. However, the other six cities that claim the same honor would probably disagree. It is one of Turkey's major seaports and the home of the 2nd largest Army and Navy bases. Most recently, Izmir was given to the Greeks at the end of World War I but was taken over by Turkey in 1922.

The city itself is beautiful, and those of the crew who did go ashore had an enjoyable time taking pictures and visiting the various monuments. Liberty in general was just what you made of it.

ISTANBUL, TURKEY

The city of Istanbul stands on the southern extremity of the Bosphorus, upon a hilly promontory that runs out from the European side of the Straits toward the Asiatic bank. Istanbul was first known as the city of Byzantine, and was founded by the Dorians in the 660 B.C. When the Persians entered Europe, the settlement fell to their arms and was destroyed. It was rebuilt and for a long period was in alliance with Athens, retaining its right of self-government under Alexander the Great. Constantine renamed the city Constantinople in the year 330, and from that day it has been one of the greatest cities of the world. Due to quarrels of various factions in the year 552, the city was almost destroyed. In the years following, the city suffered severely from many civil and foreign wars. The Avars, Persians, Arabs, and Bulars all besieged the city and in the year 860, and again in 1048, a Russian fleet forced its way through the Bosphorus with hostile intent. In the year 1204 the Latin Crusades turned aside, and in alliance with Venice, captured the city, sacked it, desecrated its holy places, and created out of the empire, a Latin Eastern Empire and a number of minor states. In 1453 Constantinople fell to the Turks under Mohammed the Conqueror,

and was made the chief city of a still greater Ottoman Empire. It remained as the capital until the first quarter of the 20th century. In the year 1924, the new Turkish Republic moved its capital from Constantinople to Ankara, and officially renamed the city Istanbul. With respect to its influence over the course of human affairs, Istanbul is rivaled only by Athens, Rome, and Jerusalem, and is now the cultural and educational center of Turkey.

There are a number of places to see in Istanbul, most of them grouped around the Aya Sophia, built as a memorial to the wife of Constantine. Within easy walking distance is the Blue Mosque, one of the hundreds scattered throughout Istanbul. Then there is the old Hippodrome, the ancient meeting place and sports arena, built by Constantine a century and a half ago. A short distance from Aya Sophia is Egyptian Bazaar, an open market place which caters mainly to the tourist trade who are willing to pay the exorbitant prices asked. There are a number of clubs scattered about the center of town, but the prices in general were high compared to other Med. ports, and the recreation was limited. However, some good bargains in Meerschaum pipes could be found at a fraction of the cost in America.

The February trip to Istanbul was otherwise peaceful, except for the sinking of #3 motor launch. In coming from the liberty landing on the afternoon of the 18th, it collided with a ferry, and sank. Luck held and there were no causalities, but no one escaped a dunking and a few men were taken to sick bay suffering from exposure. Prompt action of the ship's boats, and local native craft is credited with keeping the injury at a minimum, for the strong currents running through the Bosphorus makes swimming almost impossible.

SUDA BAY, CRETE

On 9 November 1950, the chief of staff, ComCruLant and his party came aboard, and the *Columbus* got underway for her Operational Readiness Inspection. Various drills were held in the morning, gunnery and full power drills in the afternoon. We returned to Suda Bay the same evening and received our Administrative Inspection the following day.

Though very frequented by the *Columbus*, Suda Bay, Crete was poor as a liberty port. There was nothing to see or do, and the majority of the crew caught up on their sleep and letters home. Recreation parties took up some of the slack with softball games and mountain climbing on a nearby hill. It was a *Columbus* man, Buck Read of CS Division, who set a record by topping the hill in 1 hour and 35 minutes.

When in Suda Bay, one could always depend on many inspections and drills.

1951

Augusta Bay, Sicily
Augusta Bay, Sicily, similar to Crete in many ways was very often a mainstay for the "74."

Tours were conducted to the very famous city of Syracuse nearly twenty miles away. The Greek and Roman theaters, which were built during their occupations, proved very photogenic to the camera fiend. Excavations of these ancient structures are still being carried on.

Other recreation consisted mostly of softball games, but the majority of the crew spent their liberty aboard ship.

TRIESTE

Situated at the head of the Gulf of Trieste on the Istrian Peninsula, on the north end of the Adriatic Sea, the city of Trieste rises picturesquely from the water in an amphitheater formed by the sloping escarpments of the Korst Plateau. The

The ship's band, 1951. Courtesy of Bob Heberling.

R.E. Beattie in Naples, Italy, 22 April 1951.

old section of the town with its castle of San Giusto, stands upon the hills and has its old crooked streets carrying memories of the past centuries which date back as early as 178 B.C. The new town connected by the broad and beautiful Via del Corso, the busiest street, is modern in every respect and contains many popular shopping places and restaurants.

Most typical as a seaport, Trieste has hosted more than 34,350 ships annually with imports, such as coal, coffee, and tobacco. Good wine, fruit and olive oil are the most important natural products.

The people of the world know much of Trieste because of its strategic locale and importance in World War II and it is good to see the city arising from some of its ashes of war to become once again an enterprising city of Italy. Within the port were the remains of many sinkings, yet most of the wreckage is being cleared away rapidly and by now probably is complete.

The U.S. Army maintains large warehousing establishments, cared for by the Quartermaster Corps, as well as ample airstrips and repair facilities. A station hospital of 200 beds is also maintained by the Army.

Points of interest in Trieste include the numerous and very excellent U.S. Army operated establishments. The best club, by far, was "The Hangar Club" which provided spacious gymnasium, refreshment stand, indoor recreational facilities, recreation rooms and movie area. Sightseeing around the town included such spots as the Miramar Castle. There is also an old Roman arch called the "Arch di Riccardo," named after Richard, the Lion-Hearted, in the spot where the king allegedly, was imprisoned while returning from one of the Crusades. The San Guyisto Castle contained some interesting relics. Inhabitants of the city number some 238,000.

NAPLES, ITALY

Though our first trip to Naples was brief, there was sufficient time to learn a little about the city. Perhaps the first thing that impressed the crew was the towering majesty of Mount Vesuvius. Its cloud-capped 4,000 feet guards the Bay of Napoli. Conversely, the next impression came from the dozens of peddlers that swarmed around the liberty party as they went ashore.

Naples was founded by the Greeks, but after an earthquake shook it, and half of the city slid into the sea, the Romans moved in and took over. The port itself is second only to Genoa in importance and was the base of major Italian warships during the last war. Many of the city's attractions were destroyed or damaged by the war, but there are still many points of interest for the shutterbug. There are about 300 churches and chapels, the most beautiful being the Cathedral of St. Janarius, the patron saint of Naples. There are also a number of museums, three or four ancient castles, the Royal Palace, the University, the San Carlo Opera House, and the Catacombs. And, of course, no tour would be complete without a stop at the cameo factory. Add dozens of clubs and bars, shake with some fine Italian food, and you have another good liberty port—even though most of the Sixth Fleet does hit it at the same time.

On subsequent stops at Naples, tours were conducted to Rome, but there are a number of interesting places but a short distance from the city.

The summer resort of Sorrento lies about 30 miles southeast of Naples and the Island of Capri, about 20 miles southwest. It was on Capri that Caesar spent the last years of his life. The most outstanding attraction of Capri is, of course, its caves - the most famous being the Blue Grotto. It derives its name from the effect of the sunlight which filters into the cavern and tints the water and walls a pale blue.

Another famous spot is the ancient city of Pompei, which lies at the foot of Mount Vesuvius. It is one of five cities buried when Vesuvius erupted in 79 A.D. Excavation of the city began in 1748, and now most of the city has been uncovered.

Many of us will remember February 1951 and our few days of "shore duty." Liberty boats on the 4th found it rough going because of high seas and strong winds, and that night when the men returned to the landing, they found that boats to all the ships outside the breakwater had been cancelled. Hours passed and the weather grew steadily worse, and finally the word came to load the men onto buses and distribute them among the various hotels in Naples. Naturally, there were too many men for the limited space available, and a trip through the hotels that night found sailors sleeping in the lobbies, on the stairs, in the halls and jammed by the dozens in rooms. There were also a few optimistic souls who slept in some box cars at the landing. There were still no boats the next morning and just about everyone headed for the Seamen's Club and a hot cup of coffee. Around noon they were herded back to the landing, and those whose ships had come inside the breakwater returned. *Columbus* men were spread about the various ships, to wait until the morning of the 7th when liberty boats resumed schedule. We got aboard just in time to load stores—oh well, "be it ever so humble, there is no place like home."

TARANTO, ITALY

One of the four major naval bases in Italy, Taranto, in the instep of the "Italian Boot" forms the southern anchorage for her fleet.

The disaster inflicted on the Italian Navy by the British in 1941 is well known. British planes from the "Illustrious" flew over the Italian Fleet, apparently quite secure in the harbor, and broke the back of Italian sea power in a few hours.

Taranto is one of the cleanest cities visited in the Mediterranean. It is rather small and the streets are very narrow. With a population of about 100,000, she does not have the air of a big city as some of the other ports have. Amusements are few, and luxurious bars and hotels are non-existent. There are a few sidewalk cafes that offer a pleasant place from which to view the Tarantios. Shopping is limited with most of the products coming from the northern cities. The city is not industrial, nor does it have any native handicraft that is worthy to mention. Three Naval schools are maintained here, and Italian courtesies are many but not lavish. Not far from the fleet landing one can find modern club-hotels, which serve cognac, gin, and beer at reasonable prices.

Father's Day was celebrated by inviting a group of Italian orphans to a party aboard ship. It was hard to tell who had the most fun, the children or the foster fathers.

VENICE, ITALY

Although it would be impossible to list all of the attractions Venice has to offer the sightseer, there are a few of the better known that should be mentioned. From the liberty landing it was but a few short blocks to the center of Venetian life at the Piazza Di San Marco (St. Mark's Square), filled with people and pigeons. On three sides it is enclosed with symmetrical colonnades, from which extend numerous cafe tables. On the fourth side is the fabulous

Basilica of St. Mark, the patron saint of Venice. The roof is a great cluster of golden domes of various sizes, and is adorned with 500 columns of rare oriental marbles, inside and out. The building is covered with mosaics of gilded glass and semi-precious stones. On your left as you leave the church is the 14th century Campanile. Above the brick shaft, 162 feet high, is a limestone bell chamber which affords a wonderful view of the city. Directly across the Piazza from the Campanile, over an archway leading into the maze of the city itself, is the Torre Del Orlo-Gio, the principal feature of which is a trick clock. The bronze giants called the Mori or Moors, each armed with a sledgehammer, have been striking the hours on a large bell for the past 450 years. There are a number of palaces to visit, perhaps the most famous being the Palazzo Ducale (Ducal Palace). This striking building has seen as much magnificence, cruelty, lavish generosity, low intrigue, catastrophe, and prosperity as any building this side of Hades. The Grand Canal, the main drag of Venice is a rubber-neck's paradise, with another dozen famous and beautiful spots to see.

GENOA, ITALY

This is the first visit of the *Columbus* to this port of call since the midshipmen cruise in 1948.

Nobody knows just when the city was founded. It was a very long time before the birth of Christ at any rate. The name Genoa is probably derived from the Greek word Zenos or stranger, and the early civilization of the city is due to the contact of the primitive Ligurian inhabitants with Greek and Phoenician traders.

It is both a medieval and modern city, crowded and bustling. The old part of the city is full of narrow winding streets with stairs and bridges and hemmed in by old buildings, dating from the middle ages. Carved doorways, often with wrought iron grills or gates open into inner courtyards. Great Renaissance palaces loom over one as he passes through those crooked alleys, and rear their lofty walls far above his head as they elbow neighboring palaces. One soon notices that homes or dwelling places have black street numbers, and place of business and offices have red ones. The parts of the city have broad roads and well spaced dwellings and give the appearance of a modern city as we know it.

Yet, it can be said, Genoa is pre-eminently a city of palaces. These range from the medieval homes of Genoese families in the old quarter of the town to the magnificent 16th and 17th century mansions which line the Via Garibaldi. It is of special interest to note that the year 12 October 1950 to 12 October 1951 is the "Fifth Centenary Celebration of Christopher Columbus." The exhibition in progress at St. George's palace showed much of the history of Columbus' times.

Genoa has very important metallurgical and engineering industries which are mainly connected with ship-building. The refining and processing of vegetable and seed oils, which are mainly imported, is a considerable industry. The soap and food industry, cotton manufactures, especially hosiery, tanning and leather industries (gloves), paint factories, cement works and quarries give a further picture of the Genoese at their work.

Nearby points of interest include the Staglieno Cemetery for its world-famous tombstones, also Tomb of Giuseppi Mazzini, Nervi Promenade, Galley of Modern Art, Pegli Park and Headquarters of Civil Naval Museum.

The heart of the city lies in a triangle bounded by the harbor, the Via Garibaldi and the Via Carlo Felice. It is filled with crooked streets, towering buildings, and many churches. It is in these old churches that you will really find something worthwhile.

While in Genoa a tour was made to Pisa and Florence. Pisa is world famous for its "Leaning Tower." Incessant land-slides seem to be the explanation of this oddity.

Florence like Genoa is both modern and medieval with the picturesque characteristics that such a combination has to offer. Many museums and art galleries are available to the visitor. Some of the world famous masterpieces can be seen in this old Italian city. Florence also boasts of having the only bridge in Europe that has buildings and stores on it. The great cultural awaking that finally shook Europe from its stagnant sleep of the Middle Ages started here.

ROME, ITALY

Many of the crew were fortunate enough to take one of the exciting tours offered each time the ship visited Naples. Just a few hours away by the excellent Rapido service, the Italian capital was within easy range of the sailor's camera and pocketbook. This trip offered five days of relaxation in one of the city's modern hotels and an opportunity to see the very cradle of our modern civilization.

The efficient Italian train arrives in one of the most modern and large stations which can be found throughout the world, and it is a surprise indeed to see what lies only a few blocks away. There is the old Roman Forum, originally a market place and center of trade but finally the center of religious and political life of the Romans. At each step, the tourist sees history written in marble. Not much further stands the stately Coliseum, marvelously preserved and mammoth even by modern day standards. It covers six acres, is one-third of a mile in circumference and 150 feet high. This structure is a grim reminder of the second and third centuries when thousands of Christians were martyred on its bloody stage. Another notorious history book picture is the Arch of Constantine which poses even more majestically than its photographs imply.

The famous Pantheon built in 27 B.C. in commemoration of the victory over Anthony and Cleopatra is the most perfect Roman temple. Since 609 the Pantheon has been a Christian church and within its walls are the tombs of two Italian kings and many famous painters including Raphael. It is a circular structure with a diameter of 143 feet at the bottom, and its huge dome has a 28' opening at the top. The Pantheon is used today as a church as it has done for 13 centuries and is truly a monument to Roman architecture.

As the tour progresses, the works of the Renaissance are unfolded, with the wondrous accomplishments of Raphael, Bernini, and Michelangelo. The most magnificent building in the world, St. Peters Cathedral strikes the pilgrim breathless with its beauty, size and perfection of proportion. One entrance to the Cathedral is sealed with concrete and has a large cross painted on it. This, one of the four Holy Doors (Porta Santa) which are opened only during the Holy Year, which is every 25 years. The other doors are in the ancient beautiful churches of Santa Maria Maggione, Basilica of St. John, and St. Paul's outside the walls which also is visited. The Vatican, a city with a city cannot be denied the distinction as being the most imposing palace in the world.

Here, with its 80 grand staircases and 200 smaller ones, its 20 courts, and its 11,000 halls, chapels, rooms, and apartments one can see the world's grandest collection of paintings, sculptures, tapestries, and relics. Here also is Michelangelo's amazing work on the ceiling of the Sistine Chapel, Raphael's "The Transfiguration and Coronation of the Virgin," and thousands of works by the world's greatest artists.

Mussolini's residence, the Palazzo Venecia tempts everyone to train his camera on the balcony from which the "Il Duce" made his violent speeches not too long ago.

Rome is often called the city of Fountains, and the tourist can easily understand this after he has walked several blocks and sees as many fountains. The largest and most celebrated of them is the Fontana Di Treni, and by tradition if one throws a penny into it on the eve before leaving the city then fate will have him return with a year.

Not far away is the magnificent Monument to Victory Emmanuel II which took 26 years to complete.

The visit to the Holy City is highlighted when Pope Pius grants an audience and the Holy Father makes an inspiring speech in very good English.

LaSPEZIA, ITALY

The port of LaSpezia lies at the head of the Gulf of Spezia on the Liqurian Coast, 43 miles east-southeast of Genoa, and 40 miles north north-west of Leghorn. The gulf is large and surrounded by mountains.

Before the war of 1940, LaSpezia was the largest Italian naval operating base, and had developed to some extent as a commercial port. Approximately 70 percent of the port facilities were destroyed by the Germans, but damages are almost completely rebuilt. The town is built up through two valleys, and is split in the center by a ridge, reaching almost to the waterfront in a north-south direction. To the east of this ridge are the freight yards, small factories and workers' homes. To the west is the business district and dock yards. Because of the war damage and insufficient outside illumination the town now has a drab appearance especially at night.

There are several good restaurants including Ristorante Martini and Ristorante Ruffin. Prices in restaurants and bar are reasonable.

LaSpezia itself has little of interest, but the surrounding countryside is very beautiful and offers much to the "shutterbug." The village of Lerici, four miles to the south is an interesting little place and a popular summer resort. It has an old castle and good examples of medieval architecture.

LISBON, PORTUGAL

Lisbon the capital and largest city of Portugal is situated magnificently on the north bank of the Tagus River. Few ports are more beautiful as you approach from the sea.

The center of activity in Lisbon itself is the Rossio, a great central square until the 18th century the scene of public executions, bull fights, and all sorts of activity. Today it is crowded with all kinds of traffic, noisy, bright, animated. The west side is lined with cafes. You can get a good view of the casual life of the city from this vantage point.

During our time in Lisbon sightseeing tours were conducted daily to Fatima and Lisbon and environs and many of the ship's company availed themselves of them. These tours included the Jardin Boranico which is an excellent example of a garden-park; it will be of interest chiefly to those who care for sub-tropical flowers and plants.

The Museum de Arte Antiga is a small museum with a good collection of paintings and gold and silver plate.

The most popular of the tours was the one to the small village of Fatima where the Blessed Virgin had appeared on three different occasions to three Portuguese shepherd children. Those who make the tour saw the place where the Virgin had appeared and also the beautiful church which the blessed Virgin requested to be built. It is now nearing completion.

Another must on everyone's list was the bull-fight which was held on Sunday, September 23 in honor of the U.S. Navy.

With its pageant of color and some of the best bullfighters from Spain and Portugal, it provided us with one of the most exciting events we have seen while on this cruise.

The souvenir hunters were out as usual and came back with such articles as gold and silver, filigree, hammered copper, cork ice buckets and other cork novelties. Local handicraft, Madeira and local embroidery or linen and cotton.

Bargaining was in effect except in the principal downtown shops.

HOMEWARD BOUND

While we were in LaSpezia, Italy, the sewing machine in the Bunting Repair Locker started whirling and the job order for creating a "homeward bound" pennant was begun. The man behind the machine was John A. McMahon, QMS2, USNR, who had received the "go ahead" signal from Ensign McCain and St. Germaine.

The use of the homeward bound pennant is traditional. A vessel which has been on duty in foreign waters outside the continental limits of the United States continuously for a period of one year or more flies the "homeward bound" pennant upon getting underway to proceed to a port in the United States. The overall length of the pennant is normally one foot for each officer and man who has been on duty outside the United States in excess of one year. Our pennant is 520 feet long with one star in the blue field indicating the time outside the USA. This blue portion containing the star will be presented to the Commanding Officer upon arrival in the United States and the remainder will be divided equally among the officers and men of the ship's company.

Much interest was created in leaving Lisbon when the pennant was unfurled to the blue skies and gentle breezes assisted by five helium filled balloons. The "shutter-bugs" were out in full force.

1952

SCOTLAND

As the music of the ship's band drifted across the harbor, the *Columbus* slipped from its berth in Boston's Charlestown Navy Yard and began its fourth European cruise. The date was 25 August 1952.

It was a beautiful day, the sun shining brightly and hardly a cloud in sight. And that's the way it stayed during most of the 16 day trip across the Atlantic.

Our first port of call was Helensburgh, Scotland, in the Firth of Clyde, where an immense NATO fleet was anchored in preparation for the forthcoming "Operation Mainbrace." As we first passed through the colorful banks fringing the Clyde, "twas mony on eye cauld nae belyve wha thy saw." The flowing landscape of "Bonnie Scotland," with her massive forests and proud castles looming out at intervals high above the stately pines, was truly impressive.

Near Helensburgh, the banks of the Clyde recede and form a large bay. A major portion of our task force proceeded to their respective anchorage there and dropped anchor. *Columbus* sailors found the town to be a scenic little resort with tree-lined streets and picturesque churches and homes.

However, a majority of the crew traveled to Glasgow for liberty, a distance of 21 miles. The city's mighty shipyard, its throngs of people, busy shops and hum of ambitious industry all lent an air of greatness and purpose. The ruddy complexions of the pretty lassies reflected the healthy consequence of Scottish air and the men wore countenances of rugged rural vitality: yet, these were city folk.

English, naturally, is the native language of the Scots but the thick accent the people possess gave many sailors a bad time. The people were cordial, though, and welcomed us warmly.

Newspapers were filled with stories of the impending exercises and carried many pictures of American sailors seeing the sights of Glasgow. One paper quoted a taxi driver as saying that, "They must have learned about English money from their wartime brothers. The tips are good but nothing like during the war." The city's dance halls were jammed and reported their biggest nights since the war.

It was a wonderful opportunity for relaxation following the many days we had spent at sea after leaving the States. And it gave us an equally good opportunity to get in shape for the then forthcoming "Operation Mainbrace."

After leaving Helensburgh on 13 September, we steamed in the North Atlantic and headed for the northwest coast of Norway. It was our job, as a unit of the Blue armada to find the orange naval force. This was "Operation Mainbrace," the largest joint naval exercise ever held. The navies of Britain, France, Canada, the Netherlands, Belgium, Norway, Denmark, New Zealand and the U.S. utilized the services of 85,000 men and 160 ships in waging the maneuvers over an area of a half million square miles.

One of the highlights of the exercise was the mythical sinking of an enemy raider, the HMCS *Quebec*, by the *Columbus*. Even though the *Quebec* tried to pose as a friendly ship by using radio code employed by the Blue forces, Captain Campbell received a "well done" for his keen judgment in disregarding the trick and for the subsequent sinking.

The operation carried us north of the Arctic Circle, into the Royal Domain of the Polar Bear, and that made each of us a member of the Order of Bluenoses. But as it turned out, our noses hadn't even begun to turn blue. We kept going until we reached a point about 1300 miles from the North Pole before returning to Rosyth, Scotland, to embark Admiral Lynde D. McCormick, USN, Supreme Allied Commander, Atlantic.

NORWAY

After embarking SACLANT at Rosyth, we returned to "Mainbrace" to spend the remaining five days of the operation before proceeding to Oslo, Norway. The flagships *Wisconsin, Olympus, Salerno Bay,* and HMS *Eagle* were present at Oslo and NATO leaders held conferences aboard them to talk over the recently completed exercise.

Even though it rained almost every day we were there, the crew enjoyed the visit to Norway a great deal. The trip up the Oslo Fjord (pronounced fiord) was an experience that will be hard to forget. Its shores, lined with rocky cliffs interspersed with sheltered bays and stretches of level land, reflect the rugged beauty of the entire country. The 80 mile trip from Skaggerak to Oslo, at the head of the fjord, took about six hours and every minute on deck that morning was an enjoyable one for "salt" and "boot" alike.

Even though we anchored over three miles from the fleet landing, the liberty "hounds" throughout the visit. The first thing to catch the eye of the lens jockeys when they hit the beach was the magnificent new town hall building on the waterfront. In contrast to some ports, the waterfront in Oslo is not an undesirable area. In fact, some of its better shops and businesses are located on Radhuset, near the town hall. That building, a handsome 13 story affair, covers a full city block and is a veritable museum of modern Norwegian arts and crafts. Cast in concrete and covered with a veneer of hand-molded brick, its exterior is richly ornamented with detail work, bas-relief and statuary in hewn stone. Twenty years, including the period of the German occupation, were required to complete the structure.

A large percentage of the people spoke English well, so it was not hard to find such points of interest as the Viking ships used by Leif Erikson and other explorers over 1,000 years ago; Kon-Tiki Museum, where the balsa raft used in 1947 to make the historic 4,300 mile trip across the Pacific is on display; Frogner Park, where sculptural projects of one man covers 74 acres of land; and the Roy Palace, at the head of the city's main thoroughfare, Karl Johans gate.

With a population of approximately half a million people, Oslo is the largest city in Norway and nearly half of the merchant fleet is centered there. Bearing in mind that Norwegian merchant shipping ranks third in the world, one can quickly realize that Oslo is the chief seaport of a seafaring nation.

Many tours were arranged in Oslo, including one to the mountains which would have been particularly good except for the inclement weather. Those who selected the city tour reported that it was far above average.

As one might imagine, a city with all these advantages makes an excellent location for the nation's capital. And therefore, Oslo has been the capital since 1814. Founded in 1060, the city was completely leveled by fire in 1624 and was re-planned and built up by King Christian IV on a site west of the original city. It took eight years to build the new town.

The country remained neutral during World War I and from September 1939 to April 1940 tried painstakingly to do the same thing as Hitler marched into one country after another in Europe. German forces invaded Norwegian soil on 9 April 1940, however, and the German minister at Oslo demanded that the country be handed over. When the government refused to submit to the demands, the invading armies swept across the country in two months, despite stubborn resistance. The king and the government fled to London and declared their intention of carrying on the war from there. Early in November 1944, Russian armies liberated parts of northern Norway from German occupation and she was officially freed of occupation on 8 May 1945. Now the country is a participant in the Marshall Plan and a member of the Atlantic Pact, which she joined in spite of a protest from the Soviet Union that it was an "unfriendly" move. Trygve Lie, the country's foreign minister became the first Secretary General of the United Nations.

The courageous and hardy people of Norway are a symbol for the free people of the world. Regardless of the fact that they are a small country in both size and population, they refused to surrender to the Nazis without a fight and will not be dictated to by the nearby Kremlin today.

These were the kind of people we met when the *Columbus* visited Oslo from 25-29 September. We'll remember it as a good city, inhabited by good people.

PORTUGAL

"*Columbus* Ahoy," came the resounding roar from the ship we were relieving. As we steamed into the port of Lisbon, Portugal, the crew of the *Baltimore* turned out a gala welcoming committee for the ship that was filling her bill in the Sixth Fleet. Flags flew, posters were plastered from the forecastle to the fantail, some energetic members of the *Baltimore* crew clowned with feminine togs, and from the general attitude of the Baltimore sailors, it was obvious they were happy to be heading home.

Lisbon, according to an informal poll, ranks high in popularity among the sailors aboard. It isn't too difficult to understand why. The city affords, a varied selection of entertainment, rivaling nearly any port in the Mediterranean. Many large movie houses feature American movies. While we were there such films as *Frances Goes to West Point, Quo Vadis,* and *The Three Musketeers,* were playing.

The numerous parks and gardens which can be seen from almost any portion of the city relate a tale of a people who have a great deal of pride and affection for the city in which they live. The climate is mild and equable throughout the year, thereby securing favorable conditions for the growth of nature's finery. Just about every place where even a little grass is growing, you can find flowers planted. Cobblestone streets and orange-colored roofs seem to be the trademarks of the city also.

The inhabitants are friendly to all and the street life of the city is full of interest. The bare-footed fishwives bearing flat trays of fish on their heads; the bakers, bending beneath a heavy load of bread slung in a huge basket over their shoulders; the knife grinders, and the calls of the fruit vendors all contribute to the bustle of this colorful city.

The tours that were provided proved themselves to be of great interest and worth. Fatima and the Holy Shrines indicating the sites of the visitation of Our Lady of Fatima offered many sailors an opportunity to see the actual vista of a miracle they'd read and heard of all their lives. The tours to Sintra where the palaces and castles of ancient Portuguese royalty stand; where the relics of a dead era live perpetually on, instilled in us an experience that we won't soon forget.

Even though the regular bull-fight season had ended when we reached Lisbon early in October, a special fight was arranged for the fleet. For those sailors who had never seen a bull-fight before, the ancient sport proved to be as interesting as it was centuries ago. Many of the sailors present were so enthused that they relinquished all claim to their hats as they flung them into the arena, in honor of the brave matadors.

In Portuguese style fighting, the bull is fought by a man in 18th century costume mounted on a beautiful, spirited horse, often worth over $10,000. The bull's horns are padded with straw and straps. Men on foot with capes help maneuver the bull into position where he can charge the horseman, who tries each time he is charged, to place a decorated barb between the shoulder blades of the bull. The matador's skill is judged by the accuracy of the barb's placement. Unlike Spanish bullfighting, the animal is never killed in Portugal.

Far more popular with the people as a whole are the many romaries, fiestas, and market-days. Romaries are pilgrimages to Catholic shrines, in which religious duties are combined with secular pleasures on an outdoor holiday, and compare with old-fashioned English county fairs. Brilliantly colored costumes are worn on these days.

One of the "main drags" of Lisbon, the Avenida de Liberdade, is regarded as one of the finest avenues of Europe. Its tree-shaded sidewalk cafes and expensive restaurants are a favorite haunt of the city's society people. Less than a five minute walk from the Avenida, with all its wealth and prosperity, beggars and peddlers abound in the Alfama district, however. There amid narrow, steep and winding streets and alleys is found the "seamier" side of Lisbon. The people there "still maintain the medieval aspect which other parts of the city have lost," to quote the guide who accompanied at least one of the city tours by *Columbus* personnel.

Columbus sailors touring the Vatican and Rome, have audience with Pope Pius XII at Castle Vandorfo, 1952. Courtesy of Ronald Dolinsky.

Various other units of the Sixth Fleet were tied up in Lisbon during the *Columbus'* visit, either being relieved to go back to the States or joining the Med Fleet. It was the early morning (in fact, before sunrise) of 9 October 1952, that the *Columbus* left its berth at Alcantara dock in Lisbon and steamed down the Tagus River to the Atlantic on its way to a week of fleet exercises before stopping at Augusta, Sicily, for replenishment.

GENOA - NAPLES, ITALY

Columbus men had an opportunity on this cruise to explore the "boot" of Italy from top to bottom. Beginning in October with the "toe" Augusta, Sicily, the ship then visited Genoa in the north and later on, Naples, which lies in the central part of the country.

Probably one of the best liked ports on the entire cruise was Genoa, the birthplace of the discoverer of our country, Christopher Columbus. The ship found her precarious way through the narrow harbor and moored, Mediterranean style, close by the Maritime Building on 29 October.

Those sailors who had been to Genoa before were quick to get ashore and renew old friendships while the "first cruise" men soon found the city to be everything that is was said to be.

Genoa is both a medieval and modern city, crowded and bustling. The old part of the city is full of narrow, winding streets, often with stairs and bridges, and hemmed in by lofty old buildings dating back to the Middle Ages. It is a strange sight to see these alleys, left over from a forgotten age, filled with small grocery stores, restaurants, and other places of busi-

ness, with neon signs over their doors. Often an alley only eight or ten feet wide is an important thoroughfare crowded with people at almost any hour.

Perhaps the center of town, at least one of the busiest places in Genoa, is the Piazza de Ferrari. A square with a beautiful fountain in its center, it seems as though all the city's street cars congregate there. Traffic is quite congested as the narrow side walks cannot adequately take care of the pedestrian traffic during the daytime hours, and the vehicular traffic has also outgrown its streets. Many imposing buildings border the Piazza and the smart shopping district, of which the Via Settembre takes up a large part, is located right off of it.

We'll remember Genoa for the familiar bridge at the ship's fantail where the local people lined up each day to watch us at work(?). Actually, we'll remember it more for our frequent glimpses to see how many fair maids were there.

Columbus left Genoa on 3 November to meet other units of the fleet and started "Operation Longstep," which was smaller than "Mainbrace" but still the largest joint exercise in the Med since the war. That carried us to the eastern end of the sea, near Turkey, and when the two week exercise was completed we visited Istanbul. After stopping in Greece and Lebanon, the ship came back east again and made a call at Naples. We reached there on 4 December and remained until the 10th.

The country's third largest city, Naples, disputes with Istanbul the claim of occupying the most beautiful site in the Med. The old Italian saying "Vedi Napoli e poi muori," means, "See Naples and then die," is so familiar to tourists of all nations that it is understood by everyone. In fact, it conveys the fascination of this unparalleled city so well that it seems to reassume and exalt all that make a stay in Italy desirable.

Mount Vesuvius, famous volcano overlooking the city, is famous all over the world even though it has erupted only once in the past 23 years. The last time it was active was in 1945 when it caused only slight damage and killed comparatively few people.

Perhaps a more impressing, or should we say depressing, feature of the city in the eyes of the average sailor are the hordes of persistent street merchants and guides plying their trade. Naples seemed to have more than its share of them, trying to sell everything from cheap jewelry to imported seashells.

Built at the base and on the slopes of a ridge of hills rising from the Bay of Naples, the city occupies one of the most beautiful sites the ship visited on the entire cruise. The bay extending from Cape Miseno in the north to the Sorrento peninsula in the south, is dominated by Vesuvius and dotted with towns and villas. Near its entrance are the islands of Capri, Ischia, and Procida. A beautiful view of the city and the bay is possible from the cameo factory that is an almost inevitable stop on any guided tour in the city.

The people are definitely "American Navy conscious" because of the CINCSOUTH flag stationed permanently at Naples on board the *Adirondack*. That, coupled with the fact that almost every Sixth Fleet unit is made with several ships, makes the people much more accustomed to seeing U.S. servicemen than in many other Med. ports.

In WWII the city suffered tremendous damage. The industrial suburbs were heavily bombed by the Allies, but the worst destruc-

tion was wrought by the retreating Germans in 1943. The harbor section, now one of the best in Europe, was demolished, entire blocks disappeared, and part of the rich archives and libraries were burned.

Several overnight tours from both Genoa and Naples were conducted to Switzerland, Paris, Florence, Venice and Rome. As in the past, they were greatly enjoyed and can be termed highly successful ventures both by the men and the ship. It was in Naples, also, where the crew braved a chilly evening to watch a talented USO troupe perform on the pier alongside the *Columbus*.

Even though Sicily is an island, it is actually a part of Italy and our visit there must be included in the story of Italian ports on the *Columbus'* itinerary.

Sandwiched between our Lisbon and Geno calls was an eight-day replenishment stop at Augusta Bay. Far from a good city for liberty, the stay there did afford a different kind of recreation with the daily beach parties that were held. Many took advantage of them to stretch their legs and most of the so-called ballplayers got a sore arm tossing the ball around.

Mt. Etna, one of the famous mountains of the earth, stands only a few miles away and seems to be one of the few things of interest there.

So you can see, the *Columbus* did get a well-rounded view of every port of "the boot" on this cruise. The loyal "sons of Italy" who are attached to the ship, and there are many, really

Courtesy of E. Manista

Courtesy of E. Manista

"got a kick" out of each trip ashore as they visited relatives and had a chance to try out the language they'd heard at home.

And even for those who couldn't speak the language, sunny Italy was a country where "a good time was had by all."

TURKEY

The skyline of Istanbul, Turkey, where we arrived on 14 November 1952, was different than that of any other port we had visited previously. The many Moslem churches, called mosques, with their finger-like minarets reaching skyward made it a city in wide contrast with those we'd seen in the western part of the Med.

Anchored in the Bosphorous as she was, the ship enjoyed the unique position of having a different continent on each side. Off the port side was Europe while Asia was less than a mile to starboard.

The swift current in the Bosphorous makes boating rather difficult. Skillful work by the boat crews, however, prevented any serious injury or damage during our stay there.

Cultural and educational center of Turkey, Istanbul's influence over the course of human affairs is rivaled only by Athens, Rome, and Jerusalem. Roman law, Greek literature and the theology of the Christian church are closely associated with its history.

An amazing piece of architecture is the Mosque of Sultan Ahmet, better known as the Blue Mosque. Famous for its beautiful blue tiles and six minarets, it was built between 1609 and 1616, a time when the only mosque with six minarets was at Mecca. Sultan Ahmet silenced the objections to his sixth minaret by ordering a seventh for Mecca and keeping the sixth at his own mosque. Legend says the sultan was so impatient to see it completed that he came every Friday and worked in the midst of his laborers.

The modernization of Turkey was started by the Young Turks in 1908 when they forced the grant of a constitution. Sultan Abdul Hamid was deposed the following year. After the foreign military occupation of Turkey during WWI ended, the Turks under Ataturk cleared the country of its enemies and assured its complete independence with the treaty of Lausanne, July 1923. The Republic was proclaimed in October. The Sultanate and Caliphate were abolished and all members of the Ottoman Imperial Family left the country. The authorities of the new Republic, under the guidance of a surpassing genius, have brought about a surprising evolution in the outlook, morals and customs of the a great Asiatic nation now enrolled, with deliberation and without reserve, in the family of world states.

We'll remember with pleasure the excellent USO canteen in Istanbul which was staffed by cooperative American men and women living in the city. A touring USO troupe entertained during our visit there and were helped out each night by the able Sixth Fleet dance band.

Several basketball games were arranged between local teams and the squads of various ships present which created a great deal of interest. And this was the case despite the fact that the navy teams usually held the upper hand.

As was the case in several ports, a party one afternoon for children from one of the local orphanages. About 60 youngsters with chaperons were treated to a tour of the ship, followed by movies and refreshments in one of the mess compartments.

Yes, Turkey was different all right, but our visit to Istanbul was one we enjoyed and will remember always.

GREECE

If you're an average sailor, you'll quickly remember that in Athens, Greece, there was a USO that gave away food and drinks free. What you probably won't remember is the name of the nearby hill on top of which are a lot of broken-down stone buildings.

But if you remember or not, Athens is a city whose history dates back before Christ. The Greeks erected temples there to the various gods in the magnificent 5th century B.C. Time has dealt hard with the Acropolis but man has dealt worse. Over the ages he has used it as a handy quarry, breaking up its statues and reliefs for stone to build new walls. He stored gunpowder in some of the temples, including the Parthenon, and it blew up. Later, when man's respect for the Acropolis returned, he carted off some of its finest sculptures to the museums of Europe in sheer artistic greed. But the attrition is done, and a great bulk of the works on the Acropolis survive, still radiant with bygone perfection.

The country is chiefly an agricultural one, with little manufacturing. With American aid, however, industrial output last year was almost 20 percent better than the prewar level. Agricultural production has surpassed former output, also.

Greece rejected a surrender ultimatum from Italy in October 1940, and when attacked she threw the Italians back into Albania. Nazi support resulted in the defeat and occupation of the country by Germans, Italians and Bulgarians. By the end of 1944, the invaders withdrew. At the war's end, Communists tried to seize power and civil war resulted. They brought help from the Marshall Plan and a special investigation by the U.N. ECA help stimulated economic recovery and civil strife was proclaimed at an end on 16 October 1949.

The crew was to have "manned the rail" for a visit on board of King Paul and Queen Fredericka during our stay there but choppy seas forced a cancellation. One of the American Express tours, however, gave a few sailors a glimpse of the Royal Palace at any rate.

The USO canteen, which was mentioned earlier, was one of the better ones encountered in the Med. Located on one of the main streets of the city, it provided ample room for the large fleet present and there was music and dancing every night in addition to free chow.

A good port for the "tourist" sailor, and the "Good-time Charlie" was Athens, Greece.

FRANCE

France, the land of beautiful women and wonderful wine, once more opened its hearts and home to the sailors of the *Columbus* when the ship visited Toulon and old, familiar Villefranche on this cruise. We were in Toulon from 11-15 December and then went to the Ville for the holidays from 19 December to 5 January.

As on previous visits to Ville, many found their way to Nice for liberty, the perfume factory for bargains, and Monte Carlo for sightseeing and picture taking. While in Toulon there was little in the way of recreation, since the port seemed to compare on a small scale to Norfolk as a sailor's town. The visits to the French battleship *Richelieu* for dinner and supper each day did a great deal for morale, however.

The people of Villefranche and the Riviera sector did their best to make our Christmas and New Year celebrations a happy occasion. Most of the night spots and many of the shops were decorated and in at least one Nice store there was a St. Nicholas on hand in person. A large group of French children were entertained on board at a Christmas party, where they watched movies, enjoyed dinner and received a small gift.

Ville is a small but rather attractive town, rising in terraces along the rocky shore. The old town with staircase streets and dark archways is typical of the 18th century seaports. The harbor is one of the best between Marseille and Genoa. Situated some three or four miles from Nice, Villefranche is provided with frequent service by electric tramways and buses.

Nearby Nice, a city of little more than 200,000, is a playground for European and American vacationers during the summer. Located on the beautiful Riviera as it is, the city makes an ideal resort. The surrounding area has many beautiful regions to be explored. A continuous series of tramways follows the coast from Nice to Mentone, the most beautiful part of the French Riviera. The Grande Corniche, which is part of the great military road constructed by Napoleon I in 1806 and connects the two towns, is also an exceptionally fine drive. The distance is about 19 miles and it touches neither town nor village except La Turbie. It follows the rugged outline of the mountain face, high above the coast, and commands on the south a lovely and constantly varying panorama of the sea with its bays and promontories.

Monte Carlo, a world-famous gambling center despite the fact that the town has only a population of 9,000, is located in the tiny principality of Monaco. The entire area of Monaco is only 8-1/2 square miles, but its mild climate and magnificent scenery in addition to its gambling have made it a tourist resort and international conference city of wide renown.

Our stay in France was graced by very good weather for the time of the year, even though it wasn't quite warm enough to enjoy the sandy beaches of Nice and nearby resorts. We still had to take along peacoats, but for mid-winter it was, shall we say, warmer than Boston.

For one and all, it was a visit worth remembering. One the like of which comes all too seldom in a sailor's life.

BEIRUT, LEBANON

Lebanon is practically a brand new country, having celebrated its ninth anniversary of independence from French rule just a week before we arrived on 26 November. Stopping in Beirut with the *Columbus* was the carrier *Roosevelt* and two "cans," but still there were plenty of "swabbies" in the city and the USO canteen was crowded to capacity every night. Many Americans living in the city invited sailors to their homes also and these proposals were invariably accepted eagerly.

Beirut was a good town for sightseeing, for it is a crossroads for air routes and old caravan routes. It holds a fair sample of the whole Arab world, together with the best of the new world, showing mingled influence of Arabs, Turks, French, British, and, as a glance at the autos choking the city will prove, Americans.

The ancient ruins of Baalbek, about an hour's ride from the city provided one of the best sights for the sailors who usually took the one-day tours in every port. Not only did the town contain the greatest and most photogenic Roman temple ruins in the Middle East, but the tour also included a trip across Mt. Lebanon and into the great inland Bekaa valley between Lebanon and Syria - a really unforgettable trip through the most picturesque region of all the Arab countries.

In downtown Beirut, probably the most familiar spot was alBorj, which is a long, narrow square with large and impressive palm trees waving overhead. But other sections that many sailors found of interest included the gold market, a wide street flanked on either side with dealers in gold coins and jewelry. Much of the jewelry is also made there. In addition, the big, open air fruit, vegetable and poultry market off Parliament Square was an intriguing spot to see.

The co-educational American University, which has been of importance in the Middle East since the 1860s, sponsored a dance and social hour for the fleet several afternoons during the visit. This gave the men a rare opportunity to meet some fellow Americans, thousands of miles from home.

Although perhaps not the best port we visited, Beirut proved to be above average for the purpose of liberty and recreation.

SPAIN

Without a doubt one of the ports most enjoyed on the cruise was Barcelona, Spain. A great many men termed it the best we visited but, of course, there were others who stuck faithfully by their beloved France.

No doubt about it, though, Barcelona offered just about anything the liberty-loving sailor could ask for. Wine, women and song were in abundance and there were plenty of worthwhile souvenirs to be purchased at very reasonable prices. For those who like to just "see the lights," there was an excellent overnight trip to Madrid and a ski tour to the mountains in addition to the city tour.

Several hundred people came aboard each day to look over the ship and no doubt our visit fostered a great deal of good will. It seems fewer ships visit Spain than most of the other Mediterranean ports and the people are not accustomed to having American sailors around. Consequently, we saw few instances of "price-hiking" and it was possible to buy such things as leather goods, jewelry and clothes at costs especially low. There were instances in which five-course meals cost as little as one dollar.

It was toward the end of the cruise, 9-15 January to be exact, that the *Columbus* stopped in Barcelona along with the *Everglades*, one submarine and two destroyers.

Barcelona is the center of the chief textile manufacturing region of Spain. In addition, there are important manufacturers of foodstuffs and engineering products as well as aircraft facilities.

Spain was neutral in World War II but its relation with the Axis and its Fascist character alienated the Western Allies. Spain was excluded from the UN in 1946 and the US, France and Britain recommended the withdrawal of Franco. Also in 1946 Poland, supported by the Soviet Union, demanded breaking of relations with Spain by all UN members and in December of that year the UN recommended the withdrawal of ambassadors from the country. This was heeded by the US and major powers, but disregarded by Argentina, which cemented closer relations Spain. The International Trade Conferences denied Spain admission.

After 1948 the West saw dangers to itself in Communist agitation. On the initiative of Latin American nations and the Arab League, the UN General Assembly removed the ban on Spain. The US and Spain exchanged ambassadors and the first canvass for possible American air bases in Spanish territory was made.

ALGIERS AND TANGIER, NORTH AFRICA

North Africa, especially Algiers, where the *Columbus* visited from 16-22 January, is a place where the old world seems to meet the new. A great deal of ancient customs and culture of the Arabs remains despite the fact that WWII accomplished much toward the westernization of that area.

The Acropolis, Athens, Greece, 1954. Courtesy of Ronald Dolinsky.

The world-famous Casbah of Algiers is a place of absolute filth, degradation and poverty, yet it never ceases to attract tourists and it somehow lends an air of mystery and enchantment all its own. Hedy Lamar and Charles Boyer made a movie there not many years ago.

Algiers, it could be said, is made up of two distinct cities. The Arab section, made up mostly of the Casbah, and the European or western area downtown are two widely varying sectors. The European section is made up of fine shops, eating places and entertainment spots on streets not unlike those in our own large cities. Neon lights are abundant and the bustling crowds along the main avenues remind one of the "store night" back home.

It was in that port that the *Newport News* relieved the *Columbus* and "El Supremo" did such a great job of welcoming it to the Med. Everyone agreed that the *Columbus* outdid the relieving ceremony which we received in Lisbon last October. The entire starboard side covered with gaily painted banners and signs, Admiral "El Supremo" Johnston and his court, and the weirdly uniformed crew did much to put the *Newport News* crew right in the spirit of the day (from our point of view).

We had expected to stay in Algiers until ready to return to the States but a last minute change in plans took us to Tangier to finish our Med. cruise. The ship was there from 23-26 January.

Tangier is located in an international colony controlled by four countries. Its strategic location at the very gateway to the Mediterranean has always made it a desirable possession of any country. It is a melting pot for people of Europe, Asia, Africa and even the Western Hemisphere and a large amount of trade is carried on there despite the fact that the harbor is a small one, filled mostly with small fishing boats. Smuggling black-market goods into Southern Europe seems to be one of the main occupations at present.

Liberty was enjoyed in both cities, but by the time we reached North Africa a large number of men were thinking only of the States and consequently saving money for home and leave.

1953

Admiral Cassady left the ship in January 1953 when *Columbus* returned to the United States. In the course of the Mediterranean Cruise, informal visits were made to 12 ports in Europe and Africa. Dignitaries from various countries, including the President of the Republic of Lebanon were among the long lists of notables to visit on board. The cruiser returned to the Boston Naval Shipyard on 3 February 1953.

On 9 March, she sailed to Guantanamo Bay for gunnery exercises and various drills as part of an extensive training program. Coveted Navy "E" awards were won by all three of *Columbus'* turrets. En route to Boston, the ship conducted special tests with the ammunition ship *Great Sitkin* (AE-17), to determine the effectiveness of the constant tension winch. She arrived in Boston on 11 April 1953 for a small scale leave and up-keep period. 2 May found the *Columbus* at sea again, this time as fire support ship for amphibious maneuvers off Onslow Beach, North Carolina. En route to Boston arriving 15 May, the cruiser spent four days in New York City.

In the period 17 May to July, the cruiser conducted several Navy Reserve Training Cruises and underwent her scheduled Operational Readiness Inspection.

Columbus sailed from Boston on 14 July, arriving two days later at Norfolk, Virginia for the Midshipmen Cruise "Charlie." A total of 364 NROTC Midshipmen boarded the cruiser for a six week training cruise. Six civilian guests including educators and newspaper publishers also came aboard for the trip. On 20 July, *Columbus*, with ten other ships, including the light cruiser USS *Roanoke* (CL-145), carrying RADM Richard P. Glass, Cruise Commander, left for the Caribbean area.

The Midshipmen were on board the *Columbus* until 28 August for training in various phases of naval operations including classroom instructions as well as actual experience working with the officers and men of the ship's company. During the cruise, liberty was enjoyed in Colon, Panama; Trinidad, British West Indies; and the US Naval Base, Guantanamo Bay, Cuba.

Dispatching her NROTC Midshipmen in Norfolk on 28 August, *Columbus* proceeded and arrived in Boston on 1 September. She remained in Boston until 17 September when she departed for Guantanamo Bay for more gunnery exercises. From 21-25 September she participated in NAGEX 1-54, a fire support exercise conducted at Culebra Island, Puerto Rico.

In later exercises, Navy "E"s were earned by eight 3-inch gun mounts and two 3-inch battery directors. At Culebra, where *Columbus* scored 99.2 points out of a possible 100 in the best night illumination firing ever witnessed by Culebra observers, she completed her drills and returned to Boston on 15 October for a leave and upkeep period which lasted until 2 November.

In the latter part of November, RADM Richard L. Denison, Commander Cruiser Division Four, boarded the ship to make *Columbus* his flagship until 21 December.

1954

In January, *Columbus* again embarked for Guantanamo Bay for "Operation Springboard," a three week' series of operational readiness exercises, involving other ships of the Atlantic Fleet, designed to test the preparedness of the individual units - operating alone and as a group.

On 28 January, two days after the *Columbus* went into dry-dock in the Boston Naval Shipyard, Captain Blinn VanMater, USN, relieved Captain Luther K. Reynolds, USN as Commanding Officer.

The yard period ended 21 June and with its completion could be seen a tremendous re-outfitting and remodeling job. New equipment for increased battle efficiency and new furniture and fittings for more comfort brought the cruiser up-to-date as one of the most modern ships in her class. The interior of the ship saw many changes, too, with complete revamping of the crew's messing and lounge areas.

On 21 June 1954, *Columbus* headed south to Cuban waters for a six weeks' refresher cruise. Mid-term battle problems, an administrative inspection, and operational readiness inspection, independent ship's exercises, and instruction by the Fleet Training Group were some of the more important operations designed to train and test the ship.

On the last two days of July, the heavy cruiser put in to St. Thomas, Virgin Islands for a brief visit. En route to Boston, *Columbus* visited New York City for six days, giving all hands ample opportunity to enjoy a well-deserved liberty after a good showing in the Caribbean.

Scenes from Greece, November 1954. Courtesy of Ronald Dolinsky.

Boarding the Columbus for a Midshipman's Cruise, Norfolk, VA, Summer 1954. Gene Ellis at far right.

Columbus then returned to Boston for a short leave period before departing on a five month tour of duty in the Mediterranean.

On 7 September 1954, the heavy cruiser departed her homeport of Boston with RADM D.C. Varian, Commander Destroyer Flotilla Two, for a five month tour of duty with the U.S. Sixth Fleet in the Mediterranean.

Columbus arrived in Lisbon, Portugal on 22 September, her first port of call prior to entering Mediterranean waters. Upon arrival, RADM Varian departed *Columbus* and broke his flag in USS *McCard* (DD-882).

On 27 September, *Columbus* left Lisbon and headed eastward into the Mediterranean.

During her months in these foreign waters, she was flagship to RADM Arleigh A. Burke, Commander Cruiser Division Six and his relief RADM Edward N. Parker. *Columbus* also had a change of commanding officers when, in Izmir, Turkey, Captain J.D.L. Grant assumed command.

Columbus' operating schedule between ports was heavy and she was an important agent in the Italic, Hellenic, and Turkish Skies Operations.

Another important assignment given all U.S. ships operating with the Sixth Fleet - that of good will ambassadors - was successfully completed by the *Columbus*. In each port visited, *Columbus'* officers and men played host to various orphanages and prior to leaving the Mediterranean area, represented the U.S. Armed Forces in the presentation of a huge Christmas Food Gift to several charitable institutions of Cagliari, Sardinia.

During her five months cruise, CA-74 visited and made friends in Lisbon, Algiers, Genoa, Marseille, Athens, Izmir, Leghorn, Naples, Toulon, Palma and Gibraltar.

At the foot of the "Great Rock" (Gibraltar), *Columbus* was relieved of her Mediterranean duties by the USS *Iowa* (BB-61). The *Columbus* was scheduled to go home.

1955

The cruiser returned to the United States at the end of January 1955 for a month's stay in her homeport of Boston prior to departing on another assignment along the Atlantic sea coast.

In March 1955, Columbus steamed into the Caribbean waters and made a good-will visit to Havana, Cuba. The Columbus is commanded by Captain J.D.L. Grant of Cocoa-Rockledge, FL.

The USS Columbus earned the Navy Occupation Service Medal, Pacific, for the periods 8 to 11 January, 26 February to 2 April, and 24 May to 1 June. She earned the China Service Medal for the periods 13 to 25 January, and 7 February 1946 to 23 May 1947. The ship also earned the Navy Occupation Service Medal, Europe, for the periods 27 June to 13 July 1948, 23 September to 28 October 1948, 30 October 1948 to 13 August 1949, 22 June 1950 to 26 September 1951, 30 October 1952 to January 1953, and 20 September 1954 to 17 January 1955.

Columbus, together with other elements of the Atlantic Fleet, embarked 6 June on "Midshipman Cruise Able" which took them to ports in Spain, England and Cuba.

As of 8 November the Columbus changed duty from the Atlantic to the Pacific Fleet. Her new homeport changed to Long Beach, CA.

1956

On 5 January 1956 USS *Columbus* (CA-74) departed Long Beach, California and employed for a normal tour of rotational duty in WESTPAC. The movement to the Far Eastern waters was made in company with Cruiser Division Three under the command of RADM F.D. McCorkle. En route *Columbus* stopped at Pearl Harbor, T.H., for two days before proceeding to Yokosuka, Japan. The division arrived on 26 January.

On 10 February Captain George C. Seay, USN, relieved Captain J.D.L. Grant, USN, of command of *Columbus*. The next day, RADM F.D. McCorkle, Commander Cruiser Division Three, embarked *Columbus*, departed Yokosuka for initial operations with the Seventh Fleet as a participant in NAVMARLEX off of Muko Jima and Iwo Jima. Commanding Officer of the *Columbus* was CTU 90.3.1 during this NAVMARLEX. On 20 February, following detachment, *Columbus* proceeded to Buckner Bay, Okinawa, arriving 24 February. On 27 February she proceeded to Hong Kong B.C.C., arriving on 2 March, and departing 8 March, to rendezvous with Task Force 77 for operations in the South China Sea.

On 11 March, while steaming in the company of Task Force 77, *Columbus*, as guide, was involved in a collision with the USS *Floyd B. Parks* (DD-884) at 0359. Damage to the *Columbus* was relatively minor and she escorted the *Parks* into Subic Day, P.I., for repairs.

Having completed repairs and made ready for sea, *Columbus* got underway for Zamboanga, P.I., on 28 March. The heavy cruiser anchored in the Basilan Straits on 31 March and remained there until 4 April when the ship again got underway for Manila, P.I. On 6 April *Columbus* anchored in Manila Bay for three days liberty. After a brief return to Subic Bay, P.I., *Columbus* rendezvoused with Task Force 77 for fleet exercises. During these operations, the heavy cruiser spent a large portion of the time employed on picket ship station. Having completed exercises, *Columbus* proceeded to Nagasaki, Japan, arriving there 27 April for a three day visit, participating in the Annual Port Festival. 30 April found the heavy cruiser proceeding toward a rendezvous with other Seventh Fleet units for Task Force operations. These operations completed, *Columbus* moored at India Pier, U.S. Naval Base, Sasebo, Japan, on 5 May for a period of two days. On 9 May she returned to Yokosuka, Japan, for a routine upkeep period.

The *Columbus* departed Yokosuka on 22 May, en route to rendezvous with the Task Force 77. After several days of operations and exercises, during which she was again employed as a picket ship, she anchored at Buckner Bay, Okinawa, in the early morning of 2 June. On the same day Captain G. Wales, USN, Commanding Officer of the USS *Worcester* (CL-144), relieved RADM F.D.

Valencia, Spain, Summer 1955 Midshipman Cruise, King Division Shipmates. Top Row : R. Eichenlaub, Lloyd Kingery. Bottom Row: Unknown, Dean Whiting, R. Schwagler. Courtesy of Lloyd Kingery.

Nagasaki, Japan, April 27, 1956. Courtesy of Billy Kirby.

McCorkle, USN, as Commander Cruiser Division Three and hoisted his broad command pennant in *Worcester*.

The relieving ceremonies having been completed and after two days liberty, the *Columbus* got underway for Port Swettenham, Malaya, in connection with a good-will visit of courtesy to that country. During a short stop at Subic Bay, P.I., RADM C.K. Bergin, USN Commander Destroyer Flotilla Western Pacific, broke his flag in the *Columbus*. On 13 June the heavy cruiser, in company with the USS *Insherwood* (DD-520) and the USS *Braine* (DD-630), which had joined shortly after departure from Subic Bay, arrived at Port Swettenham. On 15 June *Columbus* got underway continuing her visit to Malaya. The vessel anchored at Penang on 16 June. On 18 June RADM C.K. Bergin, USN, shifted his flag to *Braine,* and *Columbus* parted company with *Braine* and *Isherwood*, and proceeded to Guam, Mariana Islands, independently.

After refueling at Singapore, B.C.C., the ship arrived at Guam Island on 25 June. At Singapore the USS *Roanoke* (CL—145) relieved USS *Columbus* (CA-74) of Seventh Fleet duties and the *Columbus* got underway for Continental United States via Pearl Harbor, T.H.

Arriving at Pearl Harbor, T.H., on 1 July, *Columbus* departed on 3 July as a unit of Task Unit 52.3.4 in company with the USS *Helena* (CA-75). Following arrival at Long Beach, California on 8 July *Columbus* was assigned a leave and upkeep period of approximately one month.

From 6 August to 24 September the *Columbus* participated in Type Training off the Southern California coast and provided shore bombardment services at San Clemente Island for the Fleet Gunnery Support School.

The *Columbus* got underway for Naval Ammunition Depot, Mare Island, CA, on 24 September for the purpose of offloading ammunition prior to entering the San Francisco Naval Shipyard for a regular overhaul period. Having completed the off-loading of ammunition, she proceeded toward Hunter's Point Shipyard, arriving there on 26 September.

For the remainder of the calendar year, *Columbus* was at San Francisco Naval Shipyard, undergoing regular overhaul.

1957

On 1 January 1957 the USS *Columbus* was in the Hunter's Point Naval Shipyard in San Francisco, California finishing up her regular shipyard overhaul. She departed on 17 January and arrived back in her home port, Long Beach on 18 January. The rest of the month was spent in type training off the Southern California coast, and then on 4 February she reported to the Commander Fleet Training Group in San Diego for refresher training. Her four weeks were completed on 8 March and from then until 26 March the *Columbus* again operated in type training exercises out of Long Beach. Two important events took place during this period which should be noted. On 15 March Captain George C. Seay was relieved as Commanding Officer by Captain Gordon A. Uehling, and on 22 March Commander Cruiser Division Three, RADM U.S.G. Sharp Jr. shifted his flag from the USS *Helena* to the USS *Columbus*.

On 10 April 1957 the *Columbus* departed Long Beach, California and deployed for a normal tour of rotational duty in the Western Pacific. On 16 April *Columbus*, in company with

Cruiser Division Three, arrived in Pearl Harbor. From there the *Columbus* with Destroyer Division 212 went south to Melbourne, Australia to participate in the Annual Coral Sea Celebrations, stopping on 29 April in Suva, the capital of the Fiji Islands.

From Melbourne regular ports of call were visited with the exception of a stop in Manus, a member of the Admiralty chain. On 20 May *Columbus* arrived in Guam. Four days later she de-

Scenes of the conversion, 1959-1961

parted for Muko Shima and several days of shore bombardment exercises, moving on to Yokosuka on 1 June. On 12 June she proceeded to rendezvous with other Seventh Fleet units for Task Force operations. Following detachment *Columbus* stopped in Kobe, Japan for two days and on 30 June proceeded to Hong Kong B.C.C. arriving on 5 July. She departed on 12 July for more Task Force operations off Okinawa, and this time stopped in Keelung, Taiwan for a one day good-will visit. From there she went to Sasebo, Japan, 24 July; Nagasaki, Japan on 3 August; and arrived back at Kobe on 16 August. On Saturday, 17 August 1957 RADM M.H. Hubbard relieved RADM U.S.G. Sharp Jr. as Commander Cruiser Division Three.

Typhoon Agnes interrupted the stay at Kobe and the *Columbus* again put to sea, arriving back in port on 23 August, this time in Buckner Bay, Okinawa. From there she returned to Yokosuka for a two week restricted shipyard availability, leaving on 20 September for Chinhae, South Korea. En route she went through the Shimonoseki Straits and arrived in South Korea on 23 September. A last stop was made in Yokohoma, where Cruiser Division Three was relieved by Cruiser Division Five, and on 7 October the *Columbus* returned to CONUS reaching Long Beach on 19 October.

The remainder of the year was spent in leave and upkeep except for two weeks in December when the *Columbus* participated in the striking fleet exercises and in type training.

1958

January 1958 to July 1958 found the *Columbus* operating out of her normal home port of Long Beach, engaging in type training and other exercises on the West Coast.

On 4 April 1958 Captain G.A. Uehling was relieved as Commanding Officer by Captain Ralph C. Johnson.

On 16 July the *Columbus* deployed for a normal tour of duty in Western Pacific waters. The ports visited by the ship on this tour included Pearl Harbor; Guam, M.I.; Keelun, Taiwan; Kaohsiung, Taiwan; Yokosuka, Japan: Subic Bay, P.I.; Manila, P.I.; Hong Kong, B.C.C.; and Sasebo, Japan.

On this tour, the *Columbus*, as a unit of the Seventh Fleet, operated in the Taiwan Straits in support of Chinese Nationalist ships delivering supplies to the offshore islands of Quemoy and Matsu.

On 12 December 1958, RADM Miles H. Hubbard was relieved by RADM Vernon L. Lowrance as Commander of Cruiser Division Three, and on 19 December 1958, Captain Johnson was relieved as Commanding Officer by Captain Thomas H. Morton.

The year of 1958 came to a close with the *Columbus* in port in Sasebo, Japan.

1959–1961

The USS Columbus is at Bremerton, Washington being converted from Heavy Cruiser (CA-74) to the Missile Cruiser (CG-12).

1962

Crew members who served aboard the heavy cruiser USS *Columbus* before she underwent conversion to become a guided missile cruiser at the Puget Sound Naval Shipyard, Bremerton, Washington, will never recognize her as being the same ship.

Columbus, due to be commissioned at appropriate ceremonies to be held at 2:30 p.m., Saturday, 1 December, in Drydock #6, Puget Sound Naval Shipyard, has been completely "face-lifted," from bow to stern, from keel to the top of the mast. The only remaining parts of the "old" *Columbus* are the engineering systems and the hull itself. Even the hull designation number has been changed, from CA-74 to CG-12.

The entire superstructure was removed by yard workmen to make way for a new superstructure bristling with guided missile launchers and radar antenna. This new superstructure, along with the new "mack" (a new word combining "mast" and "stack"), gives the *Columbus* a strange, radical appearance - the ship is now seemingly top-heavy, however, this is not the case. Almost exclusive use of aluminum for superstructure fabrication cuts the topside weight considerably.

From the keel to the top of the mast, the *Columbus* measures 217' 6" higher than aircraft carriers of the *Coral Sea* class. Her overall length is 673 feet.

The mast, which is atop the forward "mack," is collapsible, making it possible for the ship to steam into almost any seaport in the world. Due to the low spans of some bridges at the entrances to harbors, such as New York City's "Hell's Gate Bridge," it would have been impossible for the *Columbus* to enter port without the collapsible mast.

As a heavy cruiser, the *Columbus'* armament consisted of nine 8"/55's as the main battery and twelve 5"/38's for anti-aircraft. The "new" *Columbus* is armed with three missile systems: two for anti-aircraft work and one for antisubmarine warfare. Two separate twin TALOS launchers are mounted on the port and starboard sides of the ship. The antisubmarine rocket propelled torpedo ASROC gives the *Columbus* outstanding long-range antisubmarine capabilities. The only "guns" aboard the *Columbus* are various small arms and one 40mm saluting battery.

Inclement weather is no longer a problem to the officers and men standing watch on the bridge of the *Columbus*. The entire bridge area has been enclosed with glass windows affording unrestricted visibility in all directions. What amounts to a miniature reproduction of the combat information center is located on the bridge, providing the commanding officer with an accurate, up-to-the-minute "picture" of the developing combat situation.

The *Columbus* has been redesigned to accommodate a larger afloat flag officer's staff. All of these requirements have been met through the use of spaces in the "mack." Additional spaces in the "mack" are devoted entirely to radar, communications, and other facilities essential not only to the efficient operation of the ship, but necessary for the functioning of the Admiral's staff. In addition, to facilitate rapid movement from the main deck to the eighth level above the main deck (the bridge), a personnel elevator with room for six persons has been installed.

A completely different type crew is required for manning the new *Columbus*. Guided missile technicians replace many gunner's mates to handle the intricate procedures for launching and maintaining the exotic guided missiles and guidance systems. A greater number of men in the electronics, communications and radar fields are required due to the greatly expanded communications and radar facilities.

Living conditions for officers and enlisted men are vastly improved. All Department Heads are provided with individual staterooms, and junior officers double up in staterooms as large as those for commanding officers on destroyers. All of the quarters are furnished with the newest type shipboard furniture including transom bunks, individual desks and lockers and stateroom telephones.

Enlisted berthing spaces are greatly modernized for habitability. Bunks are no longer stacked in tiers of four and five. The majority are double bunks with a few in tiers of three. Lockers are not to be seen in the compartments. The tops of the bunks lift up to reveal each man's locker beneath his foam rubber mattress. Bunks are separated by aluminum partitions to afford more individual privacy. Each bunk also has an individual reading lamp. All berthing compartments have adjacent toilet and shower facilities. And, perhaps best of all, from the crew's standpoint, all working and living spaces are air conditioned.

The ship's own radio station can pipe continuous music, news and other type programs into each compartment of the ship. These accommodations are in addition to the four-chair barber shop, the ship's retail store and the always popular soda fountain.

Also introduced aboard the *Columbus* is a Central Control Station. This station combines all of the engineering watches in a central part of the ship, away from the noise and confusion of the engine rooms. During the ship's drills this area will be bustling with activity with the engineering watches and numerous telephone talkers assembled to watch the many dials and instrument panels giving readings direct from the engineering spaces.

The *Columbus*, although a cruiser, also has an Air Department. Two helicopters are housed aboard for personnel transfer and sea rescue purposes. They are kept astern, below decks in a hangar which also houses complete maintenance facilities. To get the helicopters to the main deck for takeoff, an elevator similar to those on aircraft carriers is used.

A full complement of doctors and hospital corpsmen are carried for caring for the sick and injured. A seven-bed hospital ward is provided in addition to an isolation ward. Also available in the medical department is a modern operating room to be used in case of emergencies at sea. Many spaces, such as the barber shop and chief petty officer's lounge may be converted into emergency medical stations during wartime.

The *Columbus* is the third cruiser being converted to a guided missile cruiser. The USS *Albany* is undergoing conversion at Boston, and the USS *Chicago* is being converted at San Francisco. Recommissioning date for the Albany was 3 November 1962, and the *Chicago*, February 1964.

1963

During 1963, *Columbus* was further modernized with the addition of the AN/SPS-30 long range air search radar and two single-mounted five-inch 38-cal. guns. The Combat Information Center was reorganized for greater efficiency.

Movements included a four month cruise to the San Diego area between April and July. Missile firings with the Pacific Missile Range were conducted and the ship participated in the 1963 Presidential review. In November *Columbus* departed Bremerton, Washington for the last time, arriving at her new home port for acceptance trails and training. During December the ship was host to the Honorable Paul Nitze, who replaced Fred Korth as Secretary of the Navy.

CDR R.K. Rosemont relieved CDR W.R. Munroe as Executive Officer in July.

1964

No narrative history available. See Chronological history.

1965

During her tour in the Western Pacific, 5 August 1964 to 6 February 1965, *Columbus* operated extensively in the South China Sea. As a result of these operations during the period 3 September to 16 October, all personnel who were on board at least six days of that period were awarded the Armed Forces Expeditionary Medal. *Columbus* visited the islands of Hawaii, Guam, Midway and the Philippines; the country of Japan and the British Crown Colony of Hong Kong.

In March 1965 *Columbus* was back in her homeport and on 19 March 1965 was host to a Public Affairs Cruise for 68 members of various Navy League councils in the Southern California area. Events that day included a missile run-out demonstration and AA firing by the guided missile destroyer *Robison*, the burial-at-sea ceremony of a retired Navy Chief Petty Officer and a refueling demonstration with the oiler *Ashtabula*.

On 22 March 1965 Secretary of Defense Robert McNamara announced that as a result of competitive firing *Columbus* was awarded three "E's." Two of the awards were earned by a TALOS director and one by a TARTAR director. He also announced that *Columbus* was scheduled to be transferred to the Atlantic Fleet early in 1966.

One hundred sixty-one *Columbus* men were advanced in rate during the period of 16 May through 16 October 1965, as the result of the February exams, a total of almost 50% of all those crew members who took the tests.

During the period of 14 June through 3 August 1965, the *"Tall Lady"* hosted a Midshipmen Cruise. The ports Seattle, Washington; San Francisco, California; and Pearl Harbor, Hawaii were visited. Of the 210 Midshipmen on board, some were NROTC students from various universities around the United States while others were from the U.S. Naval Academy in Annapolis, Maryland.

From 3 August through 30 October 1965, *Columbus* participated in only two major fleet exercises. The first of which was "Operation Ragweed." This at-sea operation, which lasted a week, was followed shortly by a similar operation called "Baseline." Their primary missions were to test the operational readiness of units of the Pacific Fleet.

1 November 1965, found the *"Tall Lady"* en route to the San Francisco Naval Shipyard for her regular repair period and restricted availability. During this period *Columbus* received a new Executive Officer when Commander Victor G. Warriner relieved Commander R.D. Wood on 15 November. One hundred and ninety-three cruiser men were advanced in rate during the period of 16 November to 16 April as a result of the August servicewide examinations. Of this total over 31 percent of those crew members who took the tests were advanced. Rear Admiral John McNay Taylor, Commander Western Sea Frontier, presented 132 certificates to *Columbus* men at a Meritorious Mast on 23 November. *Columbus* departed San Francisco and the Naval Shipyard on 11 December to return to her homeport of San Diego were she remained throughout the Christmas holiday period until leaving her old homeport for the last time. Her new homeport was to be Norfolk, Virginia to join units of the Atlantic Fleet.

1966

COMMAND ORGANIZATION AND RELATIONS

On Friday, 4 March, while *Columbus* was underway from New York City to Norfolk, Virginia, Captain Lewis J. Stecher Jr. relieved Captain Royal K. Joslin as Commanding Officer. Captain Stecher came to *Columbus* from Washington D.C., where he served as Project Manager of the TARTAR Missile System, within the Surface Missile System Organization. Captain Joslin, who had commanded *Columbus* since 12 October 1964, reported to Washington D.C. where he was assigned to the Office of the Chief of Naval Operations.

Columbus changed homeports early in the year, leaving San Diego, California on 10 January and arriving in Norfolk, Virginia on 21 February, departing the First Fleet for the Second Fleet and the control of Cruisers-Destroyers Pacific for Cruisers-Destroyers Atlantic.

Columbus' mission as a guided missile cruiser is to be capable of independent or combined operations against air, surface or subsurface threats. Her functions are: to provide area defense for a task force with guided missiles; to destroy ships, air and shore targets by use of existing missile systems; to operate and support helicopters; to control aircraft; to operate aggressively against and destroy submarines; to provide facilities and accommodations for task group commander and his staff. *Columbus* acted as flagship for Commander CruiserDestroyer Flotilla EIGHT from 21 February until 25 November when the USS *Shangri La* (CVA-38) temporarily became the Flagship.

Columbus' complement at the end of the year included 970 enlisted men and 70 officers. Among these were three officers and seven enlisted men attached to Helicopter Support Squadron - 45, with their aircraft, a UH-2B, number 152204.

OPERATIONS

Columbus departed her homeport of San Diego, California on 10 January 1966 and began her cruise to Norfolk, Virginia. Her first port of call en route was Acapulco, Mexico where she happily languished for three days. Upon entering the Harbor of Acapulco on 14 January, a 21 gun salute was rendered. During her stay *Columbus* conducted general visiting and a total of 1,508 visitors were brought aboard. Upon departing Acapulco, Mexico, *Columbus* circled the harbor giving a farewell to the Mexicans and steamed southward to Balboa, Panama. During the transit man overboard drills and General Quarters drills were conducted. Upon entering Balboa on 21 January, a surprise NORAD AAWEX was conducted. *Columbus* encountered high density raids from aircraft and received a "well done" from Commanding General Norad, as she detected all raids and simulated opposing same with missiles. Liberty was granted for the crew in Balboa on 21 January.

Columbus commenced the transit of the Panama Canal on 22 January with a group of 50 military personnel and dependents embarked. While in the fresh water of Lake Gatun *Columbus* activated her water washdown system. After disembarking her passengers *Columbus* sailed northeast for Kingston, Jamaica arriving on 24 January for a three day stay during which period liberty was granted to the crew. On 27 January *Columbus* sailed to Guantanamo Bay, Cuba and arrived the same day. During the period 27-31 January conferences were conducted with the fleet training group in preparation for underway refresher training. The arrival inspection was conducted 28 January and the underway training was conducted from 1-9 February. On 9 February *Columbus* conducted an Operational Readiness Inspection of the USS *Albany* (CG-10). On 10 February *Columbus* received the battle problem given by the Fleet Training Group.

Columbus departed Guantanamo Bay on 11 February and arrived at Roosevelt Roads, Puerto Rico the next day. Fire control system alignment was conducted until 15 February when *Columbus* got underway for the Atlantic Fleet Weapons Range. On 16 February *Columbus* fired three TALOS missiles, one of which scored fired with one success, a single TARTAR missile was also fired but was scored a failure. On 18 February after an overnight say in St. Thomas, Virgin Islands, *Columbus* fired two TALOS and two TARTAR missiles with one success being achieved by a TARTAR, for a total of 8 TALOS fired with 2 "kills" and TARTAR fired with one "kill."

After the missile firings on the 18th *Columbus* sailed for Norfolk, Virginia and arrived at her new homeport on the 21st. Upon arrival *Columbus* moored next to the USS *Albany* (CG-10) and commenced embarking Commander Cruiser-Destroyer Flotilla Eight and his staff from the *Albany*. *Columbus* left Norfolk on 24 February and arrived in Newport, Rhode Island on the 25th and remained there for three days, during which time Captain Lewis J. Stecher Jr., prospective Commanding Officer, reported aboard.

Columbus departed Newport on 28 February for New York City, arriving on 1 March. *Columbus* stayed in New York for three days during which time liberty was granted. *Columbus* departed New York on 4 March and at 1300 that day Captain Lewis J. Stecher Jr. relieved Captain Royal K. Joslin as Commanding Officer. *Columbus* arrived in Norfolk on 5 March and the period 5 March to 21 March was a leave and upkeep period. *Columbus* got underway for the Virginia Capes operating area on 21 March for ASW training with the USS *Atule* (SS-403) which included firing practice units of ASROC and deck launched torpedoes. *Columbus* returned to Norfolk on 1 April for a leave and upkeep period until 25 April when she got underway for Yorktown, Virginia where missiles and ammunition were loaded, until 26 April when she returned to Norfolk. On 2 May, in company with the USS *Yarnell* and USS *Runner*, *Columbus* got underway for the Caribbean, conducting training exercises in the Virginia Capes Operating Area en route. *Columbus* pulled into Roosevelt Roads, Puerto Rico on 7 May and remained until 9 May when she got underway for the Atlantic Fleet Weapons Range to conduct missile firings. On the 9th and 10th of May five TARTAR and two TALOS missiles were fired. The five TARTAR shots resulted in four "kills" and one missile failure. Four of the TARTARS were fired in two-missile salvoes utilizing both launchers. These are considered the first two-missile salvoes armed with warheads that have been fired. One of the two TALOS fired resulted in a kill.

Upon completion of the missile firings on 11 May, *Columbus* anchored at St. Thomas, Virgin Islands and remained until 13 May when she returned to Norfolk, arriving on the 16th. On the 19th *Columbus* was underway again for New York City and a three day stay from 20 through 23 of May, during which time general visiting was conducted and liberty was granted for the crew. *Columbus* returned to Norfolk and remained there from 24 May to 8 June when she steamed to Annapolis to embark 273 Midshipmen for their annual training cruise. *Columbus* returned to Norfolk from 10-14 June when she got underway to participate in Operation Beach Time as a unit of Task Group 23.2 with a simulated mission to neutralize the airfield at Roosevelt Roads, Puerto Rico with a nuclear missiles strike. *Columbus'* Marine Detachment was attached to COMPHIDGRU TWO for the exercise and sent to the beach to enact the part of the rebel forces. The Detachment received a Let-

ter of Appreciation from COMPHIBGRU TWO for their part in the exercise. *Columbus* operated independently as a single strike unit to conduct a surprise strike on Roosevelt Roads Air Station while the remainder of Task Group 23.2 conducted deception operations. *Columbus* conducted the simulated attacks on the objective on 18 June. The ship was evaluated as "effective" in her role as she was not detected by opposing forces. *Columbus* anchored at St. Thomas on 18 June and remained there until the 20th when she got underway for the Atlantic Fleet Weapons Range. On the 20th and 21st of June she fired three TALOS and two TARTAR missiles at the range with one TARTAR and one TALOS scoring hits. After completion of missile firings, *Columbus* departed the weapons range for Yorktown, Virginia. Anti-Air Warfare exercises were conducted in support of Operation Beach Time en route. *Columbus* arrived at Yorktown on 27 June and commenced transferring missiles. Missile transfer was completed the same day and *Columbus* departed for Norfolk arriving that evening.

Columbus remained in port from 27 June to 21 July conducting training for the midshipmen and preparing for her annual Admin and POM inspection. On 21 July the ship got underway for Annapolis with the USS *Forest Royal* (DD-872) to exchange the midshipmen still on board for a new group of 26 first-class midshipmen. *Columbus* arrived on 22 July and departed Annapolis the same day for Baltimore, Maryland for a three day port visit which included large crowds who turned out for general visiting. *Columbus* departed Baltimore on 25 July and arrived in Norfolk the same day.

On 1 August RADM John D. Bulkeley relieved RADM Fred G. Bennett as Commander Cruiser-Destroyer Flotilla Eight. During the period immediately preceding the change of command ceremony held on the fantail, *Columbus* underwent her annual Admin and POM inspection given by the USS *Newport News*. *Columbus* received a numerical grade of 94 and an adjective grade of "Outstanding."

On 4 August *Columbus* departed Norfolk for a NATO exercise in the North Atlantic known as Operation Straight Laced. During this time electronic silence was set with the exception of the Raytheon 1500B "Pathfinder" radar. Task Group 401.3 was formed on 5 August. *Columbus* rendezvoused with the USS *Newport News* (CA-148) with COMSTRIKLANT (COMSECONDFLT) embarked. Electronic silence was lifted 12 August to evaluate the effect of prolonged periods of inactivity on the weapons system performance. Electronic silence was reset the same day. *Columbus* rendezvoused with the HMS *Ark Royal* and the HMS *London* on 13 August. The Strike Force commenced simulated strikes against Norway on 15 August with *Columbus* in AAW picket station. At 1100 on 15 August a Soviet TU 116 (Badger), aircraft was visually sighted by *Columbus*. On 16 August a Soviet "BEAR" aircraft was visually identified. On the same day *Columbus* was shadowed by a Soviet AGI VAL during fueling operations in the vicinity of 63-06 N, 01-18W from 1200 to 1230.

Columbus arrived in Rotterdam, The Netherlands on 21 August for an in-port period which lasted until 26 August. During the visit liberty was granted for the crew and general visiting was conducted. Several receptions for *Columbus* officers were held, including a reception by the Burgermeister followed by a "Taptoe" performed by the Dutch Royal Marine Corps. *Columbus* departed Rotterdam on 26 August for Norfolk, Virginia via the English Channel. The ship encountered high winds and heavy seas on 1 September and diverted South to avoid worse weather and arrived in Norfolk on 3 September.

Columbus departed Norfolk on 27 September for deployment to the SIXTH Fleet in the Mediterranean, via Roosevelt Roads,

Puerto Rico, St. Thomas and the Atlantic Fleet Weapons Range. Task Group 25.7 was formed at this time. *Columbus* arrived at Roosevelt Roads on 30 September and aligned weapons systems until 3 October when missile firings were conducted at the Atlantic Fleet Weapons Range. Two TARTAR missiles were fired on the third and both were successful. On the fourth, four TALOS missiles were fired with one "kill." *Columbus* anchored at St. Thomas for the night of 4 October, getting underway the following morning for the Atlantic transit.

The Straits of Gibraltar were passed on 14 October and *Columbus* reported for duty with the Sixth Fleet. On 15 October *Columbus* moored alongside the USS *Albany* (CG-10) at Pollensa Bay, Majorca and commenced the process of relieving. COMCRUDESPLOT EIGHT assumed duties as CTG 60.2 at this time. *Columbus* left Pollensa Bay on the 15th and steamed across the Tyrrhenian Sea conducting exercises en route to Naples. During the transit, *Columbus* encountered the Soviet *Agi Lossman* during fueling operations. The *Agi* steamed a parallel course on *Columbus'* port beam at a distance of 500 yards.

On 22 October *Columbus* "Med Moored" for the first time in her history as CG-12 at Naples, Italy. *Columbus* was in-port from 22-31 October during which time liberty was granted for the crew and normal maintenance of equipment was continued. *Columbus* departed Naples for Valletta, Malta on the 31st with operations in the Tyrrhenian Sea scheduled en route. *Columbus* arrived at Valletta on 8 November and departed on the 14th for Catania, Sicily where she arrived the same day. Local television and newspaper coverage was given to *Columbus'* visit to both ports and receptions were warm and friendly.

Columbus departed Catania on 17 November and continued her operations with Task Group 60.2e in the Tyrrhenian and Ionian Seas until 25 November when she pulled into the training anchorage in Navplion, Greece. During the stay at Navplion *Columbus* conducted normal in-port training and general maintenance. *Columbus* departed Navplion on 28 November and steamed across the Aegean Sea to Izmir, Turkey arriving on 30 November. In Izmir receptions were held by the American Consul General, VADM Sarikey of the Turkish Navy and by the *Columbus* wardroom. The visit received wide coverage in the local press and on radio. *Columbus* departed Izmir on 7 December for operations in the Aegean Sea en route to the training anchorage at Navplion but was diverted by search and rescue operations for possible survivors of the SS *Heraklion* of Greek registry reported sunk about 180 miles south of Athens, Greece. On 9 December *Columbus* maneuvered to investigate a floating refrigerator van for possible survivors. Finding none, the van was turned over to the Greek tug 1740. *Columbus* found no survivors of the tragedy but did recover several bodies. Search operations were broken off on the 9th and *Columbus* continued to the training anchorage arriving on 12 December. *Columbus* departed Navplion on emergency sortie exercise on 15 December en route Exercise "Quick Train."

On 17 December *Columbus* arrived in Piraeus, Greece, the port city of Athens for a 10 day visit. General visiting was conducted during the Christmas holidays, and despite inclement weather which made boating difficult more than 150 Greeks visited the ship. *Columbus* departed Piraeus on 27 December and crossed the Ionian Sea to Taranto, Italy, arriving on the 30th. A luncheon hosted by the Commander-in-Chief, Ionian Sea and Taranto Channel was attended by Captain Stecher on the 31st. *Columbus* closed out the year celebrating New Years with the residents of Taranto.

SPECIAL TOPICS

On 27 September the first helicopter detachment in the history of *Columbus* as a Guided Missile Cruiser was embarked for the remainder of the year. Detachment 45 of Helicopter Support Squadron Four. The detachment included one UH-2B aircraft, three officer pilots and seven enlisted men. During the year the helicopter was launched from *Columbus'* flight deck a total of 99 times, averaging 30 hours of flight time per month. During the course of the year the ship participated in 211 separate helicopter evolutions.

Columbus refueled 18 small boats during 1966, transferring a total of 838,827 gallons of Navy Special Fuel Oil to them. In turn, *Columbus* was refueled underway a total of 31 times. *Columbus* also conducted two major underway replenishments, one in November in the Tyrrhenian Sea and one in December in the Ionian Sea. One of which included a Vertrep and one at night, both firsts for *Columbus*.

While deployed in the Mediterranean during 1966 *Columbus* expended over 700 mail hours in rendering outside repair assistance to the smaller ships in company. This work included such things as accomplishing emergency repairs on a destroyer's only motor whaleboat, rewinding electric motors, welding and machine shop work, electronic repair and troubleshooting both radar and weapons components. In many cases the repair material/parts needed were furnished by *Columbus* either on a loan basis or as an outright gift depending on the need, the cost and the circumstances.

Major jobs performed on the ship during calendar year 1966 included the installation of new equipment in the ship's laundry and extensive work accomplished to give *Columbus* a helicopter refueling capability. The ship's laundry was refurbished with the addition of three new 50 lb. dryers and one new 100 lb. washer. Three old 40 lb. dryers and two old 50 lb. washers were removed. This program was accomplished in about one and necessitated cutting a large hole in the skin of the ship on the port side adjacent to the laundry. With the exception of continued problems with burnt out clutches in the three old 50 lb. washers still in use, the laundry has operated almost trouble free since its overhaul in September 1966.

Columbus steamed a total of 50,184 engine miles in 1966 without a single major disabling engineering casualty. However, Number Two main engine has given some problems during the year. It's the only engine which does not consistently make its required full power RPM. In September 1966 the Norfolk Naval Shipyard lifted the turbine nozzle control valves, cleaned and readjusted them. This has given some relief and number two engine is considered dependable but the loss of RPM, although only in the neighborhood of 5 to 10 RPM low, still makes it questionable when attempting to conduct a full power run.

During the year *Columbus'* TALOS battery fired a total of 17 missiles, six of these missiles were RIM-8F, seven were RIM-8E and four were RIM-8G. Five of these firings were complete successes, one of which was a direct hit. A second firing of note was a RIM-8F missile fired against a 10M(2) augmented BQM34A target, intercept was at 232.0 KYDS and 54.)KFT. This missile was a constructive hit fired in the "W" mode and acknowledged by Fleet Missile Systems Analysis and Evaluation Group, Corona to be the longest range TALOS success on record. The firing was conducted on 17 February at the Atlantic Fleet Weapons range. The TALOS battery was fully operational all year, however the Fire Control Systems have not been modified to include the CCM modifications known as ORDALT 5290.

Columbus' TARTAR Battery conducted 12 missile firings. Eight of her shots were complete successes, three were failures one missile was a dud. Four of the missiles fired were part of a two-missile salvo in early May utilizing missiles armed with warheads. These are considered the first two missiles salvos armed with warheads that has been fired. While in Rotterdam from 21 August to 26 August, the four TARTAR systems were all rendered inoperative. The fresh water of the port loosened marine growth and sea shells in the fire main which collected and clogged the valve regulating the salt water coolant flow of the TARTAR radars. The valve was removed, cleaned and temporarily replaced. Ship's Force later accomplished modifications to this system so that a similar occurrence would not cause the same casualty. with *Columbus'* modifications, the salt was coolant flow for each TARTAR radar can now be isolated.

In the field of Anti-Submarine Warfare, *Columbus* conducted a successful competitive ASROC firing on 25 March. On 27 March she conducted a successful AWTT firing. On 1 November, *Columbus* fired two deck launched and one ASROC torpedo in a competitive exercise and was credited with a direct hit on the submarine by one of the deck launched torpedoes. During this exercise the ship had no trouble in maintaining sonar contact in excess of 10,000 yards. The ASW picture was marred somewhat however by a fathometer casualty on 17 January which resulted from a burned-out blower motor which caused the entire cabinet to heat up resulting in wire deterioration, failure of the main power switch, transformer and high voltage capacitors. Although repairs were made, damage was so extensive that it was only brought up to about 50% capacity in the recorder section. The fathometer remains a suspect piece of equipment which receives constant attention.

During the period 28 June to 3 August, *Columbus* moved the AN/WLR-1 ECM tuners from the 05 level to the 012 level as a part of the ECM improvement program. This greatly reduced the wave guide length between the antenna and the tuners, and greatly enhanced the reception capability of *Columbus*. Both AN/SPS-30 radar antennas were overhauled during this period to insure their readiness for deployment. *Columbus* also installed a Raytheon Model 1500B Pathfinder Radar on 1 August to enable her to have a radar signature similar to a large merchant vessel for the North Atlantic transit to Rotterdam.

Columbus' communications personnel sent out more than 22,000 messages during the year for both the ship and the flag embarked. They handled in excess of 46,000 messages coming to the ship.

The stores division of the Supply Department on board *Columbus* controlled approximately 60,000 line items during the year. It expended $58,000 for equipage, $227,000 for repair parts and $167,000 for consumables for a total of $452,000. The food services division operated the general mess at a cost of $356,351 while serving approximately one million meals to the crew. Its sales to private messes totaled $60,180. The sales and services division totaled $270,065 in sales through a remodeled ship's store. New equipment included two new soft drink vending machines which were purchased with profits generated from all retail activities. A large scale foreign merchandise and special order program was also undertaken during *Columbus'* Mediterranean deployment. Approximately $71,000 worth of merchandise was sold under these programs. Disbursing paid a total payroll of $2,034,988; made shore patrol payments of $67,451; travel claim payments of $81,042; their gross disbursements totaled $2,591,457.

While deployed in the Mediterranean the Chaplain organized and hosted parties for orphans on board ship which included general tour of the ship with missile demonstrations, a cartoon showing in the ship's theater, an ice cream and cake party and the distribution of toys and gifts obtained through Project "Handclasp." These parties were always a large success and were held in Malta, Catania, Izmir, and Piraeus. The Chaplain also organized tours of foreign ports for ship's personnel.

While in the Mediterranean the ship carried out a community relations project involving groups of volunteer workers who performed painting and repair jobs on orphanages, schools, youth centers and the like. The program was highly successful and a large group of volunteers were kept busy in Malta, Catania, Izmir and Piraeus.

Late in the year a ship's musical combo was organized on a spare time basis. Instruments were obtained from Commander Cruiser-Destroyer Force, Atlantic and the group played at benefit performances in Izmir and Piraeus-Athens. They were extremely well received, particularly by the younger crowds.

On 8 December, *Columbus*, in company with the USS *Shangri La* (CVA-38) and the USS *Belknap* (DLG-18) and other units of Task Group 60.2 proceeded to an area some 180 miles south of Athens, Greece to take part in a rescue and assistance detail in search of survivors of the SS *Heraklion*, a ship of Greek registry which sank with more than 200 people aboard. Though *Columbus* and other ships searched for more than a day, no survivors were found, only bodies, debris and wreckage.

During the year *Columbus* performed 24,749.8 man hours of work that was documented by the MDCS system. In addition she ended the year with 16,479 man hours of work on the deferred list to be accomplished by ship's force, tender or shipyard. *Columbus* has been out of overhaul going on her fifth year. The deferred work list points out clearly that the extreme age of the engineering plant coupled with the increased demands brought about by the installed missile systems is creating special problems. There should be some provisions to increase the OPTAR of ships in *Columbus'* situation. An alternate solution would be to provide extensive RAV or TAV periods once each year after the third year out of overhaul.

Shipalts CG-10 and CG-38 should be accomplished as soon as possible. CG-10 is the relocation of the M.P. air dehydrators from number one fireroom and the after engineroom to a more suitable place where high temperatures and contaminated air are eliminated. In the past these dehydrators have caused difficulty through overheating and cutting off the line, creating a loss of air pressure to the radar wave guides. CG-38 is the installation of a vacuum drag system from the L.P. drain tanks in the forward and after enginerooms to the main and auxiliary condensers. At present electric drain pumps are used. There are four drain pumps, two for each engineroom, and at least one of these pumps is out of commission 95% of the time. During the recent deployment there were 17 Occasions when a drain pump failed. it has caused trouble on full power runs by allowing the L.P. drains to run over into the bilge when a drain pump fails.

On 16 August 1966 in the open ocean between Norway and Iceland, *Columbus* had an opportunity to track a Soviet BISON aircraft with the AN/SPG-49B Fire Control Radar. Automatic Gain Control (AGG) information was recorded for use in obtaining this type aircraft's radar reflectivity.

Upon receipt of intelligence information indicating the possibility of potential enemy target in the vicinity the tracking radar should make preparation to track these targets. The preparation should consist of those procedures outlined in TALOS System Newsletter 4.1-10 of 19 May 1964 which is reply to *Columbus'* report which indicates that *Columbus* has been the only ship to obtain and submit this essential data.

Poor Man's Tactical Data System was devised on board *Columbus* as an instrument to improve the tracking and designation of air contacts in an attempt to obtain the fastest reaction time possible in a non-NTDS environment. The system has brought about closer coordination between Weapons and CIC functions and over the past year has proved to be extremely effective against high density air raids.

1967

On 3 January 1967, while in Taranto, Italy, RADM J.D. Bulkeley broke his flag as COMCRUDESFLOT Eight aboard the *Columbus*, where he was to remain until 9 June 1967 when he was relieved by RADM J.F. Calvert. On 27 October, RADM Calvert shifted his flag to the USS *Tidewater*, and returned to the *Columbus* on 10 November.

On 5 October, Captain William A. Arthur relieved Captain Lewis J. Stecher Jr. as Commanding Officer. Captain Arthur came to *Columbus* from Washington, where he served as Manager, Advanced Systems in the Office of the Director, Surface Missile Systems Project.

Columbus kept Norfolk, Virginia as her home port throughout 1967, and gained a reputation for excellence early in her East Coast career. *Columbus'* mission as a guided missile cruiser is to be capable of independent or combined operations against air, surface, or sub-surface threats. Her functions are: to provide area defense for a task force with guided missiles; to destroy ship, air and shore targets by use of existing missile systems; to operate and support helicopters; to control aircraft; to operate aggressively against and destroy submarines; to provide facilities and accommodations for task group commander and his staff.

Columbus' complement at the end of the year included 933 men, a decrease of 37 from the previous year, and 61 officers, a decrease of nine from the previous year.

The New Year found the *Columbus* at Taranto, Italy, shortly after which she got underway for sea operations and Golfe Juan, France. On 3 January, RADM J.D. Bulkeley broke his flag on *Columbus* as Commander Cruiser-Destroyer Flotilla Eight. Underway for Golfe Juan, *Columbus* conducted a competitive Z-12GM. *Columbus* interrupted her port visit for a trip to the French Ceres Missile Range, where in company with the USS *Lawrence* (DDG4) and the USS *Belknap* (DLG-26), she participated in a missile shoot. *Columbus* fired one TALOS missile and achieved a successful intercept.

The last week in January found *Columbus* active in ASW and electronics exercises. While moored at Marseille, France from 2-6 February, *Columbus* conducted a Z-20-C, again competitively. 7 February found the *"Tall Lady"* participating in exercise Lafayette 3-67. *Columbus* anchored at Livomo, Italy on 17 February and enjoyed a port visit until 26 February when she got underway for Porto Conte. She arrived there on 28 February and prepared for an ORI conducted by RADM J.D. Bulkeley. The result was an 88.08 numerical grade with an adjective of excellent.

After ORI, *Columbus* got underway for an at-sea replenishment and a port visit to Palma, Mallorca. On 12 March, the *"Tall Lady"* departed for CONUS, arriving in Norfolk, Virginia on 20 March.

Columbus spent her first month back in a leave-and-upkeep status after her first deployment to the Mediterranean. On 16 April she got underway for participation in exercise Clovehitch III which included ASW, electronic and gunnery exercises.

During Clovehitch III *Columbus* fired two TALOS and two TARTAR missiles. The TALOS firings showed one success and

one failure. In the failure, telemetering indicated that the boost phase as normal, but at 36 seconds, excessive beam ride errors resulted in large wing movements for the remainder of the flight. Data flow ceased at 98 seconds and the flight was terminated at 117 seconds by command destruct. The successful firing terminated after 267 seconds of flight time, which gives *Columbus* the long range physical intercept record for this system.

Both TARTAR firings were classified as failures. The first started as a normal launch, but after failure of the speed gate circuit to begin sweeping, the missile flew a ballistic trajectory until sea impact at 64.6 seconds. The other failure was normal until 3.68 seconds when the missile began to roll, precluding target acquisition. TLM indicated auto-pilot failure and the flight terminated with sea-impact after 10.8 seconds.

Due to an accident caused by heavy seas, *Columbus* TALOS launching ability was reduced by 50 percent for and extended period of time. Upon termination of Clovehitch III *Columbus* returned to Norfolk, Virginia for another period of leave-and-upkeep through 31 May.

Columbus got underway for a dependents day cruise on 10 June, which found her operating in the Virginia Cape's area. She performed maneuvering exercises, air exercises and gunnery exercises for the benefit of the dependents.

After receiving her complement of Midshipmen for the Atlantic Fleet Midshipman Training Squadron Exercise, *Columbus* departed Norfolk on 12 June for three weeks of underway training. This training found the Middies receiving active on-the-job training in all aspects of shipboard life. The *Columbus* team participated in Z-12-CM exercises, and was involved in a TESTEX off the coast of Florida.

On 20 and 21 June, *Columbus* fired 10 missiles, seven TARTAR and three TALOS. She also fired a Quality Assurance Service Test (QAST) TALOS and three other TALOS in a special test program designated F/O 235. Of the seven TALOS firings, none of them was declared a success. However, all of the firings were at the extreme ends of the missile envelope, and there was excessive telemetering from the several ships present. Three of the firings were classified as undetermined. Of the four "failures," one achieved skin-to-skin contact, but since there was no firing pulse, the flight must be rated a failure. Another "failure" resulted as the missile saw no video and self-destructed after 7.6 seconds. Still another "failure" came as a result of excessive TLM at the ship's ground station. The remaining abort was due to the launcher's failure to indicate "Rail Clear," and the resultant lack of guidance program.

The *"Tall Lady"* fared much better in her TARTAR firings. Of the seven TARTARS fired, she scored four successes. One of the three misfires resulted in the missile blowing up about five seconds after launch. The other two failures were due to poor telemetering.

After this heavy missile workout, the crew and Midshipmen enjoyed a brief stay in sunny New Orleans, Louisiana. *Columbus* departed New Orleans and arrived at Norfolk on 8 July and remained there until 24 July when she got underway for type training and Operation Lashout. Late on 26 July, Operation Lashout commenced and *Columbus* exercised her anti-air, surface, and sub-surface capabilities in conjunction with NATO forces. LASHOUT terminated 2 August, and *Columbus* continued on to Annapolis, Maryland, where she offloaded Midshipmen and returned to Norfolk. The in-port period from 5-17 August was utilized in preparation for the upcoming Multiship Missilex in the Atlantic Fleet Weapons Range. The ECM team took advantage of this period by holding five Z-12-CM exercises. The *"Tall Lady"* got underway on the morning of the 17th, and after a stopover at the Yorktown

Naval Weapons Station, proceeded to the Weapons Range, conducting exercises en route. Upon arrival at the Range, close air-control exercises utilized the services of VC-8. In the Missilex, *Columbus* fired a total of three missiles and all were scored as hits. On one of the TALOS kills, target breakup was observed in radar. As these were the last firings of the year, it can be said that the missile systems have shown themselves to be satisfactory AAW environments. This is shown by the Weapons Department winning the Battle Efficiency "E" in recognition of outstanding performance. This achievement is even more noteworthy since the Weapons Department was operating at 60% of its allotted personnel during the competitive period.

After the Missilex, *Columbus* visited St. Thomas in the Virgin Islands for a weekend, and returned to Norfolk on 30 August. September was a month of leave and upkeep for *Columbus*. The EW team held three exercises weekly and a graded Z-20-C was held on 12 September.

On 3 October, *Columbus* got underway for a familiarization cruise for Captain William A. Arthur, which included an exercise at General Quarters, a man overboard drill, and an abandon ship drill

On 5 October, Captain William A. Arthur formally assumed command of *Columbus* during a Change of Command ceremony on the fantail of the *"Tall Lady."* Captain William A. Arthur relieved Captain Lewis J. Stecher Jr., who departed for duty within the Office of the Secretary of Defense in Washington, D.C. Captain Arthur came to Columbus from Washington, D.C., where he was the Manager, Advanced Systems in the Office of the Director, Surface Missile Systems Project.

The EW team kept up its drills, and the entire ship upped the tempo of its preparation for the Mediterranean deployment in early January of 1968. Intensive team training was gained by the AAW unit at the Fleet Anti-air Warfare Training Center at Dam Neck, Virginia, and the ASW team took advantage of the ASROC trainer at the Fleet Training Center in Norfolk. On 30 October, *Columbus* got underway for independent type training in the Virginia Capes area, and the Charleston Operating area. She held two close air intercept control exercises utilizing the services of VC-2, an F-8 squadron based at Oceana. On 6 November, *Columbus* held the *Amberjack* in sonar contact for a total of thirty-nine hours. *Columbus* returned to Norfolk on 9 November. She remained in port with the exception of pre-deployment missile load out at Yorktown. While in Norfolk, the Radar Navigation Team participated in a week-long course at the Dam Neck center, as did the AAW team. Ten exercises were conducted by the EW team in November as she kept up her rigid schedule.

On 30 November *Columbus* ADMIN inspection began, with RADM James Calvert acting as Chief Inspector. The result of the inspection was a final grade of 93.08.

In view of her projected air operations with the *Shangri-La,* the Air Intercept Controllers aboard *Columbus* improved their technique with 106 intercepts with both Crusader and Phantom aircraft.

On 18 December, the Fleet Intelligence Center Europe presented a pre-deployment briefing for designated officers, in which our position in the Mediterranean was outlined, and all intelligence aspects of the Mediterranean were discussed and reviewed.

After a final leave period for the Christmas holidays, *Columbus* was ready and willing to become a part of the professional United States Sixth Fleet in the Mediterranean.

SPECIAL TOPICS

The Deck Department continued to demonstrate her "Can Do" spirit throughout the year. Demands placed on the Deck personnel included being fueled by oilers thirty times, and fueling "small boys" seven times. The *"Tall Lady"* conducted helicopter operations, personnel transfers by high-line, and even a "Firefish" transfer at sea, with her professional approach which has become routine.

The Engineering Department of *Columbus* did her share also, steaming underway for a total of 2,444 hours. The plant consumed some 5,678,181 gallons of MSFO. Engine miles for the year totaled 37,419. In early July, the damaged ship's elevator was placed back in commission after five months of ladder climbing. The damaged cables were repaired with the help of the Norfolk Naval Shipyard. In August a major operation was required to transfer a two-and-a-half ton motor generator set from the eighth deck to the main deck. Numerous accesses had to be enlarged in order to hoist the motor generator out of the ship for rewinding. Another long-standing casualty was corrected in August when the number two high pressure air compressor was replaced. A new compressor was necessary due to lack of replacement parts for the damaged one. During the summer months, the Engineering Department made extensive modifications to the Wardroom, living compartments and working spaces aboard the *Columbus*. Late in the year, replacement of parts of the 150 lime automatic telephone exchange was accomplished at a cost to the government of $10,000. This improved the exchange efficiency from 33 to 66 percent.

The Communication's people transmitted and received over 30,000 encrypted messages during 1967. Basically, Communications are hampered in two aspects only. Both UHF and HF antennas need complete overhauling, and while the ship's force carries out a strict PMS, the tempo of communications operations limits the opportunities to secure the antennas for repair. Also, the patch panels, both transmit and receive, have not been overhauled since 1962, and are in dire need of extensive modernization.

Columbus' Supply Department handled numerous transactions during the year. Total consumables and repair parts consumed totaled over a half a million dollars. $320,162.53 worth of food was consumed. Ship's store sales totaled a quarter of a million dollars, and gross disbursements for the year came to over two and one half million dollars. These figures combine to form a grand total of $3,716,079.97 worth of transactions.

The Medical Department reported the following figures for the year.

Total Admissions to Sick List	96
Total inpatient Sick Days	406
Average Inpatient Sick Days	4.22
Admissions to Sick List and Transferred to other Treatment Facility	12
Patients referred for admissions to other Armed Force Treatment Facility	20
Total Sick Call Visits	3,593
Total Prescriptions Filled – Pharmacy	7,602
Total Clinical Laboratory Procedures	9,750
Total X-ray Examinations	899
Total Complete Physical Examinations	504
Total Screening Physical Examinations	1,914
Total Tuberculin Skin Test (PPD)	1,112

1968

Departing Norfolk, Virginia on 3 January *Columbus* sailed for a 7-month Mediterranean deployment as a unit of the Sixth Fleet and flagship of COMCRUDESFLOT 8/CTG 60.2, RADM James F. Calvert. On 3 January three TALOS missiles were fired in the Virginia Capes Operating Area. Two missiles were duds caused by launcher misfiring and the third self-destructed after launch for unknown reasons. One TARTAR missile was also fired but was rated undetermined due to telemetering noise. On 10 January, following a transit marked by heavy weather, *Columbus* arrived in Rota, Spain to officially report as a unit of Sixth Fleet. During a brief 2-day turnover period, *Columbus* relieved USS *Topeka* (CLG-8) as flagship of Commander Task Group 60.2.

Columbus departed Rota on 13 January for an independent transit to Palma, Mallorca, Spain. Early on the morning of 15 January *Columbus* completed a rendezvous with *Shangri-La, Standley,* and *Goodrich* to form Task Unit 60.2.9. With *Columbus* as guide, the unit formed a column and steamed smartly into Palma while rendering a 21-gun salute that was returned by Fort San Carlos Battery.

Departing Palma on 22 January, *Columbus* proceeded towards Salto Di Quirra Missile Range on the southeastern tip of Sardinia, conducting anti-submarine warfare drills with USS *Irex* en route. On the morning of 24 January *Columbus* participated in Missilex 8-68. One TARTAR missile was fired but the firing was considered a failure due to loss of missile thrust.

During the days following the missile exercise *Columbus* conducted various anti-air warfare, electronic warfare, and antisubmarine warfare exercises with various units of Task Group 60.2.

13 January found *Columbus* med-moored at Naples, Italy for a routine visit which lasted until 7 February when she left for multiship antisubmarine warfare operations. On 12 February, after several days of exercises, *Columbus* took on more than 80 tons of food and stores, in addition to fuel and mail, during a major underway replenishment.

After several more days of at-sea operations, *Columbus*, in company with other Task Group 60.2 units, anchored in Soudha Bay, Crete on 16 February, for a well earned period of rest. Taranto, Italy had been originally scheduled as the port of call for this period, but was cancelled due to an outbreak of meningitis in that city. Limited liberty and recreational facilities in Soudha were fully utilized. During the inport period, COMCRUDESFLOT 8 conducted a surprise personnel and administrative inspection of *Columbus*.

On 20 February, due to a cumulative effect of derangement's to the main propulsion system, the entire system was CASREPT (Casualty Reported).

On 23 February with repairs to the engineering plant completed, *Columbus* steamed from Soudha Bay and began preparations for participation in Missilex 9-68 to be conducted 28 February. This exercise was also conducted at the Salto Di Quirra Missile Range. One TARTAR missile was fired at a high flying drone and was considered a success with a miss distance determined by telemetry to be only 15 feet.

On 1 March, *Columbus* anchored at Lovo Santo, Corsica to await the start of NATO exercise Fairgame VI which began on 3 March. During the exercise *Columbus* was unit of NATO Task Force 502 and assumed an anti-air warfare disposition. During the closing phase of Fairgame VI, *Columbus* attempted to simulate the electronic emissions characteristic of *Shangri-La*. These were intended to deceive pilots from *F.D. Roosevelt,* attached to opposing forces, into making unknowing attacks on *Columbus*, thereby drawing them within *Columbus'* missile range.

Unexpected difficulties required the departure of *W.A. Lee* on 8 March, making it necessary for *Columbus* to become the rescue destroyer for *Shangri-La.* Fairgame VI ended on 10 March.

Columbus arrived at Valletta, Malta on-13 March and *Columbus* personnel enjoyed the excellent facilities and warm hospitality of the city until 23 March.

Prior to returning to Soudha Bay on 29 March *Columbus* conducted several Weapons Department exercises and fired 16 rounds of 5" 38 ammunition during a gunnery exercise on 25 March. At Soudha limited facilities were again used to the fullest extent until 1 March when *Columbus* got underway by emergency sortie plan.

Antisubmarine warfare drills were the order of the day in conjunction with opportunities for *Columbus* to improve anti-air warfare defenses by detection of *Shangri-La* aircraft returning from air strikes against Filfla Rock acting as strike units against the *Columbus*.

On 4 April, a helicopter from *Essex* making a routine landing on *Columbus'* fantail rolled forward upon touchdown causing its rotor blades to strike COLUMBUS' after TALOS missile launcher. The accident was attributed to pilot error in failing to lock the helo's brakes upon touchdown. There were no injuries to personnel and slight damage to the missile launcher.

The helicopter was unable to take off and remained on *Columbus* until offloaded in Athens, Greece.

On 5 April a major underway replenishment was conducted with the helicopter on the fantail preventing *Columbus* from participating in vertical replenishment.

On 8 April *Columbus* dropped anchor in Athens, Greece for a 7-day stay. *Columbus* men maintained their excellent conduct record while enjoying the many facilities and the warm hospitality of the Greek people.

After Athens, *Columbus* continued a fast paced training schedule of antisubmarine warfare exercises until 20 April when she moored at Messina, Sicily. The port was friendly but lacked the facilities desirable for large liberty parties.

Exercise Dawn Patrol commenced on 29 April. Phase I, designated "Dark Night," was conducted as a combined antiair/antisubmarine warfare exercise under NATO control in a peacetime environment. "Enemy" submarines, surface ships and airforce were to create incidents which would lead to an emergency termination of the exercise and reversion of units to national control. This was accomplished on 1 May.

Phase II was conducted in an atmosphere of slowly increasing tensions between the ORANGE and BLUE forces, and further developed as various situations presented themselves. *Columbus'* primary mission was to provide air defense for Shangri-La. She discharged this responsibility by staying within 15 miles of the carrier, and on 2 May a second opportunity presented itself to demonstrate *Columbus'* anti-air warfare capabilities when air opposition was received from the *Roosevelt.* On 3 May, *Columbus* chopped to NATO forces and continued her assignment. Phase II ended on 4 May and Phase III began the same day and was a redeployment phase for repositioning of ships and was conducted in a non-exercise status.

After experiencing difficulties with her evaporators, *Columbus* took on 22,000 gallons of potable and feed water from the oiler Pawcatuck on 5 May. *Columbus* was unable to participate immediately in the closing phase of Dawn Patrol due to the seriousness of her evaporators condition. She went to anchorage at Soudha Bay, Crete on 6 May for emergency repairs. The engineering force worked long hours during the following two days in order to enable *Columbus* to participate in the final days of Dawn Patrol. At 1630, 8 May, *Columbus* rejoined Dawn Patrol, resuming her station within 15 miles of the carrier.

Dawn Patrol ended on 10 May, and was considered to be of only marginal value as a training exercise because of the very limited activity in which *Columbus* was involved.

At 0800, 11 May, *Columbus* dropped anchor at Athens, Greece for the post-exercise critique and a well deserved 3-day period of rest and relaxation.

When *Columbus* got underway at 1700, 14 May, it was for Valletta, Malta instead of Palma, Spain, as previously scheduled. The change was made to afford *Columbus* nine days of tender availability alongside USS *Shenandoah*. During this availability *Columbus* completely shut down her engineering plant and went cold iron for the first time in six years.

Valletta was once again enjoyed by *Columbus* men because of the friendly populace, plentiful recreational facilities, sightseeing, shopping opportunities, and minimal language difficulties.

Departing Malta on 25 May with a much-improved engineering plant *Columbus'* assignment was to provide anti-air warfare protection for Exercise Poopdeck which was conducted 27-29 May with the Spanish Air Force.

On 30 and 31 May *Columbus* moored in the harbor at La Spezia, Italy for a 6-day visit. Because of its location and the accessibility to such historic Italian cities as Genoa, Pisa, Florence, and Rome, the visit was enjoyable. While in La Spezia, 24 First Class Midshipmen embarked for a 6-week training cruise.

Getting underway on 10 June *Columbus* proceeded to Gaeta, Italy, the homeport of USS *Little Rock* (CLG-4), flagship of Commander Sixth Fleet. The purpose of this visit was to conduct an Administrative/Material Inspection of *Little Rock*. The inspection commenced immediately upon *Columbus'* arrival on 11 June.

On 17 June, *Columbus* got underway for Gaeta for her last operational sea period of the deployment. She conducted various maneuvering, air intercept control and antisubmarine warfare exercises before joining other units in the Mediterranean to celebrate the Sixth Fleet's Anniversary in Operation Flapex (Fleet Anniversary Parade Exercise).

The period 22-24 June was used in rehearsing the exercise with the final performance taking place, on 25 June. To commemorate the occasion the assembled groups conducted all-day air power, surface and sub-surface exercises to demonstrate the fleet's capabilities as a peacekeeping force. *Columbus* fired an ASROC and conducted joint antisubmarine warfare tactics with P-3 aircraft against the submarine, USS *Runner*.

In addition to press and television coverage, Flapex was relieved by General Lyman K. Lemnitzer, USA, Supreme Allied Commander, Europe, and Commander in Chief, U.S. European Command. Also present were Admiral Horatio Rivero, USN, Commander in Chief, Southern Forces, Europe, and Vice Admiral William D. Martin, Commander Sixth Fleet.

After the celebration, *Columbus* proceeded to Barcelona, Spain for a final rest and recreation visit before departing for the United States. The ship arrived in Barcelona on 28 June.

Barcelona proved to be a fitting climax after a long, hard cruise. There was much last minute shopping, sightseeing, and, for the strong-hearted, there was Spain's number one spectacle, the bullfight.

On 6 July, *Columbus* got underway for Malaga, Spain and turnover with the USS *Topeka* on 9 July. *Topeka* arrived at 0800, 9 July, and by 1430, with enthusiastic efforts by all hands, the turnover was completed and the *Tall Lady* left for home, with a few hours in Rota early the next day to top-off fuel and load

fresh food. By 0900 the Navigator of *Columbus* had set the course of 271 deg. T, destination Norfolk, Virginia.

On 16 July, after having been away for 195 days, *Columbus* moored to Pier 51 Norfolk Naval Base. This also signaled the end of the 6-week Midshipmen cruise and the 24 First Class Midshipmen embarked in La Spezia, Italy departed the *Columbus* with greater knowledge and fond memories.

In preparation for a restricted availability at Norfolk Naval Shipyard, Portsmouth, Virginia, *Columbus* got underway on 19 July for Naval Weapons Station, Yorktown, Virginia, to offload missiles and ammunition. Two days later, this task was accomplished and the ship returned to Norfolk.

On 29 July, *Columbus* was towed by tugs, down river to Portsmouth, to commence her restricted availability (RAV).

Columbus commenced an 11-week RAV on 1 August, lasting through 21 October. Most of the effort was directed at revitalizing the engineering plant in preparation for redeployment in December.

On 21 October *Columbus* left Norfolk Naval Shipyard for a 2-day sea trial, after which she proceeded to Naval Weapons Station, Yorktown to onload missiles, torpedoes, and conventional ammunition. The time between 23 October and mid-November was spent in and out of Norfolk conducting various tests and exercises.

Columbus sailed to Newport, Rhode Island to onload COMCRUDESFLOT TEN'S equipment on 15 November. The last two weeks of November were spent pierside in Norfolk making final preparations for deployment.

COMCRUDESFLOT TEN, RADM Mans L. Johnson, broke his flag in *Columbus* on 1 December.

On 2 December, *Columbus* cast off her lines and deployed to the Mediterranean and duty with the Sixth Fleet. Arriving in Rota, Spain on 9 December, *Columbus* once again relieved USS *Topeka* (CLG-8), as flagship of Commander Task Group 60.2.

Departing Rota on 10 December, *Columbus* spent her first liberty in Genoa, Italy, arriving 13 December. After three cold, wet days in that port, she left on 17 December and participated in Exercise Lafayette 2-69 with the French Air Force.

Arriving in Villefranche-sur-mer, *Columbus* dropped anchor in that harbor and celebrated Christmas and New Year's there.

SPECIAL TOPICS

The cumulative effect of derangement to main propulsion system, leading to the casrepting of the entire system on 20 February are delineated as follows:

Derangement commenced with Number One Boiler out of commission for routine fireside/waterside cleaning. Number 1B forced draft blower was out of commission awaiting a lube oil pump housing. On 12 February a Class BRAVO fire occurred behind Number Two Boiler, both inside and outside the boiler air casing. The fire was extinguished quickly, reflashed momentarily, then remained out. At the time, because of the smoke problem and possibility of serious damage, Number Two Boiler was secured and procedures to cross-connect the plant were initiated, a seemingly routine evolution in light of the many recent casualty control exercises conducted. At this time all auxiliary machinery operating in the forward plant began to lose steam. Investigation revealed that one of the auxiliary steam cross-connect valves could not be opened. As a result, ship's propulsion was reduced to a one boiler and two engine capability. Since auxiliary steam could not be provided by cross-connecting the plant, it was necessary to relight fires under Number Two Boiler without making more than a visual inspection of the exterior boiler casing for damage. The boiler was slowly brought back up to pressure and placed on the line for normal split plant operation. Conditions were normal, although all capability to cross-connect auxiliary steam was still lost. Immediate steps were instituted to isolate and repair the defective valve, however, it was found that additional valves were leaking through which prevented isolation of this valve to allow safe repairs while the ship was underway. Also during this casualty period while lighting off Number Three ship's service generator it started to overspeed due to a bent pin in the throttle linkage. The operator immediately regulated the steam line stop valve to control the speed of the generator. Number Two emergency diesel generator was placed on the line to permit repairs to be made to the throttle. This throttle valve had operated properly the previous day during casualty control exercises. The uncorrected casualty on Number One Boiler along with the new problem with the auxiliary cross-connect valve had a deleterious effect on the flexibility of the main propulsion plant.

On two occasions, 13 and 15 February, Number Three Shaft had to be locked due to major lube oil leaks. In both cases the cause was ruptured lube oil overflow recirculating line which had to be removed and rebuilt. Since vibration was deemed to be a major cause, the line had been rigidly braced and reinforced to prevent recurrence. Two similar casualties had occurred on Number Two Main Engine in January. After the correction of the casualties, difficulty was experienced in unlocking shafts. In each case it was necessary for the ship to be stopped before the shaft could be unlocked. Since the shaft was secured for a period of 2 to 3 hours each time that repairs were being made, it is suspected that the turbine rotor was slightly bowed and would not turn over properly until the load was taken from it. Once the shaft was unlocked normal tests and operation continued without further difficulty.

On 13 February, an oil leak developed on the reduction gear housing of Number Three ship service turbo generator. In order to replace the defective oil seal it was necessary to lift the reduction gear casing. After the casing was lifted all bearings were leaded and the shaft bearing surface cleaned. The generator was placed back in commission on 16 February.

On 13 February, the defective steam valve was opened up and repaired. It was found that the valve seat had broken away from the stem thus making the valve inoperable. The other valves that were found to be leaking through were not repaired due to time limitations. At the same time, Number Two Boiler casing was opened up to allow for inspection of the fire damage. The apparent cause of the fire was an accumulation of lube oil which had been picked up by the forced draft blower and forced into the air casing. This oil had accumulated on the lagging and boiler casing over a period of time and had finally ignited. No damage to the Boiler casing or internal fittings was found. The affected area was wiped down and the boiler was placed back in service. By the morning of 14 February the Main Propulsion Plant was fully operable with the exception of Number 1B Forced Draft Blower.

On 14 February, en route to Soudha Bay, Crete, problems were experienced with high salinity in the Feed System. By the time the cause was found and isolated, enough chloride had collected in one boiler to make it necessary to take it off the line and dump it. The cause was found to be two leaks in the galley steam table heating system which allowed fresh water to be drained back into the L.P. Drain System. After correcting this situation a further problem with salinity in the feed system

started occurring at an alarming rate. It must be understood that heretofore salinity had been a constant problem due to the deteriorated state of the steam drains running through the bilges. At this point the problem started to grow in proportion and investigation indicated that of 12 feed bottoms, four of them (two each in Number Two and Four Firerooms) comprising about one-third of the feed water capacity were salty. Also at this time the salinity in another boiler was high enough to cause it to be taken off the line and dumped. Because Number One Boiler could not operate at full capacity it was necessary to steam On Number Three Boiler and Number Four Boiler with all but the auxiliary steam system split out. Investigation of the feed tanks resulted in finding two bilge sumps that had deteriorated to such an extent as to require replacement because both were admitting bilge water directly into the tanks. In addition, two other tanks were found to have from two to four holes up to 2 inches in diameter in their tank tops. In order to patch these tanks it was necessary to open Number Two Boiler and Number Four Boiler air casings, and the manhole covers, and to remove a fuel oil service pump from its foundation. By replacing another, plus patching numerous other smaller holes, the Shipfitters and Boiler Tenders, with around-the-clock work, were able to restore the tanks to usable condition by noon on 22 February. In order to forestall further deterioration, the air box casings of Number Two Boiler and of Number Four Boiler were scaled down and re-preserved while the other work was in progress.

On 20 February, while at anchorage in Soudha Bay, Crete, and as the work was being done one of the feed tanks, Number Three Main Engine was placed out of commission to permit repairs to a flange on the auxiliary steam line to the condensate pump. This work included building up an area with weld and refacing the flange. In addition to this, two sections of H.P. Drain line in Number Two Fireroom and the Forward Engineroom, respectively, developed serious leaks. In order to repair these new leaks it was necessary to secure all operating machinery forward of Number Three Fireroom. This, until completion of the repair on the auxiliary steam line, left the ship with a one-boiler and two-engine capability. The cumulative effect of these derangement's along with the feed tank problems resulted in a CASREPT of the entire Main Propulsion System. Since electrical load was being carried by Number One and Number Three Ship's Service Turbo Generators at the time the H.P. Drain leaks developed, it was necessary to shift the load to the after generators prior to securing all of the machinery forward. As Number Four Ship's Service Generator was being brought on the line in parallel with the other generators, the circuit breaker would not close. The turbine was secured and the generator disconnects were opened on the bus to permit repairs. The circuit breaker was operated satisfactorily in manual on the dead bus. Control power was the "Jury-Rigged" into the control power fuses of the circuit breaker from an external source. (Normal control power comes from the generator itself but it was secured.) With control power from another source the circuit breaker was operated satisfactorily in manual and also in power operation. The Generator was then brought up to speed and successfully paralleled with the other generators. The apparent reason for the sticking circuit breaker was that during the cleaning of the breaker, while conducting a routine switchboard cleaning the previous night, the breaker had been operated several times manually to see if all the mechanisms were operating correctly. During this operation apparently the breaker was moved to an over-travel condition which depressed a limit switch. This limit switch in turn prevented the normal operation of the control power circuit.

As Number Four Ship's Service Turbo Generator was running parallel, it was determined that a voltage regulator on Number Three Ship's Service Turbo Generator was causing erratic reactive power recirculation problems. The generator was secured and the automatic voltage regulator reactor was removed for repair. It was found that a ball bearing that is inserted in a finger in the reactor control had come out of place, thereby causing a variable resistance in the field control circuit. This in turn caused the voltage to vary considerably and caused the generator to take excessive current and unbalanced the power factor. After this repair the generator was successfully placed on the line with no difficulty. While neither of the generator problems were significant in themselves, they did delay the start of repairs to the H.P. Drain Lines by nearly 5 hours. As a matter of note, all four main switchboards received their annual cleaning during this in-port period. By noon on 22 February the plant was restored to an operable condition and it was possible to send out a CASCOR on the Main Propulsion System.

1968

MEDITERRANEAN CRUISE STATISTICS

Liberty Ports Visited	12
Liberty Days	78
Personnel on Liberty	21,060
Liberty Cancellations	23
Formal Reports	3
Personnel Received for Duty	84
Personnel Transferred	136
Ports in which tours were conducted	9
Tours Conducted	70
Columbus Men attending tours	1,509
Times Alongside Another Ship	96
Refueling	43
Fueling Other Ships	4
Rearming	18
Replenishment	6
Highlining	25
Pounds of provisions received at sea	1,000,000
Supply Requisitions processed	5,212
Meals served	484,000
Beef	48,000 lbs.
Flour	12,000 lbs.
Milk	26,000 gallons
Value of Ship's Store Sales	$317,000.00
Foreign Merchandise Sold	$168,000.00
Toothpaste sold	3,800 tubes
Soap	11,000 bars
Cigarettes	21,000 cartons
Stereo Taps	3,750 rolls
Cokes	333,000 drinks
Gross Disbursements by Disbursing	$1,410,000.00
Foreign Currency Sold to Crew	$130,000.00
Allotments Processed	650
Fuel Oil Burned	6,276,367 gallons
Miles Steamed	38,337

1969

New Year's Day 1969 found *Columbus* in Villefranche, France, one month into a five-and-one-half month deployment to the Sixth Fleet.

On 3 January, *Columbus* got underway for operations with TG 60.2 and participation in Operation PHIBLEX. This was a five-day amphibious operation in which *Columbus* served as an AAW picket ship. We learned later in that week that our scheduled port visit to Valletta had been canceled and that the ship would proceed to Athens, Greece for a week's visit.

The ship anchored at Orimos Faliron in Athens on 13 January. During the next week, the crew of *Columbus* established three precedents which would be continued through over 20 port visits during the next twelve months. First, the ship participated in tours of Athens and the surrounding countryside. These tours proved extremely popular and were continued with a prodigious total at the year's end. Second, *Columbus'* athletic teams were never more active than in 1969. In bowling, basketball, soccer, and football, teams from *Columbus* competed with foreign teams as well as with teams from other units of the Sixth Fleet. Thirdly, *Columbus* crewmen began an excellent shore conduct record, which would remain enviable throughout the year.

On 20 January, *Columbus* was underway for a two-week-at-sea period which included anchorage in Taranto, Italy and Pollensia Bay, Mallorca. During this period, the ship operated extensively with Task Group 60.2. AZ-9-AA, Z-7-U, Z-8-U, Z-12-CM, and two Z-13-GMs were exercises conducted during this at-sea period. Further, the ship participated in two periods ASW free-play and a low-flyer missile radar tracking exercise.

During this period, RADM E.W. Dobie Jr., relieved RADM M.L. Johnston as COMCRUDESFLOT TWO.

For a well-deserved rest, *Columbus* arrived in Barcelona, Spain, on 3 February for a seven-day visit. While moored there, RADM Dobie shifted his flag from USS *Shangri-La* to USS *Columbus*.

Columbus left Barcelona on 10 February for more operations with TG 60.2. She participated in ASW exercise, Operation Poopdeck 2-69, and a surface gunshot. Poopdeck was an airwarfare exercise in which our aircraft conducted simulated strikes against defended land installations in Spain. *Columbus* provided long and short range surface-to-air missile and ASW support for the carrier.

They arrived in Golfe Juan, France, for a seven-day visit on 17 February. From this date until 2 March, *Columbus* was almost entirely in port as the Golfe Juan visit was followed by a five day visit to Gaeta, Italy, homeport of USS *Little Rock,* Sixth Fleet flagship. On 26 February, the ship conducted an Administrative/Material inspection of the *Little Rock*.

From 2 March, *Columbus* was again at sea with 60.2 conducting AAW and ASW operations in connection with Operation National Week. *Columbus* was primarily employed as an AAW picket ship.

On 7 March, the ship med-moored in Naples, Italy, for a 10-day visit. Both the exchange facilities at the NATO installation there, and the U.S. Navy exchange saw extensive use by the crewmen of the *Columbus*.

The ship left Naples on 17 March, arriving in Gaeta, Italy, on the same day, to commence an Operational Readiness Inspection of the *Little Rock*. The first day of inspection was composed of selected in-port readiness exercises. The second day the *Little Rock* got underway for at-sea exercises in Combat Information, Weapons Control, Navigation and seamanship. The final day was spent conducting a battle problem and a critique for the entire inspection.

Columbus sailed from Gaeta on 19 March for a five-day-at-sea period which saw RADM P.B. Armstrong relieve RADM M.L. Johnston as COMCRUDESFLOT TEN. The ship conducted a KOMAR exercise in which our effectiveness to combat small high speed surface craft was tested. We also conducted two Z-13-GM and a Z-2-CI during this time.

The *"Tall Lady"* arrived in Athens for the second of three trips to that port during 1969 on 24 March, just in time for the celebration of Greek Independence Day on 25 March.

We sailed again on 29 March for TG 60.2 operations, and more experience in aircraft and weapons control. The ship conducted a LOWFLEX in which our weapons systems were tested against attacking waves of low-flyers. Two Z-12-CMs, a Z-13-GM, and an AWEX 40T were also conducted.

On 2 April, the ship fired two TARTAR missiles against drone targets on the Malta Missile Range. One shot was a missile equipped with a telemetering instrument package, while the other was a live warhead shot. The latter destroyed the incoming drone.

From 3-11 April, the ship was moored in Grand Harbour at Valletta, Malta for an eight-day visit to the site of the historic World War II Battle of Malta.

Columbus got underway from Malta for her last major at-sea period of this particular deployment. She was at sea for approximately three weeks with a two-and-one-half day visit to Souda Bay, Crete. During the first week the ship participated in ASW training exercises, surface and AAW gunnery shots and our monthly logistic deployment. After the Souda Bay anchorage, the ship took part in the NATO exercise Dawn Patrol with surface units and aircraft of Turkey, Greece, Italy, and Spain. Dawn Patrol is designed to simulate the political and military actions likely in case of actual hostilities in the Mediterranean area. The simulated increase in political tensions, in which readiness conditions are upgraded, was closely followed by the commencement of simulated hostilities. *Columbus* served, during the major portion of this exercise, as an AAW picket ship for TG 60.2. Admiral Armstrong shifted his flag to the USS *Shangri-La* during this period.

Following *Dawn Patrol, Columbus* arrived in Palma, Mallorca, for a four-day breather prior to our departure for Rota, Spain, and turnover with USS *Galveston.*

Columbus sailed for Newport, Rhode Island, on 7 May. In mid-transit, the ship was informed that it would participate in a Second Fleet exercise coined Country Constable. As more information was received, it became clear that the ship would be on display before the President of the United States. *Columbus* arrived in Newport a day before schedule, off-loaded the staff of COMCRUDESFLOT TEN, and then proceeded to the Virginia Capes Missile Range. On 16 May, *Columbus* fired two TALOS missiles for President Nixon, the second achieving a direct hit against incoming drone, and then proceeded to the homeport of *Columbus*, Norfolk, Virginia.

On 16 May, the ship began a month's leave and upkeep period. At the beginning of this period, a complete inspection of the ship's weapons systems was conducted by a team from Nossolant, and at the end, the ship went to Yorktown for three days to offload her missiles. She returned to the Norfolk Naval Shipyard in Portsmouth, Virginia, to begin a 10-week RAV.

While in Portsmouth, the ship received extensive work on her engineering plant, weapons systems and communications equipment. Dock trials, which had been delayed for several days, took place on 21 August. A full sea detail was set and the trials were conducted satisfactorily.

Columbus got underway from Norfolk Naval Shipyard for sea trials on 25 August. All engines and running gears were checked

out on the way to the Naval Weapons Station in Yorktown. Weapons were on-loaded for three days. On 29 August, she sailed from Yorktown for Norfolk, tying up to Pier 7, at the Norfolk Naval Shipyard.

After a weekend at home, the ship was once again underway for training exercises off the Virginia Capes operating area. This five-day period was of great value to the crew as a refresher course in the operations the ship would be required to conduct daily in the upcoming deployment to the Sixth Fleet.

On 15 September, the ship's annual Nuclear Weapons Technical Proficiency Inspection began and lasted for three days. The senior chief inspector was RADM Chase, COMCRUDESFLOT FOUR. The ship received a grade of "good" on the inspection.

Columbus set sail from Norfolk, for the final time in 1969, on the Morning of 7 October. She began the first leg of a five-and-one-half month deployment with a trip to Newport, Rhode Island, to on-load the staff of COMCRUDESFLOT TWO, and RADM E.W. Dobie Jr.

The ship made the crossing without incident, arriving Rota, Spain, to commence turnover with the USS *Galveston* on 16 October. RADM Dobie relieved RADM Spreen, COMCRUDESFLOT EIGHT.

Columbus left Rota on 17 October to join TG 60.2. She was scheduled for a week's operations and then her first port visit was in Villefranche, France. However, this visit was canceled as the ship was ordered to station off Libya during the crisis during the fall of 1969. During this period, the ship had several visitors. RADM Roberts of the Royal Navy visited the ship on 22 October, and the Honorable John H. Chaffee, Secretary of the Navy, accompanied VADM David C. Richardson, COMSIXTHFLEET, in an inspection of the ship on 5 November. Numerous at-sea training exercises were conducted during this time.

After over a month, the ship received her first real liberty in Barcelona, Spain as the *Columbus* visited the famous Spanish resort city from 12-22 November.

Following the Barcelona visit, the ship conducted at-sea operations with units of TG 60.2 for five days then arrived in Valletta, Malta, for a ten day visit.

Columbus was at sea from 5-19 December in TG 60.2 operations. On 19 December, the *"Tall Lady"* with four other Sixth Fleet units, paid a visit to Izmir, Turkey. The visit received wide press coverage in newspapers all over the world. Major student demonstrations were held during the visit. Crewmen of the *Columbus* demonstrated their ability as diplomats as well as sailors.

The ship remained anchored in Athens, Greece, for the remainder of 1969, after arriving 22 December.

1970

Columbus spent six months out of the year 1970 on duty with the Sixth Fleet, completing in March a tour begun in October of 1969 and starting another, her fifth deployment in as many years, in late August. The record compiled by *Columbus* was notable in every respect and reflected the high level of training maintained at all levels. This was especially evident in the performance of personnel manning the weapons systems during MISSILEX 4-71, when *Columbus* scored three direct hits against air targets, one with TARTAR, and two with TALOS. The TALOS shots were skin-to-skin knockdowns and the second was especially notable in that it utilized the launcher from one system and the guidance equipment from the other—a technique successful only when the systems are in perfect alignment.

During the deployment ending March 6, *Columbus* served as flagship for COMCRUDESFLOT TWO, RADM Earnest W. Dobie. COMCRUDESFLOT EIGHT, RADM Roger E. Spreen, broke his flag in *Columbus* for the autumn deployment, shifting to USS *Independence* (CVA-62) at the beginning of the contingency operation in connection with Operation Fig Hill in September and early October. For her service in the eastern Mediterranean, remaining on Bravo Station for one stretch of 33 days, *Columbus* was awarded the Meritorious Unit Commendation.

Columbus received the COMCRUDESFLOT EIGHT Electronic Warfare Excellence Award for her achievements in this important field during the competitive year ending 30 June 1970.

Columbus had an unusual opportunity to boost the morale of her men and their families through participation in the very first Navy-wide Holiday Dependents Air Charter Program. During her port visit to Villefranche at Christmas time, *Columbus* sent 92 men home to spend the holidays with their families in the United States, and sponsored 98 wives, parents, and children who flew to join their husbands on the Riviera. Reactions to this programs were most favorable in all quarters, justifying the time and effort invested, and arguing strongly for its repetition in the future.

During the RAV period in the Norfolk Naval Shipyard, *Columbus* corrected the major deficiency in her engineering plant: the superheater headers. The headers were removed and reworked, and all the superheater tubes in all four boilers were replaced. Ship's force and tender personnel also accomplished major repair work on a number of pieces of auxiliary equipment.

On 14 August, Captain Robert H. Robeson Jr. relieved Captain Denis-James J. Downey as Commanding Officer. CDR William R. Yetman took over as Executive Officer from CDR Henry T. Dietrich Jr. on 7 April. At year's end *Columbus* carried 72 officers, 51 chief petty officers and 981 other enlisted men.

1971

The first days of 1971 saw *Columbus* in Villefranche, France, completing the last two months of hey six-month Mediterranean deployment. On 16 January *Columbus* transferred RADM R.E. Spreen, COMCRUDESFLOT EIGHT, from USS *Independence* to USS *John F. Kennedy* in St. Paul's Bay, Malta, and visited the island nation's capital, Valetta.

After a one week stopover in Barcelona, Spain, the *"Tall Lady"* participated in Exercise National Week VIII from 10-18 February for the return to the United States. On 22 February *Columbus* turned over SIXTHFLT equipment and publications at Rota, Spain, to await USS *Albany* as the *Tall Lady* turned her bow westward to the most anxiously awaited liberty port, Norfolk.

For six weeks after her 1 March arrival, *Columbus* remained in port with side trips to offload weapons at NWS, Yorktown, and offload fuel at Canary Island.

On 12 April *Columbus* began the trip down the Elizabeth River that would be the beginning of a six-month, $30,000,000 overhaul at Norfolk Naval Shipyard in Portsmouth, Virginia.

Sitting out of water for one of the few times in her history, *Columbus* had her hull sandblasted and painted while the ship's force and yard personnel made adjustments and repairs on *Columbus'* below-the-waterline engineering plant. While in Portsmouth, all four boilers were rebricked, a new probe fueling system was installed, main feed and fuel oil pumps were overhauled and the hanger bay elevator repaired.

Weapons Department accomplished the installation of the new CHAFFROC system, with twin-tube units mounted on each of the port and starboard sides amidships. Overhaul work was also completed on the TALOS, TARTAR and ASROC systems.

The remodeling of the crew's galley and mess decks highlighted the yard work done in the Supply Department. The galley switched from steam to primarily electric cooking and added two six-foot grills, one on each mess line, to bring hotter food to the men sooner. The three mess decks were retiled with the initials of each enlisted rating on board laid into the after mess deck, and with full color copies of the ship's emblem centered on all three. New laundry and dry cleaning equipment was also added while *Columbus* was in the yard.

New accommodation ladders were installed, and the ship's utility and motor whale boats were overhauled during the yard period.

On 3 August, Captain Harold L. Carpenter, USN, relieved Captain Robert H. Robeson Jr., USN, as Commanding Officer of *Columbus*.

The *Tall Lady* left NNSY on Columbus Day, 13 October, to retake her place as an active ship-of-the-line of the Atlantic Fleet.

November was a busy month for the *Tall Lady* as the ship tried out her new systems in the Ship's Qualification Trials in the VACAPES Operational Area. During the month, *Columbus* onloaded TALOS and TARTAR missiles at NWS Yorktown, Virginia, and gave the ship's company dependents a ride from Yorktown to Norfolk aboard the *Tall Lady* on 5 November.

On 1 December, *Columbus* departed Norfolk for Roosevelt Roads, Puerto Rico, for SQT missile firings in the Atlantic Fleet Weapons Range. *Columbus* sailors had their first liberty in a "foreign" port 10 months after leaving the Mediterranean as busloads of *Columbus* men traveled over winding bumpy roads to San Juan, Puerto Rico.

CDR Marcel B. Humber took over as Executive Officer on 24 December, relieving CDR William R. Yetman.

At year's end, *Columbus* carried 71 officers, 54 chief petty officers and 815 enlisted men.

1972

As 1972 began, the crew of the *"Tall Lady"* continued preparations in Norfolk, Virginia, for refresher training at Guantanamo Bay, Cuba. Local operations in the VACAPES and CHASN areas were filled with communications drill, anti-aircraft exercises, general quarters and gun shoots.

Refresher training began 30 January. *Columbus* men labored daily to improve scores and correct deficiencies noted by the Fleet Training Group's Training Readiness Evaluation. The weeks were filled with drills and long hours with brief respites on weekends for relaxation. Excellent weather and the base's recreation facilities permitted the crew to "get away from it all" with softball and beer at Phillips Park and FTG's Casino Night and Mardi Gras celebrations.

The oasis of *Columbus'* six weeks was a port visit to Port-au-Prince, Haiti, from 25 to 27 February. A total of 52 guests, dependents and their sponsors, stationed at Guantanamo, cruised with us to the Haitian capital for an R and R visit. The Haitian Under-Secretary for Foreign Affairs, Pierre Gousse, his family and an escort from the American Embassy toured *Columbus*.

Columbus completed her final week of training and the following note was appended to the final-training report from Commander, Fleet Training Group, "These are the strongest grades I have seen in a major combatant; I congratulate you and your crew."

The final mark for the training was a solid "Satisfactory," the highest evaluation conferred on a major combatant in years.

With refresher training ended, *Columbus* was given an immediate opportunity to put her skills to the test by refueling USS *McCaffery,* a destroyer conducting special operations in the Cienfuegos area.

On 22 March, RADM Hildreth, Commander, Cruiser-Destroyer Flotilla Four, as Nuclear Weapons Acceptance Inspection Senior Officer, conferred a "Satisfactory" on *Columbus* for her NWAI. After receiving missiles from the Naval Weapons Station at Yorktown and conducting more local operations, *Columbus* prepared for her fifth deployment to the Mediterranean since 1966.

On 29 April, *Columbus* men said their good-byes to families and steamed past the bridge-tunnels en route to the "Med." First, however, *Columbus* exercised with Task Group 27.4.1 participating in LANTREADEX 4-72 off Roosevelt Roads, Puerto Rico, and had a rare rendezvous with her sister ship USS *Albany.* After a short stay in the familiar Caribbean port, *Columbus* began her Atlantic transit on 8 May, inchopping to the Sixth Fleet at Rota, Spain, the 17th receiving turnover material from USS *Edward McDonnell.*

The first Mediterranean port-of-call was the seldom visited city of Malaga, Spain. Arriving on 19 May, *Columbus* men took advantage of ship's tours to the nearby fabled city of Granada and the popular tourist resort of Torremolinos.

Leaving Malaga on 24 May, *Columbus* transited the Straits of Gibraltar to visit exotic Tangier, Morocco, the following day. The highlight of the stay for 70 officers and enlisted men were two dinners given by Miss Barbara Hutton in her magnificent Kasbah Palace. On 26 May, *Columbus* was forced by high winds and surging seas to put to sea overnight, stranding many of the crew on the beach. Several members of the U.S. Consul-General's staff were treated to an unplanned night at sea. The ship anchored again the next day.

Columbus returned to the Mediterranean on 29 May to relieve USS *Greene* on Bystander Surveillance Operations in the Western Mediterranean. While carrying out these tasks, *Columbus* steamed across the Mediterranean with a surfaced Soviet Foxtrot submarine and a submarine tender carrying the Commander Soviet Mediterranean Squadron. A Soviet guided Missile Kresta II cruiser, the Russian tanker, *Komsomol,* a Kashin frigate and a Mirny class AG, VAL, all joined in the procession from time to time during the transit. On 1 June, *Columbus* was overflown by an IL-38 May with A.R.E. markings and later that day by several more aircraft. Italian ships *Alpino* and *Rizzo* with an Italian helicopter joined the American ships as the Russian passed through the Straits of Sicily.

Two IL-38 Mays once again overflew the ships as *Columbus* followed the Soviet ships into the Eastern Mediterranean. On 7 June, the sub tender altered course for Sollum, United Arab Republic, and *Columbus* was relieved by USS *Owens.* The following message was received from Commander, Antisubmarine Force, Six Fleet, "Upon termination of your participation in recent Bystander Operations, it is a pleasure that I commend the dedicated and professional performance of all your fine personnel. You clearly demonstrated your professional ability to be prepared for every eventuality. It has been a distinct pleasure to have you on the team. Warm regards, RADM Clifford."

On 10 June, *Columbus* moored in one of the favorite Mediterranean liberty ports, Barcelona, Spain, for a 10-day stay. Many of the crew took an overnight tour to the tiny mountain nation of Andorra while others enjoyed the bullfights and sights of Spain's second largest city. Twelve Naval Academy and ROTC midship-

men and an Iranian ensign boarded *Columbus* for MEDTRAMID training.

Columbus joined British and Italian ships for a NATO MISSILEX off the coast of Sardinia on 23 June, and several days later a Sea Power Demonstration for the NATO Defense College embarked in USS *John F. Kennedy* was conducted off the Italian coast near Naples. This evolution was repeated for the Permanent NATO Representatives on 28 June.

Toulon, France, was the *"Tall Lady's"* next port, with arrival on 29 June. *La Bourdonnais, Columbus'* host ship, sponsored a luncheon for petty officers and officers on 30 June. During the visit, *Columbus'* Wardroom hosted a cocktail party at the Officers' Club for French officers and civilian dignitaries.

Independence Day was celebrated in the French city with several luncheons and a 21-gun salute by *Columbus* at noon. *Columbus* men quickly discovered the beauty and attraction offered by the beaches on the eastern end of the French Riviera.

Columbus participated, along with British and American ships, in MISSILEX 1-73; on 10 and 11 July and debarked midshipmen in Souda Bay, Crete. At the same time, the second increment of summer training MIDTRAMID was taken aboard.

From 12-15 July, *Columbus* men enjoyed the sunny little island of Corfu, Greece, before joining elements of the Sixth Fleet for National Week XIII, which began on 17 July. *Columbus* was one of the friendly "Blue" forces engaged in simulated hostilities in the central Mediterranean. As the exercises progressed, *Columbus* took part in deceiving "Orange" enemies by successfully imitating the carrier *John F. Kennedy* and was credited with several air and surface kills. On 21 July, the final day of the exercise, the "victorious" Blue forces effectively ended the "war" and headed for Augusta Bay, Sicily, for a "hot washup."

Midshipmen were given opportunities to conn the ship as *Columbus* took part in various operations en route to Valencia, Spain, where she arrived on 30 July.

After a four-day stay, *Columbus* exercised en route to Athens, Greece, for an 18-day port visit highlighted by the dependents' charter flight from the States. A total of 79 dependents visited the cradle of western civilization with their *Columbus* men and 48 crew members took the back-haul flight home. There were tours of Athens, the historic and beautiful areas of Delphi, Mycanae, Corinth, and the Greek Islands.

USS *John F. Kennedy* and three escorts joined *Columbus* in Athens, and all departed on 26 August for more missile exercises with units of the Italian fleet.

From 31 August to 4 September, Columbus men enjoyed the popular Greek Island of Rhodes with tours of the impressive castle of the Knights of St. John as well as the hilly and narrow streets of the old town.

Proceeding from Rhodes, *Columbus* again rendezvoused with *John F. Kennedy* and destroyers as ASW exercises in the Ionian Sea, and then on to Trieste, Italy, for a port visit from 8-11 September. Columbus men enjoyed the quiet beauty of Trieste, and many made tours to the picturesque and lively city of Venice.

More ASW exercises followed as *Columbus* steamed south through the Adriatic Sea to Palma de Mallorca, Spain. The visit from 18-20 September was followed by a return to the French Riviera and Golfe Juan. The town's proximity to Cannes, Nice and Monte Carlo made it a favorite liberty port. Underway on 26 September, *Columbus* arrived at the British Crown Colony of Gibraltar, where the crew and officers hosted and were hosted to a series of parties which made "Gib" one of the highlights of the deployment.

Columbus left Gibraltar for Lisbon, Portugal, on 2 October for five days of sporadic boating due to the weather. Tours included the famed Fatima shrine, and there was that last hunt for European souvenirs. On 9 October *Columbus* completed turnover with her sister ship USS *Albany* at Rota, Spain, took in all lines and headed westward.

The Atlantic crossing proved uneventful, and, on 18 October, shortly before 1000, the first lines were put over and *Columbus* was berthed comfortably at her "home," Pier 5 NOB, and the long-awaited reunion with wives and sweethearts was underway.

Schooling and tender availability followed the post-deployment stand down period. On 5 December, *Columbus* sailed to the Weapons Station at Yorktown with 100 Naval Junior Reserve Officer Training Corps cadets from Virginia Beach's Kellam High School on board. After a missile load-out, the ship sailed for Roosevelt Roads, Puerto Rico, on 6 December for missile exercises in the Atlantic Fleet Weapons Range. After firing TALOS and TARTAR missiles, with a TALOS scorecard of two for three and one for one in TARTAR, it was back to Norfolk for the Christmas holiday stand down.

The holiday spirit onboard was expressed in several ways: on 22 December, *Columbus* hosted 100 local orphans and underprivileged children for a Christmas party; on 24 December, the *Tall Lady* served as host ship for USS *Newport News'* return from the Western Pacific and the ship's lighting display won the Norfolk Chamber of Commerce's award for "Most Original Ship" at NOB in the annual holiday competition. It was an appropriate end to a busy and very successful year.

1973

As 1973 began, USS *Columbus* was in her homeport, Norfolk, Virginia, for a holiday leave period. The crew continued routing maintenance and training in preparation for the first exercise of the year, Operation Springboard in the Caribbean. On 30 January the ship proceeded to Yorktown Naval Weapons Station for a missile loadout, then conducted ISE en route to the Caribbean. A short liberty stop at St. Thomas was followed by gunnery exercises and TALOS, TARTAR, and ASROC firings on the LANTFLT weapons range. The ship demonstrated her capabilities against surface, air and subsurface targets, climaxed by a solid hit with a practice torpedo against a submarine.

Columbus was detached from Operation Springboard on 9 February and proceeded to Port Everglades, Florida, for a visit in Fort Lauderdale. She then steamed home and remained in Norfolk from 16 February to 27 March. During this time *Columbus* was host ship for the visiting Dutch Cruiser HMNS *De Seven Provincien*.

On 28 March *Columbus* departed Norfolk to participate in Exotic Dancer VI, a joint Army-Navy-Air Force-Marine Corps exercise off the coast of North Carolina. RADM Dennis-James J. Downey, COMCRUDESFLOT EIGHT, was embarked when the ship entered the Caribbean. On 6 April, the ship underwent an Operational Readiness Inspection by COMCRUDESFLOT EIGHT.

The ship remained in-port at Norfolk from 7 April until commencement of LANTREADEX 3-73 on 29 May. On 29 May, just prior to sailing, Captain M.B. Humber was relieved as Executive Officer by Commander R.E. Helms Jr. LANTREADEX included fleet training with several foreign ships and missile firings on the LANTFLT Weapons Range.

Columbus received the "Top Tactical Operator" Award for her superior contribution during LANTREADEX 3-73. The ship then visited Roosevelt Roads, Puerto, Rico and Nassau, Bahamas from 10-12 June.

Columbus began three weeks of upkeep on 15 June in Norfolk. During the Summer she conducted onboard training for three groups of Midshipmen. In July, she returned to the Caribbean to conduct missile firings and participate in LANTREADEX 1-74. The ship was back in Yorktown on 29 July for a missile load-out, followed by in-port time in Norfolk.

Captain William H. Rowden relieved Captain Harold L. Carpenter as Commanding Officer onboard on 21 August. During the next several weeks the ship conducted type training off the Virginia Capes, participated in FORACS off Connecticut, and was host to USS *Springfield* upon the ship's return to Norfolk from the Mediterranean for decommissioning.

An INSURV was concluded on 21 September except for one phase, with *Columbus* ruled by the INSURV BOARD to be fit for further service. The crew then commenced preparations for overseas movement to the Mediterranean. On 23 October the ship completed the full-power run and crash-back phase of the INSURV, then conducted a weapons load-out at Yorktown, Virginia. A family cruise was held for 243 dependents en route to Norfolk.

Columbus departed Norfolk on 2 November for extended deployment to the Mediterranean with the U.S. Sixth Fleet. The Atlantic transit was made in company with the USS *Sellers* (DLG-11).

A brief stop was made on 9 November at Ponta Delgada, Azores, for the USS *Sellers* to refuel. *Columbus* inchopped to Sixth Fleet on 12 November just prior to entering Rota, Spain for refueling. The same day, *Columbus* departed for Augusta Bay, Sicily, where the ship conducted turnover with the USS *Belknap* (DLG-26) on 15 November.

The ship's initial Mediterranean assignment was with Task Group 60.1 operating in the eastern Mediterranean, south of Crete. From 17-21 November, *Columbus* served as long-range missile defense for the USS *Independence* (CVA-62) and Task Group 60.1.

Columbus proceeded to Izmir, Turkey, for a port visit from 22-27 November. One day's steaming in the Aegean brought the ship to Athens, Greece on 28 November where *Columbus* anchored for five days of liberty and upkeep.

On 2 December, *Columbus* was again underway for operations with Task Group 60.1 south of Crete. On 13 December, *Columbus* joined Task Group 60.2, under RADM Downey embarked in USS *Franklin D. Roosevelt* (CVA-62), while that task group proceeded to Spanish ports for the Christmas holiday period.

Columbus moored at Barcelona, Spain on 19 December along with the USS *Franklin D. Roosevelt* and other members of the task group. During the holiday period a dependents charter flight and a backhaul flight brought families together for the holidays.

1974

As 1974 began, USS *Columbus* was two months into her Sixth Fleet deployment and her crew members were enjoying a well-deserved holiday upkeep period in Barcelona, Spain. The Barcelona visit included a, dependents charter and "backhaul" flight which brought families together in Norfolk and Barcelona for the holidays.

Columbus got underway on 5 January and conducted an intelligence collection mission along the North African littoral while en route to Athens, Greece, arriving there on 16 January. *Columbus* again got underway on 24 January with other units of Task Group 60.2 and conducted inter-type training, including one ASROC and one torpedo firing and the annual Operational Readiness Exercise during five days of operations in the Aegean Sea.

Columbus arrived at Kavalla, Greece on 29 January for a five-day visit followed by a seven day visit to Thesseloniki, Greece. Departing Thessaloniki on 11 February, *Columbus* proceeded to Soudha Bay, Crete, arriving there on 12 February and joining numerous other units of the Sixth Fleet for pre-exercise planning for Exercise National Week XVI.

CO, USS *Columbus* as commander of the Orange surface forces for Exercise National Week XVI during the period 15-19 February and *Columbus* simulated a KYNDA class cruiser as the exercise ranged across the Eastern Mediterranean. In addition to USS *Columbus*, Orange surface forces included USS *Neosho* (AO-143), USS *Sellers* (DDG-11), USS *Page* (DEG-5), USS Wood (DD-715), USS *Graham County* (AGP-1176), USS *Nespelen* (AOG-55), USS *Antelope* (PG-86), USS *Ready* (PG-87), USS *Grand Rapids* (PG-98) and USS *Douglas* (PG-100).

At the conclusion of her highly successful participation in Exercise National Week XVI, *Columbus* made a brief port visit to Corfu, Greece from 21-23 February and then proceeded to the NAMFI missile range off Crete for missile firing exercise. On 26 and 27 February, *Columbus* fired two TALOS and three TARTAR missiles at MQM-74 drones, scoring one out of two hits with TALOS; all three TARTAR firings were hits.

On the evening of 27 February, *Columbus* commenced a transit from Soudha Bay, Crete to the Western Mediterranean, joining Task Group 61 in the vicinity of Porto Scudo, Sardinia for Amphibious Exercise 9-74 on 1 March. From 2 to 10 March, USS *Columbus* acted as Force Anti-Air Warfare Coordinator for CTF 71, controlling numerous friendly aircraft and engaging aggressor aircraft with her assigned interceptors, missiles and guns. During PHIBLEX 974, *Columbus* exercised her fun crews in both surface and air live firings and her air controllers conducted over 80 intercepts.

While enjoying a port visit in Naples during the period of 12 to 19 March, USS *Columbus* was directed to get underway and proceed at best speed to the Eastern Mediterranean for participation in NATO Exercise Daffodil Face. *Columbus* was underway within 12 hours of the CTF 60 Sailord and joined the NATO force operating south of Mamaris, Turkey on the evening of 22 March. During Exercise Daffodil Face, *Columbus* participated in anti-submarine, gunnery, anti-swimmer, anti-PT boat and convoy escort exercises with units of the Turkish, Greek, British, and Italian navies. Exercise ships arrived in Izmir, Turkey on 30 March for a post-exercise critique. At the critique, the Turkish commander praised *Columbus*, the only U.S. participant, for her versatility in anti-air, anti-PT boat, and anti-submarine warfare.

On 31 March, *Columbus* commenced transiting to the Western Mediterranean, again, and joined Task Group 60.2 on 2 April for a day of anti-submarine training during which an exercise ASROC and exercise torpedo were fired against the USS *Greenling*.

After a one day visit to Naples, Italy and four days of Task Group 60 operations in the Tyrrhenian Sea, *Columbus* proceeded to Genoa, Italy, arriving on 9 April. In the early morning hours of 12 April, *Columbus* sailors rescued more than 30 people from the waters of Genoa Harbor who were overboard from the capsized ocean ferry *Monica Rossotti*. Later, the same day, *Columbus* once again sailed on 12 hours notice to conduct surveillance of a large Soviet surface force operating in the Western Mediterranean with one or more submarines.

On 16 April, CTF 67 released *Columbus* from her surveillance duties to proceed to Malaga, Spain where she arrived on 17 April for a ten-day port visit. On 27 April, *Columbus* got underway for NATO Exercise Dawn Patrol 74 operations in the Straits of Gibraltar and the Eastern Atlantic. On 3 May, *Columbus* was released from exercise participation to proceed to Palma de Majorca, arriving there on 4 May. The remainder of *Columbus'* seven month Mediterranean cruise was spent en route to or in the Spanish ports of Barcelona, 11-20 May, and Rota, 23-24 May. On 25 May, after a brief turnover with USS *Conynahm* (DDG-17), *Columbus* got underway for CONUS, arriving in Norfolk on the afternoon of 31 May.

Columbus men received a well-deserved rest while in a post-deployment standdown status in port of Norfolk during the month of June. In July, *Columbus* offloaded all weapons and ammunition at NWS, Yorktown, in preparation for her forthcoming inactivation. A family day cruise was held for nearly 300 dependents on the return trip to Norfolk on 15 July.

On 2 August, Commander Raymond E. Helms Jr. relieved Captain William H. Rowden as 25th and last Commanding Officer. At the ceremony, the quest speaker, RADM Wentworth, COMCRUDESLANT, announced that the *Columbus* had won the 1974 Battle Efficiency "E."

On 8 August, *Columbus* received official notification that, in addition to the Battle Efficiency "E," she had made a clean sweep of all departmental and mission area excellence awards for cruisers in the 1974 competition. On 15 August, *Columbus* was moved by tugs to St. Helena's Annex of the Naval Inactive Ships Maintenance Facility where pre-inactivation commenced the next day with a reduced crew of 28 officers and 530 enlisted men.

1975

After 36 years of naval service, the guided missile cruiser USS *Columbus* (CG-12) will be decommissioned and transferred to the Inactive Ship Maintenance Facility, Portsmouth, Virginia. The ceremony will take place at St. Helena's Annex of the Inactive Ship Maintenance Facility on Friday, 31 January 1975 at 11 a.m.

Vice Admiral Denis-James J. Downey, Chief of Staff, Supreme Allied Commander, Atlantic, will be the quest speaker at the ceremony which will officially retire the ship from the fleet. Vice Admiral Downey commanded the *Columbus* from February 1969 to August 1970.

Among the guests will be Mrs. Edward G. Meyers of Columbus, Ohio, who christened the heavy cruiser USS *Columbus* (CA-74) in honor of that city on 30 November 1944, at the Bethlehem Steel Company's Quincy, Massachusetts shipyard. Mrs. Meyers lost two sons in combat in World War II.

COMMANDING OFFICERS

Allen Hobbs	8 June 1945 – 13 March 1946
Walter E. Moore	13 March 1946 – 22 January 1947
Milton E. Miles	22 January 1947 – 4 December 1947
John P. Cady	4 December 1947 – 7 October 1948
John M. Will	7 October 1948 – 3 October 1949
Ephraim R. McLean, Jr.	3 October 1949 – 12 September 1950
Joseph H. Wellings	12 September 1950 – 2 August 1951
Frederick B. Warder	2 August 1951 – 14 March 1952
Gordon Campbell	14 March 1952 – 26 February 1953
Luther Reynolds	26 February 1953 – 28 January 1954
Blinn VanMater	28 January 1954 – 18 November 1954
J.D.L. Grant	18 November 1954 – 10 February 1956
George C. Seay	10 February 1956 – 15 March 1957
Gordon A. Uehling	15 March 1957 – 4 April 1958
Ralph C. Johnson	4 April 1958 – 19 December 1958
Thomas H. Morton	19 December 1958 – March 1959

During the period of March 1959 through 1 December 1962, the Heavy Cruiser *Columbus* (CA-74) was decommissioned and converted to the Missile Cruiser *Columbus* (CG-12) at the Puget Sound Naval Shipyard, Bremerton, Washington.

Gideon M. Boyd	1 December 1962 – 12 October 1964
Royal K. Joslin	12 October 1964 – 4 March 1966
Lewis J. Ștecher, Jr.	4 March 1966 – 5 October 1967
William A. Arthur	5 October 1967 – 6 February 1969
Denis-James J. Downey	6 February 1969 – 14 August 1970
R.H. Robeson, Jr.	14 August 1970 – 3 August 1971
H.L. Carpenter	3 August 1971 – 21 August 1973
W.H. Rowden	21 August 1973 – 2 August 1974
Cdr. Raymond E. Helms, Jr.	2 August 1974 – 31 January 1975

FLAGS ON THE USS *COLUMBUS*

(CA-74 / CG-12)

Broke Flag			Name
17	January	1946	RDM Thomas G.W. Settle
24	January	1946	RDM Albert M. Bledsoe
16	February	1946	RDM Andrew C. Bennett
7	February	1947	RDM Willard A. Kitts III
20	August	1947	RDM Roscoe F. Good
10	July	1950	RDM Richard L. Conally
1	November	1950	RDM Robert B. Carney
25	August	1952	RDM Lynde D. McCormick
	January	1953	RDM John Howard Cassady
	November	1953	RDM Richard L. Denison
7	September	1954	RDM Donald Cord Varian
		1954	RDM Arleigh A. Burke
		1954	RDM Edward N. Parker
11	February	1956	RDM Francis D. McCorkle
2	June	1956	Captain G. Wales of CL-144 relieved F.D. McCorkle as Cmdr. Cruiser Div Three
		1956	RDM Charles K. Bergin
22	March	1957	RDM Ulysses S. Grant Sharp, Jr.
17	August	1957	RDM Miles Hunt Hubbard
12	December	1958	RDM Vernon L. Lowrance
		1964	RDM Horace V. Bird
		1964	RDM Dennis C. Lyndon
21	February	1966	RDM Fred G. Bennett
1	August	1966	RDM John D. Bulkeley
9	June	1967	RDM James Francis Calvert
1	December	1968	RDM Mans L. Johnston
		1969	RDM Ernest W. Dobie, Jr.
		1969	RDM R.B. Armstrong
			RDM Roger E. Spreen
		1973	RDM Dennis-James J. Downey

Note: From 1959 through 1962 there were no admirals on board. The ship was in the Bremerton, Washington Navy Yard being converted from a heavy cruiser to the Missile Cruiser (CG-12).

Vincent St. Marks Cathedral, 1954. Courtesy of Ronald P. Dolinsky

CHRONOLOGICAL HISTORY OF THE USS COLUMBUS

1944

30 November Hull No. 1506 was given the name USS *Columbus* and was launched.

1945

9 June Commissioned and accepted by Capt. Allen Hobbs.

6 July Started on shakedown, reduction gear went out. Returned to South Boston Navy Yard for repairs.

6 September Left Boston for shakedown cruise after necessary repairs were made.

27 October Arrived in New York City to celebrate Navy Day with other ships of the fleet.

1 November Arrived back in Boston for repairs from shakedown.

24 November Enroute Boston, MA to Guantanamo Bay, Cuba.

27 November Arrived at Guantanamo Bay.

27 November to
4 December Participated in refresher training exercises.

4 December Departed Guantanamo Bay, Cuba for Culebra Island for bombardment practice.

6 December Sighted Culebra Island.

6-7 December Conducted shore bombardment exercises.

7 December Departed for Panama Canal Zone.

10 December
– 0659 Entered Lemon Bay.

10 December
– 0737 Entered Panama Canal from Lemon Bay.

10 December
– 0748 Commenced transit through Canal, first locks, Gatum Locks.

10 December
– 1457 Completed transit through Canal and moored at Balboa, Panama Canal Zone, Panama.

13 December Departed for Pearl Harbor, T.H.

25 December Arrived Pearl Harbor–moored at Pearl Harbor, Oahu, T.H.

28 December Underway for Buckner Bay, Okinawa Bay, Okinawa. *Columbus* hit first rough seas.

31 December Crossed 180 meridian–date changed to January 2, 1946, lost January 1st

1946

9 January Anchored at Buckner Bay, Okinawa

11 January Underway for Tsingtao, China

13 January Anchored at Tsingtao, China

24 January RADM Bledsoe reported aboard as ComCruDivOne.

2 February Held searchlight display in honor of Chinese New Year.

7 February Underway for Shanghai, China.

9 February Anchored at Woosung, China

10 February Underway up Whangpoo River, then up the Yangtse, anchored at 0807 in Shanghai off Pootung Point.

13 February Rendered passing honors to Generalissimo Chiang Kai-Shek. Crew lined the rails.

15 February RADM Bledsoe was detached.

16 February RADM Bennett reported on board as ComCruDivOne as relief for RADM Bledsoe.

23 February
– 1453 Underway to Woosung, China.

23 February
– 1722 Anchored at Woosung, China.

24 February Underway for Yokosuka, Japan.

27 February Moored at Yokosuka, Japan.

13 March Captain W.E. Moore relieved Captain Allen Hobbs as Commanding Officer of the USS *Columbus*.

27 March Underway for Sasebo, Japan.

29 March Moored at Sasebo, Japan.

1 April
– 0902 Underway for Operation "Road's End, Deep Six".

1 April
– 1320 Arrived at Deep Six, commenced sinking 24 Japanese submarines by demolition and gun fire including I-58, the sub that sunk the USS *Indianapolis*, and I-402, the airplane carrying sub that is believed to have sent planes to drop incendiaries on the state of Washington.

2 April Underway for San Pedro, California.

17 April ETA, San Pedro, California. Entered dry dock for repairs and maintenance.

September Operating out of Long Beach, California, conducting weekly radar tracking of radio controlled missiles launched at Point Mugu, California.

October Celebrated Navy Day at Santa Barbara, California.

November Participated in joint Army-Navy exercise "Operation Duck" held on Southern California coast and San Clemente Island.

1 December Participated in the Fifth Fleet Maneuvers.

14 December Returned to Long Beach for Christmas and New Year's holidays.

1947

15 January Set sail for second visit to the Orient

21 January Arrived at Pearl Harbor and took on Captain Milton E. Miles

23 January Left Pearl Harbor, making a brief stop at Saipan

7 February Arrived at Shanghai, China. Became Flag Ship for Commander, Cruiser Division 3, RADM W.A. Kitts III, USN.

February Spent three weeks in training.

23 May Underway for Yokosuka, Japan on first leg back to the States.

26 May Arrived at Yokosuka, Japan. Spent six days.

1 June	Set sail for San Francisco, California.
12 June	Arrived in San Francisco. Proceeded to Mare Island for repairs. Remained until 16 July.
16 July	Sailed for Long Beach to operate with Cruiser Division 13 participating in competitive gunnery exercises at San Clemente Island.
20 August	Hoisted flag of RADM Roscoe F. Good, Commander, Cruiser Div One.
December	Spent Christmas holiday at Long Beach and remainder of the year at Puget Sound Naval Shipyard, Bremerton, Washington.

1948

January/ February	Completed sea trials and set sail for the Panama Canal to join CruDivTwo in the Atlantic Ocean.
April	Passed through the Panama Canal enroute to Norfolk, Virginia
Summer	NROTC students and Midshipmen boarded for the Midshipmen Cruise.
15 September	Left Norfolk, Virginia for European cruise.
23 September	Arrived in Gibraltar.
28 September	Departed for Venice, Italy.
2 October	Arrived in Venice.
4 October	Departed for Trieste, Italy.
4 October	Arrived in Trieste.
7 October	Departed for Bizerte, Africa.
9 October	Arrived in Bizerte.
11 October	Departed for Villefranche, France.
13 October	Arrived in Villefranche.
16 October	Departed for Algiers, Morocco.
18 October	Arrived in Algiers.
21 October	Departed for Naples, Italy.
23 October	Arrived in Naples.
26 October	Depart for Plymouth, England (homeport).

2 November	Arrived in Plymouth.
6 December	Departed for Gravesend, England.
10 December	Arrived in Gravesend.
14 December	Departed for Plymouth, England.
18 December to Jan 6, 1949	Arrived and moored in Plymouth.

1949

6 January	Departed Plymouth, England for Casablanca, Morocco.
9 January	Arrived in Casablanca.
12 January	Departed for Gibraltar.
13 January	Arrived in Gibraltar.
15 January	Departed for the Island of Malta.
17 January	Arrived at Malta.
21 January	Departed for Athens, Greece.
23 January	Arrived in Athens, Greece.
26 January	Departed for Istanbul, Turkey.
27 January	Arrived in Istanbul.
4 February	Departed for Salonika, Greece.
5 February	Arrived in Salonika.
8 February	Departed for Taranto, Italy.
10 February	Arrived in Taranto.
13 February	Departed for Tobruck, Libya.
15 February	Arrived in Tobruck.
28 February	Departed for Augusta, Sicily.
2 March	Arrived in Augusta.
3 March	Departed for Toulon, France.
6 March	Arrived in Toulon.
10 March	Departed for Gibraltar.
12 March	Arrived in Gibraltar.
12 March	Departed for Plymouth, England.
15 March	Arrived in Plymouth.
4 April	Departed for Torquay, England.
8 April	Arrived in Torquay.
11 April	Departed for Plymouth,

	England.
14 April	Arrived in Plymouth.
21 April	Departed for Tobruck, Libya.
1 May	Arrived Tobruck.
8 May	Departed for Gibraltar.
13 May	Arrived in Gibraltar.
17 May	Departed for Augusta, Italy.
22 May	Arrived in Augusta.
26 May	Departed for Villefranche, France.
28 May	Arrived in Villefranche.
7 June	Departed for Naples, Italy.
8 June	Arrived in Naples.
12 June	Departed for Tobruck, Lydia.
14 June	Arrived in Tobruck.
21 June	Departed for Tripoli, Libya.
24 June	Arrived in Tripoli.
24 June	Departed for Gibraltar.
27 June	Arrived in Gibraltar.
27 June	Departed for Plymouth, England.
30 June	Arrived in Plymouth.
12 July	Departed for Sheerness, England.
13 July	Arrived in Sheerness.
14 July	Departed for Oslo, Norway.
16 July	Arrived Oslo.
21 July	Departed for Copenhagen, Denmark.
22 July	Arrived in Copenhagen.
27 July	Departed for the Keil Canal, Germany.
28 July	Arrived in Keil Canal.
28 July	Departed for Amsterdam, Holland.
29 July	Arrived in Amsterdam.
1 August	Departed for Plymouth, England.
4 August	Arrived in Plymouth.

13 August	Departed for Gibraltar.
16 August	Arrived in Gibraltar
17 August	Departed for Tobruck, Libya.
21 August	Arrived in Tobruck.
28 August	Departed for Gibraltar.
1 September	Arrived in Gibraltar.
1 September	Departed Gibraltar.
3 September	Arrived in El Ferrol, Spain.
8 September	Departed for Plymouth, England.
10 September	Arrived in Plymouth.
10 October	Departed for Gibraltar.
13 October	Arrived in Gibraltar.
13 October	Departed for Villefranche, France.
15 October	Arrived in Villefranche.
21 October	Departed for Argostoli, Greece.
23 October	Arrived in Argostoli.
24 October	Departed for Athens, Greece.
26 October	Arrived in Athens.
29 October	Departed for Gibraltar.
2 November	Arrived in Gibraltar.
2 November	Departed for Portsmouth, England.
5 November	Arrived in Portsmouth.
5 November	Departed for Plymouth, England.
10 November	Arrived in Plymouth.
19 November	Departed for Bremerhaven, Germany.
20 November	Arrived in Bremerhaven.
21 November	Departed for Plymouth, England.
23 November	Arrived in Plymouth.
1 December	Departed for the United States.
9 December	Arrived in New York City. Going to Boston Naval Shipyard for overhaul.

1950

January to June	Overhaul in Boston Naval Shipyard.
12 June	Departed Boston.
22 June to 10 July	Inport, Plymouth, England.
11 July	Arrived Breol, France.
16 to 19 July	Antwerp, Belgium
20 to 23 July	Rotterdam, Holland
24 to 31 July	Plymouth, England
3 to 4 August	At Gibraltar
10 to 11 August	Famagusta, Cyprus
12 to 14 August	Beirut, Lebanon
16 August	Suda Bay, Crete
19 August	Valletta, Malta
20 to 21 August	Naples, Italy
22 August to 5 September	Cannes, France
9 to 13 September	Bizerte, Tunisia
15 to 19 September	Oran, Algeria
22 to 24 September	Aranci Bay, Sardinia
25 to 28 September	Villefranche, France
29 September to 1 October	Cogilari, Sardinia
2 to 5 October	Valletta, Malta
5 to 9 11 to 15 October	Augusta, Sicily
18 to 26 October	Trieste, Italy
26 to 30 October	Venice, Italy
3 November	Piraeus, Greece
4 to 13 November	Suda Bay, Crete
17 to 20 November	Izmir, Turkey

25 to 29 November	Villefranche, France
1 to 2 December	Valletta, Malta
3 to 7 December	Naples, Italy
13 December to 5 Jan 1951	Plymouth, England

1951

10 to 13 January	Villefranche, France.
20 to 22 January	Augusta, Sicily
22 to 25 January	Valletta, Malta
29 January to 2 February	Augusta, Sicily
3 to 11 February	Naples, Italy
16 to 21 February	Istanbul, Turkey
22 to 27 February	Piraeus, Greece
3 to 5 8 to 9 March	Suda Bay, Crete
10 to 14 March	Valletta, Malta
16 to 28 March	Villefranche, France
4 to 9 April	Bizerte, Tunisia
12 to 15 April	Augusta, Sicily
18 to 24 April	Naples, Italy
25 April to 2 May	Villefranche, France
5 to 8 May	Oran, Algeria
15 to 19 May	Naples, Italy
24 to 29 May	Augusta, Sicily
1 to 8 June	Piraeus, Greece
14 to 18 June	Taranto, Italy
23 to 29 June	Genoa, Italy
2 to 16 July	Villefranche, France
23 to 28 July	Istanbul, Turkey
2 to 12 August	Suda Bay, Crete
18 August to 1 September	Beaulieu, France.

8 to 12 September	LaSpezia, Italy
22 to 26 September	Lisbon, Portugal
5 October	Arrived in Norfolk, Virginia
October	Participated in LANTFLEX operations in Cuban and Eastern U.S. coastal waters. Steamed to Boston for general overhaul and armament refitting.

1952

January to May	Overhaul and armament refitting
May	Completed overhaul in Boston. Sailed for training exercises in Guantanamo Bay, Cuba.
7 July	Returned to Boston
2 August	Participated in goodwill reserve cruise to Halifax, Nova Scotia in honor of Canadian Navy Day
25 August	Departed Boston as Flagship of RDM Lynde D. McCormick, Supreme Allied Commander, Atlantic. Participated in NATO Exercise "Main Brace"
10 to 13 September	Helensburgh, Scotland
16 September	Crossed the Arctic Circle
19 and 20 September	Edinburg, Scotland
25 to 29 September	Oslo, Norway
3 to 9 October	Lisbon, Portugal
16 to 24 October	Augusta, Sicily
29 October to 3 November	Genoa, Italy
8 and 9 November	Marsaxlokk Bay, Malta
14 to 19 November	Istanbul, Turkey
20 to 24 November	Phaleron Bay, Greece
26 November to 1 December	Beirut, Lebanon

4 to 10 December	Naples, Italy
11 to 15 December	Toulon, France
19 December to 5 January 1953	Villefranche, France

1953

9 to 15 January	Barcelona, Spain
16 to 22 January	Algiers, Algeria
23 to 26 January	Tangiers, Spanish Morocco
6 February	Returned to Boston Naval Shipyard
9 March	Sailed to Guantanamo Bay for gunnery practice and drills
11 April	Arrived in Boston for small scale leave and up-keep period
2 May	At sea as fire support ship for amphibious maneuvers off North Carolina
15 May	Arrived at Boston after spending four days in New York City
17 May to July	Conducted several Naval Reserve Training cruises and underwent scheduled Operational Readiness Inspection
14 July	Left Boston
16 July	Arrived at Norfolk for Midshipmen Cruise "Charlie"
20 July	Columbus with ten other ships left for Caribbean area.
28 August	Disembarked Midshipmen in Norfolk.
1 September	Arrived in Boston
17 September	Departed for Guantanamo Bay for gunnery practice.
21 to 25 September	Participated in NAGEX 1-54 at Culebra Island, Puerto Rico
15 October	Returned to Boston for leave and up-keep period
November	RDM Richard L. Denison, Commander, Cruiser Division Four, boarded the ship until 21 December

1954

January	Embarked for Guantanamo Bay for Operation SPRINGBOARD
26 January	USS Columbus went into drydock at Boston Naval Shipyard.
28 January	Captain Blinn Vanmater relieved Captain Luther K. Reynolds as Commanding Officer
21 June	Re-outfitting and remodeling is completed. USS *Columbus* heads south to Cuban waters for six-weeks' refresher cruise.
29 July	USS Columbus put into St. Thomas, Virgin Islands
???	Visited New York City for six days
???	Returned to Boston before departing for five-month tour of duty in the Mediterranean Sea.
7 September	Departed Boston. RDM DC Varian Commander Destroyer Flotilla Two to join the Sixth Fleet in the Mediterranean Sea.
22 September	Arrived in Lisbon, Portugal. RDM Varian departed the USS *Columbus* and broke his flag in USS *McCord* (DD-882).
27 September	Departed Lisbon, Portugal

1955

January	Inport at Boston
March	Steamed to Caribbean Sea to make a good-will visit to Havana, Cuba.
6 June	Departed with part of Atlantic Fleet on "Midshipman Cruise Able" visiting ports in Spain, England and Cuba.
2 and 3 August	Inport at Annapolis, Maryland
4 August	Vacapes Operation
6 to 22 August	Inport at Boston
24 to 25 August	Vacapes Operation
27 to 29 August	Inport at Boston

30 August to 2 September	Narrabay Operation
3 to 26 September	Inport at Boston
30 September to 3 October	PEUGLDS
8 October to 8 November	Inport at Boston
12 November	Gitmo Operation
14 to 16 November	Inport at Balboa, Cristobal
19 to 22 November	Inport at Callao, Peru
25 November	Balboa
2 December to 5 January 1956	Inport at Long Beach

1956

5 January	Departed Long Beach, California. Joined Cruiser Division 3 commanded by RDM FD McCorkle.
12 January	Arrived at Pearl Harbor
14 January	Departed Pearl Harbor
26 January	Arrived Yokosuka, Japan
10 February	Captain George C. Seay relieved Captain JDL Grant as Commanding Officer
11 February	RDM FD McCorkle, embarked, departed Yokosuka for Seventh Fleet.
20 February	Proceeded to Buckner Bay, Okinawa
24 February	Arrived Buckner Bay
27 February	Departed for Hong Kong, BCC
2 March	Arrived in Hong Kong
8 March	Departed Hong Kong to rendezvous with Task Force 77 operating in the South China Sea.
11 March	While steaming with Task Force 77, the USS *Columbus*, as guide, was involved in a collision with the USS *Floyd B. Parks* (DD-884) at 0359. Damage to the *Columbus* was minor, two crewmen from Parks were listed as missing. *Columbus* escorted the Parks to

	Subic Bay P.I. for repairs.
28 March	Made ready for sea after repairs were made. Departed to Zamboanga, P.I.
31 March	Dropped anchor in Basilan Straits
4 April	Underway for Manila, P.I.
6 April	Anchored in Manila Bay
27 April	Arrived in Nagasaki, Japan
30 April	Underway to rendezvous with Task Force 77
2 June	Dropped anchor in Buckner Bay, Okinawa. Captain G. Wales relieved RDM FD McCorkle as Commander Cruiser Division Three
13 June	Underway for Port Swettenham, Malaysia on goodwill visit.
16 June	Anchored at Penang, Malaysia
18 June	RDM CK Bergin shifted his flag to the USS *Braine*. *Columbus* proceeded to Guam, Mariana Island.
25 June	Arrived at Guam Island after a fueling stop at Singapore B.C.C.
	Departed for the States.
1 July	Arrived Pearl Harbor, T.H.
3 July	Departed for U.S. as a unit of Task Group 52.3.4 with USS *Helena* (CA-75) and USS *Worcester* (CL-144)
8 July	Arrived Long Beach, CA. Leave and upkeep period for approximately one month.
6 August to 24 September	Participated in Type Training off Southern California coast and shore bombardment at San Clemente Island.
24 September	Departed for Naval Ammunition Depot Mare Island, California to offload ammunition.
26 September	Arrived at Hunter's Point Shipyard.
26 September to 31 December	In San Francisco Naval Shipyard undergoing regular overhaul.

1957

1 January to 17 January	At Hunter's Point Naval Shipyard finishing regular shipyard overhaul.
17 January	Departed for Long Beach.
18 January	Arrived in Long Beach
18 January to 31 January	Type training off the Southern California coast.
4 February	Reported to Commander Fleet Training Group, San Diego for refresher training.
8 March	Completed four week refresher training.
8 March to 26 March	Operated Type training exercises out of Long Beach
15 March	Captain Gordon A. Uehling relieved Captain George C. Seay as commanding officer.
22 March	Commander Cruiser Division Three RDM U.S.G. Sharp, Jr., shifted his flag from the USS *Helena* to the USS *Columbus*.
10 April	Departed Long Beach
16 April	Arrived Pearl Harbor with Cruiser Division Three.
April	Departed Pearl Harbor Pearl Harbor for Melbourne, Australia with Destroyer Division 212
29 April	Arrived Suva, capital of Fiji Islands.
20 May	Arrived Island of Guam
24 May	Departed Guam for Muko Shima
1 June	Arrive d Yokosuka
12 June	Proceeded to rendezvous with other Seventh Fleet units for Task Force operations.
28 June	Arrived Kobe, Japan
30 June	Proceeded to Hong Kong, B.C.C.
5 July	Arrived Hong Kong
12 July	Departed for Task Force Operations off of Okinawa, stopped in Keelung, Taiwan for a one day Goodwill visit.
24 July	Arrived Sasebo, Japan

3 August	Arrived Nagasaki, Japan
16 August	Arrived Kobe, Japan
17 August	RDM M.H. Hubbard relieved RDM U.S.G. Sharp, Jr., as Commander Cruiser Division Three
— August	Typhoon Agnes interrupted *Columbus'* stay at Kobe and ship put to sea.
23 August	Arrived in Buckner Bay, Okinawa and then returned to Yokosuka, Japan.
20 September	Departed for Chinhae, South Korea
23 September	Arrived South Korea
September 7 October	Stopped at Yokohama, Japan USS Columbus returned to CONUS
19 October	Arrived in Long Beach
20 October to 31 December	Spent in leave and upkeep except for two weeks in December participating in striking fleet exercises and Type training

1958

4 December 1957 to 20 January 1958	Inport at Long Beach, California
24 January to 3 May	Inport at Long Beach, California
9 to 13 May	Inport at Long Beach, California
14 to 19 May	Inport at San Francisco, California
20 to 22 May	SP OPAR
22 May to 9 June	Inport at Long Beach
10 to 11 June	Inport at San Diego
13 June to 16 July	Inport at Long Beach
22 to 25 July	Inport at Pearl Harbor
2 to 4 August	Inport at Guam
9 to 11 August	Inport at Keelung, Taiwan
20 to 26 August	Inport at Yokosuka, Japan

6 September	Inport at Boko Ko
9 to 10 September	In Taiwan Straits, east of Kinmon
14 to 15 September	Inport at Kaohsiung, Taiwan
20 to 21 September	Inport at Buckner Bay, Okinawa
29 September to 1 October	Inport at Kaohsiung, Taiwan
2 to 11 October	Inport at Subic Bay, Philippines
23 to 26 October	Inport at Keelung, Taiwan
4 to 13 November	Inport at Yokosuka, Japan
16 to 17 November	Inport at Bucker Bay, Okinawa
19 to 20 November	Inport at Kaohsiung, Taiwan
21 to 24 November	Inport at Manila, Philippines
6 to 8 December	Inport at Subic Bay, Philippines
10 to 17 December	Inport at Hong Kong, China
24 to 27 December	Inport at Keelung, Taiwan
28 December to 5 January 1959	Inport at Sasebo, Japan

1959

9 to 11 January	Inport at Yokosuka, Japan
16 to 23 January	Guam, Apra
6 February to 11 March	Inport at Long Beach, California
14 March	Inport at Bremerton, Washington
20 March	Placed ICIR with Bremerton Group Pacific Reserve Fleet

1960

In shipyard at Bremerton, Washington being converted from Heavy Cruiser (CA-74) to the Missile Cruiser (CG-12).

1961

In shipyard at Bremerton, Washington being converted from Heavy Cruiser (CA-74) to the Missile Cruiser (CG-12).

1962

In shipyard at Bremerton, Washington until 1 December, being converted from Heavy Cruiser (CA-74) to the Missile Cruiser (CG-12).

1963

1964

January to July	In and out of San Diego, California
5 August	Left San Diego for West-Pac Cruise
11 August	Arrived at Pearl Harbor
13 August	Departed Pearl Harbor for Midway Island
16 August	Arrived at Midway Island for fueling, then departed.
17 August	Crossed International Date Line
23 August	Arrived Guam
24 August	Left Guam
28 August	Arrived Subic Bay, Philippines
29 August	Left for tour of Manila
3 September	Left Subic Bay for patrol duty in South China Sea
24 September	Arrived in Hong Kong
28 September	Departed Hong Kong
29 September	Arrived Subic Bay, Philippines
1 October	Departed Subic Bay for Manila, arrived in Manila.
4 October	Hosted Philippine Maritime Academy cadets for the day.
5 October	Departed Manila for Yokosuka, Japan
???	Arrived Yokosuka
28 October	Departed Yokosuka, Japan for operations in the South China Sea
1 December	Arrived Buckner Bay, Okinawa

2 December	Went to sea to fire Talos and Tartar missiles and join CenPacFlt
3 December	Arrived Kagoshima, Japan
7 December	Departed Kagoshima, Japan

1965

March	Returned from the Western Pacific
19 March	Hosted 68 members of the Navy League of California for a demonstration
April	Received results of competitive firings
14 June to 3 August	Hosted a midshipman cruise
3 August to 30 October	Participated in two fleet exercises
1 November	Enroute to San Francisco Naval Shipyard
15 November	Changed Executive Officers
11 December	Departed for San Francisco Naval Shipyard homeport of San Diego, California

1966

10 January	Departed San Diego to join Second Fleet at Norfolk, Virginia
14 to 17 January	Acapulco, Mexico
21 to 22 January	Transited the Panama Canal
24 to 27 January	Inport Kingston, Jamaica
27 January to 10 February	Participated in underway training at Fleet Training Center, Guantanamo Bay, Cuba
16 to 18 February	Conducted missile firings at the Atlantic Fleet Weapons Range, St. Thomas, Virgin Islands.
21 to 24 February	Arrived Norfolk, Virginia. Embarked RDM Fred G. Bennett, Commander Cruiser-Destroyer Flotilla Eight and his staff from the USS Albany (CG-10)

25 to 28 February	Inport Newport, Rhode Island
1 to 4 March	Inport New York City
4 March	Capt. Lewis J. Strech, Jr., relieved Capt. Royal K. Joslin as Commanding Officer
5 March	Arrived Norfolk, Virginia
5 to 21 March	Period of leave and upkeep
21 March	Underway for Virginia Capes
1 April	Returned to Norfolk. Leave and upkeep period.
25 April	Underway to Yorktown, Virginia
26 April	Returned to Norfolk, Virginia
2 May	Underway for the Caribbean
7 May	Arrived Roosevelt Roads, Puerto Rico
9 to 10 May	Conducted missile firings at Atlantic Fleet Weapons Range.
11 May	Anchored St. Thomas, Virgin Islands
13 May	Underway for Norfolk, Virginia
16 May	Arrived Norfolk, Virginia
19 May	Underway for New York City
20 to 23 May	Inport at New York City
24 May to 8 June	Inport at Norfolk, Virginia
8 June	Embarked midshipmen for a training cruiser
10 to 14 June	Underway to participate in Operation BEACH TIME.
20 to 21 June	Conducted missile firings at the Atlantic Fleet Weapons Range
27 June	Arrived at Norfolk in the evening
27 June to 21 July	Remained in port and conducted midshipmen training.
21 July	Disembarked midshipmen and embarked a new group for another training cruise
22 July	Departed Annapolis and arrived Baltimore for three day port visit

1 August	RDM John D. Bulkeley relieved RDM Fred G. Bennett as Commander Cruiser-Destroyer Flotilla Eight.
4 to 19 August	Participated in NATO Exercises, Operation Straight Laced in North Atlantic
21 to 26 August	Arrived Rotterdam, Netherlands.
26 August	Underway for Norfolk, Virginia
3 September	Arrived in Norfolk.
27 September	Deployed for the Mediterranean Sea.
3 to 4 October	Conducted missile firings at Atlantic Fleet Weapons Range.
4 October	Underway for Atlantic transit to Mediterranean Sea.
14 October	Transited the Straits of Gibraltar and reported for duty in the Sixth Fleet.
15 October	Relieved the USS Albany (CG-10) at Pollensa Bay, Mallorca, and became part of Task Group 60.2, commanded by RDM John D. Bulkeley. Left Pollensa Bay.
22 to 31 October	Inport Naples, Italy
8 November	Arrived in Malta
14 November	Departed Malta for Catania, Sicily
17 November	Departed Catania, Sicily
25 November	Inport at Navplion, Greece
28 November	Departed Navplion, Greece
30 November	Arrived in Izmir, Turkey
7 December	Departed Izmir, Turkey for Search & Rescue mission
8 to 9 December	Participated in search and rescue operations in the Aegean Sea after the sinking of the Greek Liner SS Heraklion.
12 December	Arrived in Navplion, Greece
15 December	Departed Navplion for exercise "Quick Train"
17 December	Arrived in Piraeus, Greece

27 December	Departed Piraeus, Greece
30 December	Arrived Taranto, Italy

1967

1 January	Continued Mediterranean deployment
2 to 6 January	Moored in Marseille, France
7 to 9 February	Participated in Exercise Lafayette 3-67.
17 to 26 February	Anchored at Livomo, Italy
26 February	Departed Livomo, Italy
28 February	Arrived Porto Conte
2 March	Given Operational Readiness Inspection conducted by RDM J.D. Bulkeley
12 March	Departed Palma, Mallorca for CONUS
20 March	Arrived Norfolk, Virginia
20 March to 16 April	Inport Norfolk. Leave and upkeep period.
16 to 30 April	Participated in Exercise CLOVEHITCH III
30 April to 31 May	Inport Norfolk, leave and upkeep period
8 June	Embarked midshipmen for LANTMIDTRARON-67.
10 June	Conducted a dependent's day cruise
12 June	Underway for LANTMIDTRARON-67
20 to 21 June	Fired missiles
8 July	Arrived Norfolk after brief stay in New Orleans, Louisiana
24 July	Underway for Operation LASHOUT
26 July to 2 August	Participated in Operation LASHOUT
3 August	Anchored at Annapolis Roads, Maryland for offloading midshipmen.
5 August to 17 August	Inport Norfolk

17 August	Underway for Atlantic Fleet Weapons Range.
22 August	Conducted missile firing at Atlantic Fleet Weapons Range
30 August	Returned to Norfolk
September	Month of leave and upkeep
3 October	Underway for familiarization of prospective commanding officer
5 October	Captain W.A. Arthur relieved Captain L.J. Stecher, Jr. as commanding officer
30 October	Underway for Virginia Capes
6 November	Sonar contact with AMBERJACK for 39 hours
9 November	Returned to Norfolk, Virginia
30 November to 1 December	Admin Inspection of Columbus with RDM J.F. Calbert, Chief Inspector
18 December	Predeployment Intelligence Briefing given to designated officers by Fleet Intelligence Center, Europe Representatives.

1968

3 January	Departed Norfolk, Virginia for the Mediterranean Sea and SIXTH Fleet Operations.
10 January	Arrived Rota, Spain and relieved USS Topeka (CLG-8) as flagship of Commander Task Group 60.2.
13 January	Departed Rota for Palina, Spain
24 January	Participated in MISSILEX 8-68
20 February	Entire main propulsion system was CASREPT (Casualty Reported) due to cumulative effect of derangements.
22 February	Participated in MISSILEX 9-68
3 to 10 March	Exercise FAIRGAME VI
29 April to 10 May	Exercise DAWN PATROL
6 to 8 May	Withdrew from Exercise DAWN PATROL to make

	emergency repairs to evaporators in Soudha Bay, Crete
16 to 26 May	Received tender availability at Valletta, Malta
27 to 29 May	Exercise POOP DECK
30 to 31 May	Conducted an Operational Readiness Inspection of USS Little Rock (CLG-4)
4 June	Twenty-four First Class Midshipmen embarked for a six-week training cruise.
11 to 17 June	Conducted an Administrative/Material inspection of USS Little Rock (CLG-4)
25 June	Participated in SIXTH Fleet 20th Anniversary Parade Exercise (FLAGEX)
9 July	Relieved by USS Topeka (CLG-8) as flagship of Commander Task Group 60.2.
16 July	Arrived Norfolk, Virginia after completing a 195-day Mediterranean cruise.
19 to 21 July	Offloaded missiles and ammunition at Naval Weapons Station, Yorktown, Virginia, in preparation for a restricted availability.
1 August	Commenced Restricted Availability
23 to 25 October	Onloaded missiles and ammunition at Naval Weapons Station, Yorktown, Virginia
15 November	Embarked COMCRUDESFLOT 10 staff gear in Newport, Rhode Island.
1 December	COMCRUDESFLOT 10 broke his flag in Columbus at Norfolk, Virginia.
2 December	Departed Norfolk for the Mediterranean Sea and SIXTH Fleet Operations.
19 to 21 December	Exercise LAFAYETTE 2-69.
23 to 31 December	Arrived in Villefranche (surmer), France, for holiday upkeep period.
28 December	Her Serene Highness, Princess Grace of Monaco, and her son Prince Albert visited the Columbus as guests of RDM M.H.

Johnston, COMCRUDESFLOT 10.

1969

1 to 3 January	Inport, Villefranche, France
3 to 13 January	Underway, Task Group 60.2 Operations Exercise QUICKDRAW 8-69.
13 to 20 January	Inport Athens, Greece
20 to 22 January	Underway, Task Group 60.2 Operations Exercise QUICKDRAW 1-69.
23 to 31 January	Underway, Task Group 60.2.Operations LOGREP
1 to 2 February	Training anchorage, Pollensa Bay
2 to 3 February	Underway for Barcelona, Spain
3 to 10 February	Inport, Barcelona, Spain
10 to 17 February	Underway, Task Group 60.2 Operations Exercise POOPDECK 2-69
17 to 24 February	Inport, Golfe Juan, France.
24 to 25 February	Underway for Gaeta, Italy
25 February to 2 March	Inport, Gaeta, Italy, ADMAT of USS *Little Rock* (CLG-4)
2 to 7 March	Underway, Task Group 60.2 Operation QUICKDRAW 4-69
7 to 17 March	Inport, Naples, Italy
17 to 19 March	Inport, Gaeta, Italy, ORI of USS *Little Rock* (CLG-4)
19 to 24 March	Underway Task Group 60.2 Operations KOMAREX
24 to 29 March	Inport Athens, Greece
29 March to 4 April	Underway, Task Group 60.2

	Operations Malta RIMEX
4 to 11 April	Inport, Valletta, Malta
11 to 16 April	Underway, Task Group 60.2 Operations ISE
16 to 19 April	Training anchorage, Soudha Bay
29 April to 2 May	Underway, Task Group 60.2 Operations Exercise DAWN PATROL 2-69.
2 to 5 May	Inport, Palma, Mallorca.
5 to 7 May	Underway, Transit, Inport, Rota, Spain, TURNOVER with USS *Galveston* (CLG-3)
7 to 14 May	Underway, Transit, Inport, Newport, Rhode Island, disembark COMCRUDESFLOT TEN and staff
14 to 17 May	Underway, Second Fleet Operations, Exercise COUNTRY CONSTABLE, Presidential Missile Firing Demonstration
17 May to 10 June	Inport, Norfolk, Virginia, leave and upkeep.
10 June	Underway, Yorktown, Virginia
10 to 13 June	Inport, Yorktown, Virginia, weapons offload
13 June	Underway for NNSY, Portsmouth, Virginia
13 June to 25 August	Inport, NNSY, Portsmouth, Virginia
25 to 26 August	Underway, Yorktown, Virginia
26 to 28 August	Inport, Yorktown, Weapons Onload
28 August	Underway, Portsmouth, Virginia
28 August to 2 September	Underway, Post-RAV trials
8 October	Inport, Newport, Rhode Island, embarked COMDRUDESFLOT TWO
8 to 17 October	Underway for Rota, Spain
17 to 18 October	Inport, Rota, Spain, turnover with USS *Galveston* (CLG-3)

18 October to 12 November	Underway, Task Group 60.2 Operations
12 to 22 November	Inport, Barcelona, Spain
22 to 23 November	Underway for San Paolo Bay
23 November	Anchorage, San Paolo Bay
23 to 26 November	Underway, Task Group 60.2 Operations LOGREP
26 November to 5 December	Inport, Valletta, Malta
5 to 19 December	Underway, Type training
19 to 22 December	Inport, Izmir, Turkey
22 to 23 December	Underway for Athens, Greece
23 to 31 December	Inport, Athens, Greece

1970

3 January	Departed Athens, Greece, COMCRUDESFLOT TWO embarked as Commander Task Group 60.2.
7 to 11 January	Visited Palma, Mallorca.
15 to 16 January	Conducted Exercise DEEP SIX III, fired TALOS and one TARTAR missiles
17 to 21 January	Anchored in Pollensa Bay, Mallorca
22 to 31 January	Visited Palma, Mallorca
3 to 5 February	Conducted Exercise NATIONAL WEEK V.
6 to 14 February	Visited Valletta, Malta
18 February	Conducted MISSILEX, fired two TARTAR and two TALOS missiles
21 to 22 February	Anchored in Soudha Bay, Crete
24 to 27 February	Visited Naples, Italy

5 to 6 March	Conducted TURNOVER with USS *Albany* (CG-11) at Gibraltar.
18 March to 16 April	Inport, Norfolk, Virginia
17 April to 6 July	RAV, NNSY
7 to 9 July	Conducted weapons transfer at Yorktown, Virginia
9 to 16 July	Pre-deployment workup VACAPES OPAREA
16 July to 26 August	Inport, Norfolk, Virginia
10 to 12 August	NTPI, Grade 90%
14 August	Captain R.H. Roberson, Jr. relieved Captain D.J. Downey as commanding officer.
6 September	Conducted TURNOVER with USS *Albany* (CG-11) at Gibraltar, assuming duty with Task Group 60.2. COMCRUDESFLOT EIGHT embarked as Commander Task Group 60.2.
6 to 9 September	Visited Gibraltar
12 September	Arrived on Bravo Station for Contingency Operation in Eastern Mediterranean
15 September	Commander Task Group 60.2 shifted flag to USS *Independence* (CVA-62).
7 to 11 October	Visited Athens, Greece
12 to 22 October	Conducted Exercise DEEP EXPRESS
23 to 28 October	Visited Athens, Greece
7 to 15 November	Visited Taranto, Italy
23 to 30 November	Visited Naples, Italy
4 to 5 December	Conducted MISSILEX 4-71, fired two TALOS and one TARTAR missiles
8 to 14 December	Visited Barcelona, Spain
21 to 31 December	Visited Villefranche, France

1971

1 to 6 January	Visited Villefranche, France
16 to 22 January	Visited Valetta, Malta
30 January to 8 February	Visited Barcelona, Spain
10 to 18 February	Conducted Exercise NATIONAL WEEK VIII
15 February	Transferred COMCRUDESFLOT EIGHT from USS John F. Kennedy to USS Columbus. Was transferred from USS Independence to USS John F. Kennedy on January 16.
22 February	Turned over SIXTHFLT equipment and publications at Roa, Spain to await arrival of USS Albany
1 to 21 March	Inport Norfolk, Virginia
22 to 25 March	Conducted weapons transfer at NWS Yorktown, Virginia.
26 to 27 March	Conducted fuel offload at Craney Island, Virginia
28 March to 11 April	Inport Norfolk, Virginia
12 April to 13 October	Overhaul NNSY (Norfolk Naval Shipyard)
3 August	Captain H.L. Carpenter relieved Captain R.H. Roberson, Jr. as commanding officer
6 to 7 October	Conducted weapons PRT VACAPES OPAREA
14 October to 2 November	Inport Norfolk, Virginia
15 October	FY1971 Battle Efficiency and Engineering E's presented by RDM H.D. Train II, COMCRUDESFLOT EIGHT, for ADM T.B. Weschler, COMCRUDESLANT.
2 to 5 November	Loaded weapons at NWS, Yorktown, Virginia
5 November	Conducted dependent's cruise from Yorktown, Virginia to Norfolk.
6 to 14 November	Inport Norfolk.

15 to 19 November	Engineering SQT exercises, VACAPES OPAREA
20 to 21 November	Inport Norfolk, Virginia
22 to 23 November	Weapons SQT exercises, VACAPES OPAREA
24 to 30 November	Inport Norfolk
3 December	Inport Roosevelt Roads, Puerto Rico.
4 to 11 December	Conducted SQT missile firing exercises in Atlantic Fleet Weapons Range, firing 7 TALOS and 7 TARTAR missiles.
16 to 31 December	Inport Norfolk.

1972

1 to 12 January	Inport Norfolk, Virginia.
13 to 14 January	Local operations
15 to 16 January	Inport Norfolk
17 to 21 January	Local operations
22 to 26 January	Inport Norfolk
30 January to 8 March	Refresher training, Guantanamo Bay, Cuba
25 to 27 February	Inport Port-au-Prince, Haiti
11 to 26 March	Inport Norfolk
27 to 29 March	Conducted weapons transfer, Yorktown, Virginia
29 to 31 March	Local operations
1 to 29 April	Inport Norfolk.
30 April to 5 May	LANTREADEX 4-72/RIMEX 4-72
5 to 8 May	Inport Roosevelt Roads, Puerto Rico

17 to 18 May	Inport, Rota, Spain for TURN-OVER
19 to 24 May	Inport, Malaga, Spain
25 to 29 May	Inport Tangier, Morocco
30 May to 7 June	Bystander Operations
10 to 20 June	Inport Barcelona, Spain
23 June	NATO MISSILEX
28 June	NATA Sea Power demonstration
29 June to 5 July	Inport Toulon, France
10 to 11 July	MISSILEX 1-73
11 July	Anchored, Soudka Bay, Crete
12 to 15 July	Inport Corfu, Greece
17 to 21 July	Exercise NATIONAL WEEK XIII
21 to 22 July	Anchored, Augusta Bay, Sicily
29 July to 3 August	Inport Valencia, Spain
8 to 26 August	Inport Athens, Greece
28 to 29 August	NATO MISSILEX
31 August to 3 September	Inport Rhodes, Greece
5 to 6 September	ASWEX
8 to 11 September	Inport Trieste, Italy
18 to 20 September	Inport Palma de Mallorca, Spain
21 to 26 September	Inport Golfe Juan, France
29 September to 2 October	Inport Gibraltar, BCC
3 to 7 October	Inport Lisbon, Portugal
7 to 9 October	Inport Rota, Spain for TURN-OVER
18 October to 4 December	Inport Norfolk, Virginia
5 to 6 December	Conducted weapons transfer, Yorktown, Virginia

9 to 10 December	Inport Roosevelt Road, Puerto Rico
10 to 11 December	MISSILEX, Atlantic Fleet Weapons Range
15 to 31 December	Inport Norfolk, Virginia

1973

1 to 10 January	Inport Norfolk, Virginia
30 January	Weapons loadout, Naval Weapons Station, Yorktown, Virginia
31 January to 16 February	Operation SPRINGBOARD
16 February to 27 March	Inport Norfolk.
28 March to 6 April	Exercise EXOTIC DANCER VI.
7 April to 28 May	Inport Norfolk
29 May to 15 June	LANTREADEX 3-73
6 to 7 June	Inport Roosevelt Roads, Puerto Rico
10 to 12 June	Inport Nassau, Bahamas
16 to 17 June	Inport Norfolk, Virginia
18 June	Weapons loadout, Naval Weapons Station, Yorktown.
19 June to 8 July	Inport Norfolk
9 to 26 July	LANTREADEX 1-74
19 to 20 July	Inport Roosevelt Roads, Puerto Rico
27 to 29 July	Inport Norfolk
30 July to 2 August	Weapons loadout, Naval Weapons Station, Yorktown
3 to 25 August	Inport Norfolk
21 August	Captain William H. Rowden relieved Captain Harold L. Carpenter as commander officer.
27 to 30 August	Local operations, Virginia Capes Operating Area

31 August to 4 September	Local operations off Connecticut and Virginia
9 September to 23 October	Inport Norfolk
10 to 11 October	NTPI Inspection
17 to 21 October	INSURV Inspection
23 October	Local Operations at sea portion of INSURV
24 to 26 October	Weapons loadout, Naval Weapons Station, Yorktown
26 October	Dependents' cruise, Yorktown to Norfolk
2 November	Departed Norfolk for duty with SIXTH Fleet
9 November	Anchored, Ponte Delgade, Sao Miguel, Azores
12 November	Inport Rota, Spain. Inchopped SIXTH Fleet
15 November	TURNOVER with USS *Belknap*, Augusta Bay, Sicily
17 to 21 November	Operations with Task Group 60.1
22 to 27 November	Inport Izmir, Turkey
28 November to 1 December	Inport Athens, Greece
2 to 12 December	Operations with Task Group 60.1
13 to 18 December	Operations with Task Group 60.2
19 to 30 December	Inport Barcelona, Spain

1974

1 to 4 January	Inport Barcelona, Spain
5 to 6 January	Enroute to Western Mediterranean Sea
7 to 15 January	Transit to North African littoral

16 to 23 January	Inport Athens, Greece
24 to 28 January	Operational Readiness Exercise and Task Group 60.2 operations
29 January to 2 February	Inport Kavala, Neapolis, Greece
3 February	Enroute to Thessaloniki, Greece
4 to 10 February	Inport Thessaloniki, Greece
11 February	Enroute to Soudha Bay, Crete
12 to 14 February	Training anchorage, Soudha Bay, Crete
15 to 19 February	Exercise NATIONAL WEEK XVI operations
20 February	Enroute to Corfu, Greece
21 to 23 February	Inport Corfu, Greece
24 to 25 February	Enroute to Missile Firing Range
26 to 27 February	Missile firing exercise, NAMFI missile range, Crete
28 February to 10 March	Enroute Western Mediterranean and Amphibious Exercise 9-74 operations vicinity of Porto Scuda, Sardinia
11 March	Enroute to Naples, Italy
12 to 19 March	Inport Naples
20 to 22 March	Enroute to Eastern Mediterranean, brief stop for fuel at Soudha Bay, Crete

23 to 29 March	NATO exercise DAFFODIL FACE Operations
30 March	Inport Izmir, Turkey
31 March to 2 April	Task Group 60.2 operations
3 April	Inport Naples, Italy
4 to 8 April	Task Group 60 operations
9 to 11 April	Inport Genoa, Italy
12 to 18 April	HALLMARK BYSTANDER operations, Western Mediterranean Sea
17 to 26 April	Inport Malaga, Spain
27 April to 2 May	NATO Exercise DAWN PATROL operations
3 May	Enroute to Palma de Majorca, Spain
4 to 10 May	Inport Palma de Majorca, Spain
11 to 20 May	Inport Barcelona, Spain
21 to 22 May	Enroute to Rota, Spain
23 to 24 May	Inport Rota
25 to 30 May	Enroute CONUS
31 May	Arrived Naval Station, Norfolk
1 June to 7 July	Inport Naval Station, Norfolk
8 to 15 July	Weapons offload, NWS, Yorktown
15 July to 14 August	Inport Naval Station, Norfolk
2 August	CDR Raymond E. Helms, Jr. relieved Captain William H. Rowden as commanding officer
15 August	Moved *Columbus* to St. Helena's Annex to commence inactivation.

16 August to 30 January 1975	Pre-inactivation. *Columbus* status becomes "in commission; in reserve"

1975

31 January	USS *Columbus* is decommissioned at St. Helena's Annex of the Inactive Ship Maintenance Facility, Norfolk

1976

9 August	The name USS *Columbus* is stricken from the Naval Vessel Register

1977

18 August	The hull is sold, for scrapping, to the Consolidated Andy Corporation, Brownsville, Texas

1986

27 October	Construction begins on USS *Columbus* (SSN-762)

1991

07 January	Keel Laid for the new SSN-762
21 November	Initial Crew Manning Completed

1992

30 March	Crew Commenced Watchstanding in the Propulsion Plant

1994

June	Post Shipyard Availability completed in Groton, CT, shakedown operations completed.
September	USS *Columbus* is transferred to Pearl Harbor, HI and joins the U.S. Pacific Fleet Submarine Force

Villa France, 1955.

USS Columbus

Sea

Stories

GETTING EVEN

BY BOB BOWEN

Well, June 8th has come and gone once more. I can't help but remember that date each year when it comes around. I stood as a proud crewmember at the commissioning of the most modern cruiser afloat at that time. It's been 53 years now, but you don't forget an event like that.

I wonder how many of my shipmates remember April 1, 1946? We escorted 24 Japanese submarines out of Sasebo, Japan. We were part of a task force to assist in "Operation Roads End-Deep Six." Twenty two of the subs were sunk by demolition charges, the remaining two were sunk by surface fire from one of the destroyers in our group.

After I left the service, I went to work for the Southern California Gas Company for the next 40 years. In the early days of my career, there I was on an installing crew laying gas mains and services to all the new housing tracts going up. One day at lunch break we sat around shooting the breeze. The subject came up about what branch of service we had been in. I said Navy heavy cruiser. One young man piped, "I was a cruiser sailor, too." He served on the USS *Indianapolis*. I said "she was sunk." He said, "I know, I'm one of the survivors." Lyle Umenhoffer had hung on to life as his shipmates gave in to exhaustion, untreatable wounds and the ever present sharks. They had delivered the Atom Bomb that would an end to the war in the Pacific and were back to their designated area when they were sunk.

I told Lyle we helped get even in a way: the 8th sub sunk was the I-58, the sub that sunk the USS *Indianapolis*. What's the chances

of two people coming together to share an experience like that? Was it FATE? I leave you with that thought.

A BROKEN ANTENNA

BY LARRY FINN

While cruising the Pacific during early 1946, the search radar aboard the USS *Columbus* (CA-74) was found to develop a problem with it's rotational sweep. Since I was one of the electronic technicians, I was assigned the task to climb the forward mast and check out the SK antenna assembly.

This was a memorable experience for me, as the antenna platform was at least 100 feet above the main deck. My partner took a picture of me that day while on the platform, taking a break and enjoying the view from that lofty perch. Looking down as the ship rolled provided a sensational feeling, seeing water directly below.

The antenna needed major repairs that required removal when we returned to port. I took pictures of it being lifted off the platform with the aid of a land based crane.

EN ROUTE TO SHANGHAI, CHINA

BY LEON LEVY

As a radioman 3/c, I drew the 4:00 a.m. to 8:00 a.m. watch. As luck would have it, I had the duty of monitoring the most boring

Japanese submarine I-58, prior to Operation Roads End–Deep Six. Courtesy of Bud Kathan.

Lawrence Finn, 1945.

Leon Levy on Shore Patrol Duty, Shanghai, China, 1946.

radioband - the SOS circuit. Those of our shipmates that experienced monitoring this circuit know that days and days could go by without receiving a distress signal which, of course, was good news.

As I was nearing the end of my watch, I was startled to see two gold stripes by my side. The communication officer admonished me for sleeping on watch and told me to report to his wardroom at 0900 hours. When I did so he read the "riot act to me", and told me that he was putting me on report and I was to go to the MAA shack within the hour for my extra duty assignment.

Since the ship was due in Shanghai the next day, I was given two days of Shore Patrol duty in addition to standing my regular shipboard watches. At the time it was required that each ship send one shore patrolman ashore for every ten sailors on liberty.

At noon on Feb. 10, 1946, the shore patrol detail mustered on the quarterdeck for transfer to the Shanghai liberty pier. All of the Navy ships that were anchored off shore in the Yangtze River sent their liberty parties ashore in small landing craft.

At 1400 hours, the liberty parties began coming ashore and every sailor was spiffed up, friendly, happy and looking forward to having a good time in Shanghai. At the time I thought that this wasn't such a bad duty at all. Beginning 20:00 hours, most of the liberty party was due back at the ship, and this is when the action really begun.

The liberty pier had a holding pen, which confined a couple hundred people at a time. It had a swinging gate and as each ship's liberty boat would arrive at the pier the Coxswain would announce over the bull horn, "Columbus liberty boat ready to load." At that signal they would open the gates and every sailor, no matter which ship he was from, would charge down the ramp. As shore patrolmen, we lined up with our batons outstretched and our backs to the river to make sure that no one plunged in.

Since this was a real good liberty town, most shipmates returned in a not too coherent condition and were far removed from the group greeting us six hours earlier at the beginning of liberty. There were some that over indulged and were carried back to the pier, necessitating our going through their credentials to determine which ship they were from and placing them in the proper liberty boats as they came in.

Around 2300 hours things quieted down somewhat and then we had the onslaught of the locals complaining about sailors not paying for rickshaw rides, and even confiscating and destroying their rickshaws. This was a job for the local police, since these complaints were all in the Chinese language and we could not communicate with the complainers.

At any rate, around 0100 hours the Columbus Shore Patrol returned to the ship, realizing full well that we had put in a grueling 12 hours of extra duty.

Rest assured that after two days of this duty I never closed my eyes while on watch for the remainder of my Navy tour.

MEMORABLE MOMENTS & TIMES

BY TED MCGIVERON

1) Boot training at Samson, NY. Fire fighting at 65°F – sweating in front and freezing behind.

2) Drinking "Hotuey" at Gitmo Bay, Cuba – they said it was beer.

3) While shelling Colebra – Picking up food rations being outside when an 8-inch gun went off. The vacuum and noise were incredible. Didn't time that one right.

Taking a break at GITMO U.S. Naval Air Station, Enlisted Man's Club, 1953. From left: unknown, Gene Ellis, ? Myers, Reggie ?, and Richard Grasmick. Courtesy of James E. Ellis, Jr.

4) Panama City, Panama – Going to night clubs where the ladies wore evening gowns only, with zippers on the sides. Going through the Canal.

5) Pearl Harbor – All hands loading ammunition party. Failing to persuade Jim Sherrill to see an officer and get excused. He had just had a hernia operation and was still stapled together.

6) Going through a typhoon off Okinawa where some of the Old Salts got sick and scuttlebutt was that two Destroyers were in serious trouble. Never heard how they made out?

7) At Japan, taking part in Operation Deep Six, i.e. the sinking of 24 submarines, prizes of war.

8) Leaving the CA-74 at San Pedro, CA in June 1946 to board (and find out) what a cattle car was. In this case it was a coal burning train, and it was too hot to close the windows. The result was that we ate, drank and slept in soot for five days – destination being Lido Beach, Long Island, NY for discharge. After the first day it was near impossible to tell what race a person was.

sky forward. This was my regular cleaning station. From up there a person could see lots of sea life swimming around. I noticed something black come up and then go under again. I took the binoculars off of the control of sky forward and looked again. The object came up and showed the typical "horns" of a mine. I called the bridge by phone and reported the sighting.

The ship stopped and they tried at first to detonate it with Marine rifle fire, but that didn't work. They then fired a 40mm quad single fire and it detonated. The side of the ship was sprayed with shrapnel and it was a miracle that no one was hurt.

While this was going on, there were more mines sighted nearby. The skipper decided to let other properly equipped ships dispose of the mines. They set a mine watch on the bow, 24 hours a day, the rest of the way to China.

We were very fortunate not to have struck one of the mines. It was very apparent how easily a mine could sink or badly damage a ship.

SIGHTING A MINE

BY RALPH LEHDE

In the spring of 1947, somewhere west of Hawaii, we were cruising toward China. I was sitting outside on top of the turret of

A LONG DAY

BY JAMES E. ELLIS JR.

In 1954, on St. Patrick's Day, the USS *Columbus* had a detachment of sailors march in the St. Paddy's day parade in

Southtown section of Boston. They first picked all the duty petty officers of each division for that day and I was the lucky duty petty officer for the CR Division. How they selected the remainder of the group I don't know. I received word by the grapevine that Lt. Lucas was looking for me to give me the wonderful news. I tried to hide all over the ship, but he finally cornered me in Radio 2. I had not marched or carried an M1 rifle since boot camp three years earlier. Anyway, the complete unit would drill on the pier alongside the USS *Columbus* every day for two weeks before the parade. I thought we were getting real good. St. Patrick day came and we were bussed over to Southdown for the seven-mile parade route. There was a problem. It turns out there was a unit in front of us and behind us, but a band was in front of the front unit, with another band behind the back unit. The problem? The USS *Columbus* unit was picking up the drumbeat from each band and we could not keep in step. Being part Irish, I could here the mocks out in front of the bars making sarcastic comments about who in the hell were those Navy guys. Finally, after numerous stops in the parade route, the lieutenant in charge of our unit somehow got one band to quit playing. After that, we had no problems and started to receive applause and hear "that's the way to go scabies." The five-mile parade took seven hours to complete and when we got back to the *Columbus*, supper was over and we had nothing to eat. It was a long day.

A NICE MEMORY

BY R.B. HEBERLING

One of my best remembered experiences commenced the first day reporting aboard. Our MSTS ship arrived in Plymouth, England only to see that the 74 was underway, leaving the harbor. Word was passed for all *Columbus* passengers to report to the quarter deck with sea bags packed for transport to the 74. We tossed our sea bags and followed them to the deck of a local tug boat, which took us along side our new ship. She had furled a landing net over the side for our entry. Memory of this experience was renewed during our recent Rapid City reunion, where I met another shipmate who had also reported aboard that date via landing net.

Other nice memories would include an audience with the Pope while visiting Rome, and a chance meeting with the Queen of Greece at a USO club in Athens. Not to mention all my shipmates in the E X Division and other new friends I made while on board.

Bob Heberling, Chief Yeoman Raymond Brown, unknown. Courtesy of Bob Heberling.

Collision between the Columbus and the Destroyer Floyd B. Parks, 11 March 1956. Courtesy of Lloyd Kingery.

Hon. Charles S. Thomas, reviewed the exercise, conducted by Vice Adm. Robert L. Dennison, commander of the First Fleet.

One of my most memorable experiences was the collision between the heavy cruiser USS *Columbus* and the destroyer *Floyd B. Parks*. The collision occurred during night maneuvers some 250 miles off the coast of Manila in the South China Sea. It was March 11, 1956, about 4:00 a.m. I was proceeding to his watch in CIC (Combat Information Center) when the ship took a thunderous shudder, rocking the ship like taking on a huge wave. The alarms sounded and the news that 50 feet were torn from the destroyer bow. The *Columbus* was gashed in several places above the waterline. The collision resulted in two missing men, lost overboard, and three injured crewmen aboard the *Parks*. The sea tug *Munsee* was dispatched and towed the *Parks* to Subic Bay for emergency repairs, accompanied by the *Columbus*.

THE COLLISION

BY LLOYD L. KINGERY

My wife and guests were welcomed on board the USS *Columbus* by Captain George C. Seay, Commanding Officer, to witness the review of the First Fleet on Sept. 14, 1956. The *Columbus* participated in the largest fleet review since WWII. Seventy-two ships of the U.S. First Fleet and 160 Navy aircraft, including the Blue Angels, crack flight demonstration team, assembled at Long Beach, CA. The Secretary of the Navy,

USS COLUMBUS

SUBMITTED BY PAUL T. PAYNE

After serving aboard two submarines and attending Navy Diving School, I finally realized that the 'elite' in submarine duty was well, - a 'relative' term. I decided I needed to see and feel the sun, take leave once in a while, and stop pressing my whites by sleeping on them! I had realized in order to get my head out of (well you know), I needed to do things 'differently.' So, I 'non-volunteered' for subs and off I went to the

A First Fleet Review on 14 September 1956, Long Beach, CA. Guests include Lloyd & Jean Kingery (3rd couple), Dean & Shirley Whiting (4th couple), and Captain George C. Seay, Commanding Officer (middle). Courtesy of Lloyd Kingery.

Columbus. On the way to the *Columbus*, I spent almost three weeks doing nothing but washing and waxing a chief's Navy gray Plymouth station wagon (classic), and getting his money changed into pesetas for him at the exchange. Tough duty! The day I set eyes on *Columbus* I suddenly realized I was standing on the same pier that two months prior I'd been standing on next to the USS *Cutlass* (SS-478)! Tough duty again, huh? This didn't seem so bad ... The Pan Am Club, the Barcelona Club, the Texas, hmmm.

Of course, as Navy tradition has it, being non-rated I went straight to mess cooking. Now that may sound bad to some, but if you've ever had to mess cook aboard a submarine, where there's maybe four for a crew of 150, a cruiser's not bad at all! Trust me! 48 sounds better than 4!

I decided it was time to get my priorities in line, so I decided to find a good skatin' rate. I DID NOT intend to go from mess cooking to deck force. I'd had enough of chipping and painting round hulls. It didn't take an admiral to convince me of that! The post office! I found out that in there you didn't have to stand many watches, only condition three and refueling. This was no longer your typical dumb seaman! I wised up REAL quick, took out the coarse book, took the test, and was rated the first increment! I was told I made the highest score among those taking the third class test on the ship. Don't ask me how, I sure wasn't going to contest it!

I worked for a Lt. Tharp. He was a fine man and friend. He was always fair, and always had a way to get the most from you. He once told me I was an 'Opportunist.' Never sure today just how he meant that - maybe he was right though - life was good as a postal clerk. First off in ports to go pick up mail, and you got to know personally almost all 698 guys aboard, including chiefs and officers.

One Navy lesson I did learn quick. There's five guys aboard a ship you never mess with. The cook, if you want to eat; the disbursing clerk, if you wanted to get paid; the supply clerk who ran the guidank(sp), if you wanted a coke and candy bar; and the yeoman if you wanted your records to stay straight. Oh ya, I forgot one - the postal clerk! If you wanted to hear from that gal, or wanted that Playboy, you kept him on your good side! Truth is, I'd never have messed with any man's mail, but I sure wasn't going to stop them from feeling that way! It really was great being the postal clerk. For one thing, you had a job that for the most part, gave good morale to the guys. You got to know their faces and them, and you usually knew where you were actually going from one place to another before anyone else except maybe the radiomen! I had a lot of friends on *Columbus* that I'll never forget. I sure wish I could see them all right now.

I sure would like to hear from my best friend aboard *Columbus*. Though like many of us, I haven't heard from him in a long, long time. Danny Rodriquez was his name, a signalman. Danny was a Chicano from San Antonio, TX. No better friend can a guy have. Danny would have backed me up, and me him, in any fight that came along! A Chicano and a White Boy. Odd combo, but we was tight!!

All I can say is that within one year aboard *Columbus* my life had changed for the better. I wound up making third-class, received the Navy Expeditionary Medal for sub stuff, running a post office, got married, and wound up taking 68 straight days of leave! Due to sub duty (always going and being underwater), I'd saved quite a bit of leave. I still had 30 days left on the books after coming back from the honeymoon!

Replacing mount 310 that was torn off in the collision with the USS Parks. Courtesy of Bill Kirby.

In November of '73, we found ourselves due to head for the Med. But, we also found ourselves between a rock and a hard place. As we watched bombs and tanks being loaded aboard ships, and aircraft markings being painted over and sealed, we were put on alert because the second Israeli/Arab war was flaring up. We figured we were headed straight for it. But in the meantime, the Chicago's replacement had broken down. And guess who was put on a four hour alert to head for 'Nam! They wouldn't even let us on the pier without our ID's being checked! Here I was, only six months left in the Navy, and I might be going to Vietnam! What a BUMMER! It worked out that we spent six hours refueling at Rota, and off to sunny Alexandria, Egypt. We were put on condition three watches for 28 straight days! All we did was steam up and down, up and down in front of Alexandria. We were told to shoot down anything that passed the 100 mile perimeter! Now days it seems the Navy is handing out medals and ribbons for any kind of Middle East duty! I wonder if the *Columbus* ever received doodly squat for that cruise? I never did find out. I left *Columbus* in Crete for a three month school early out.

As I look back, I have fond memories of *Columbus*. She truly was an icon of her own. Remember grilling steaks on the fantail? Leaning back on the after missile house and gazing up at the stars as the exhaust fan kept you warm? Those stars in the Caribbean looked so close, you thought you could actually reach up and grab them!

Oh well, they say you can't go back... It is true. As MacArthur once said, "Old soldiers never die, they just fade away."

THE SPUD LOCKER

BY RAY E. PAYNE

Some nights while we were at sea, we would want to fix french fries. Being in the US Navy meant we had "Acquire" the spuds.

I was assigned to the Battery Locker at the time and we serviced all the batteries on the ship. Most were in our launches. We had six launches, two whale boats, the captains gig, the officers motor boat and two admiral's barges. Then there were three main gun turrets, 7.5" gun mounts and several autos.

Getting back to the spuds, we had an eight cup percolator in the Battery Locker. The hot plate it sat on was never turned off the three years plus I was on board the USS *Columbus*. We made coffee all day. The pot was filled and placed on the hot plate as soon as it was emptied. Every morning we had to get our coffee rations from the galley, as every other area did.

On the night I'm thinking about, I said I would get the spuds. Another sailor went to "find" a pound of butter to cook them in. There were two spud lockers on the main deck, one starboard and one on the port side. I chose the one on the port side because it was close to the hatch leading up to the Battery Locker.

The ship was rolling gently side to side, as always, and the night was clear and a little cool. We were in the Med. I undid the pin that held the door closed, inside I stuffed my shirt full of spuds. Just as I was about to leave, I heard a voice say, "Anyone in there?" It was one of the Master-at-Arms. This was all I needed, to get caught stealing spuds.

I knelt down as low as I could get behind the piled up cases of spuds. He called out again. Then he got down and closed the door and put the pin back in place locking me inside. What a fix.

I must have sat at that door for almost an hour when I heard a friendly voice, "Payne, are you in there?" I answered and told him to open the door. Quick as lightning we were away from there and up in the Battery Locker. They were waiting to fix the French Fries in the coffee pot. It had been washed and the butter was hot and ready to go. We peeled the spuds, sliced them and in they went. In a matter of minutes we were eating the fries and perking another pot of coffee - at 2:00 in the morning.

This sea story has been told many times and when I tell it, I can still hear that Master-at-Arms calling out. There are many more sea stories, but they are for another time.

REPAIRS AT SEA

SUBMITTED BY GERALD L. ROWE

In September 1952, the USS *Columbus* (CA-74) was operating in the North Atlantic with ships from other North Atlantic Treaty Organization (NATO) nations in the joint fleet training exercise "Main Brace." We crossed the Arctic Circle and were all properly initiated into the "Royal Order of the Blue Nose" by being dowsed with cold water by the old timers, who acted as King Neptune and his Court. At the end of this operation the *Columbus* was invited to spend three days in Oslo, Norway, before returning to the Mediterranean and normal operations with the USN Sixth Fleet. During the last part of this training exercise the SG navigation radar antenna malfunctioned. The T Division guys diagnosed the problem and knew that to fix it they would have to go up the mainmast where the antenna was located. Captain Campbell reviewed the situation with our T Division electronics officer, Lt. Bailey, and told him that he was not going to sail this heavy cruiser up that narrow 80-mile long fjord to Oslo unless he had his navigation radar working. When Lt. Bailey came back to the electronics shop, he asked if we wanted to have liberty in Oslo and if so would we go up the mast and fix the radar antenna. Of course all said, "sure we do" and "sure we would." There were some reservations about going up on that tall mast because the ship was rolling quite a bit in the North Sea wind and waves. We told our electronics officer that in order to do the work up there the ship would have to sail in a direction for minimum roll. When the captain heard this, he decided to request authorization to break formation with the other ships. That request was granted but limited to only 20 minutes before we had to get back in formation with the rest of the ships in the NATO fleet. All the tools and everything needed for the repair were gathered together and three of us went up the mast to the radar antenna. The failed parts were quickly replaced, but then the replacements had to be realigned. By use of the sound powered phones, we talked to the radar operator in CIC and with his help finally got everything correctly readjusted. Believe it or not, we were able to do this all within the 20 minutes the captain gave us. Thus Captain Campbell was able to sail the *Columbus* up that very long and narrow fjord to anchor in the Oslo harbor. Everyone had a great three days liberty in Oslo before we returned to our normal operations in the Mediterranean.

OIL ON THE DECK

SUBMITTED BY GERALD L. ROWE

In December 1952, the USS *Columbus* (CA-74) had been in port in Toulon, France for several days, and during that time T Division did some routine service of the radar antenna on the mainmast. When the ship weighed anchor and got under way all was okay until she cleared the harbor and started rolling in the choppy waves of the open Mediterranean Sea. Each time the ship rolled, a shower of oil would come down from the mast and the wind spread it all over the fantail deck. It was obvious that the radar antenna was leaking oil and had to be fixed. Two of us went up the mast to see what was wrong. We found and fixed the leak but while trying to refill the antenna gear box, the rolling of the ship caused more oil to spill and spray all over the teak wood deck and everything else aft of the mainmast. Finally all got taken care of, but the boson mate and deck hands that had to clean things up were really mad at the T Division guys for getting oil all over everything. I think that some of the T Division guys had to join the holy stone crew to help clean up the deck. Our electronics officer also caught hell about it and had to make restitution to the deck division officers.

The USS Columbus Softball Team, 1954-55. Courtesy of Peter Simmons.

Trophy presentation to the USS Columbus softball team, 1954-55. Courtesy of Peter Simmons.

THE USS COLUMBUS SOFTBALL TEAM

SUBMITTED BY JAMES G. WARNER JR. (TAKEN FROM ARTICLES POSTED IN THE COLUMBUS'S NEWSLETTER, DISCOVERER)

In 1952/53, the USS Columbus Softball Team, the "Discoverers" took the USS *Columbus* to a runner-up spot in the annual Atlantic Fleet Battleship-Cruiser Mediterranean Softball Tournament. The following was compiled from several articles which were posted in the USS *Columbus's* newsletter, known as the "Discoverer."

PORTUGAL - USS COLUMBUS VS. USS DES MOINES - SCORE 4 TO 3

The *Columbus* softball team started out the season with a bang! They were decked out in their new uniforms (blue with red and white letters) and with a zeal to win played their first game against the *Des Moines*. After 11 innings of "heads up" ball playing, sparked by the beautiful pitching of "Pop" Warner from the S-2 Division, the *Columbus* nine came out on top 4 to 3.

PORTUGAL - USS COLUMBUS VS. USS FOX - SCORE 5 TO 3 AND 6 TO 0

The *Columbus* marked up two more victories, both over the USS *Fox*, with the first game being a regulation 7 innings. "Pop" Warner chalked up number "2" backed by the sharp infield playing of Mearns - 3B, Armstrong - SS, Massey - 213, Casteligi 1B and Flaherty - Catcher. The outfield was also moving around fast with Hendrickson - RF, Beattie - CF and Albunio - LF. The score 5 to 3. In the third game, lasting nine innings, the *Fox* was shut out 6 to 0 with the fast firing "Little Pete" Simmions from the Second Division on the mound.

ITALY - USS COLUMBUS VS. USS DES MOINES - SCORE 8 TO 4

The *Columbus* nine "downed and drowned" the USS *Des Moines* yesterday afternoon by a score of 8 to 4. In the fourth straight win of the current Mediterranean season the boys turned in a beautiful spectacle of fast precision team-work in a game that was all theirs from the first pitch. Playing at the Italian Naval Base, the men "brought home the bacon" for the best ship in the fleet. "Pop" Warner was on the mound for the "Discoverers" and turned in a beautiful, one-hit game. Flaherty, the man behind the plate was up to his usual standard for excellence. "Pete" Simmions - LF, led the Columbus steam-roller with a three-run "homer" in the sixth. "Al" Albunio - SB, with three hits and a steal home, provided one of the highlights of the game. Cromer from the A Division was the "Eagle-eyed Ump" who called them like a true veteran of the big leagues.

USS COLUMBUS VS. USS WOODSON - SCORE 33 TO 0

The powerful *Columbus* softball team blasted the USS *Woodson* Sunday by a powerful score of 33 to 0. Warner, *Columbus* hurler, had a no-hit, no-run game for 6-2/3 innings, before he was reached for a single. Warner struck out 14 batters with no walks against him. Beattie, Armstrong, Louth, Niday and Lewis, each collected two hits each. The *Columbus* will play the *Quincy* this evening, with Simmions or Warner doing the Hurling.

USS COLUMBUS VS. USS QUINCY - SCORE 14 TO 0

The *Columbus* softball team continues to roll, as Saturday afternoon they came through with a 14 to 0 shutout over the USS *Quincy*. Warner once again came thru with another one hitter. Warner going all the way walking no one and striking out 14 batters. Beattie paced the *Columbus* with three hits with Massey, Armstrong and Louth getting two each.

USS COLUMBUS VS. USS NEGRA - SCORE 10 TO 0

With the usual high standard pitching of "Pop" Warner, and the hard hitting of Dick Vaughan, who is new on the *Columbus* softball bench, the *Columbus* tramped over the *Negra* to win their seventh game with only one defeat. Vaughan accounted for driving in seven runs with three hits, while "Russ" Massey knocked out a two-run homer in the sixth inning. Warner, pitching fine ball all the way gave up only three hits to the *Negra* nine and made it his sixth straight win of the Mediterranean season. The team was supposed to play the *Salerno Bay,* but the CVE boys failed to show up. The team expects to get some games in while at Genoa and with the fine spirit the boys are showing the games will be well worth turning out for.

ISTANBUL - USS COLUMBUS VS. ROBERTS COLLEGE - SCORE 18 - 8

The *Columbus* softball team in the past week has won four games. Three in Istanbul and one in Greece. Their first game with Roberts College of Istanbul proved the boys are still on the ball, by winning over the College boys 18 to 8, behind the usual good pitching of "Pop" Warner who made it his 7th straight.

ISTANBUL - USS COLUMBUS VS. USS INGERSOLL - SCORE 20 TO 0

The *Columbus* with the victory sign in their eyes went after the USS *Ingersoll* and won by the score of 20 to 0 and again "Pop" Warner was the winning pitcher. Beattie and Flaherty, both of the Executive Division, led the hitting.

The Columbus softball team. Courtesy of R.E. Beattie.

The USS Columbus Softball Team, 1954-55. Courtesy of Peter Simmons.

Istanbul - USS *Columbus* vs. USS *Leyte* - Score 9 to 7

With two easy defeats fresh in their gloves they tackled the mighty Leyte. Behind the fine hurling of "Pete" Simmions the *Columbus* Discoverer's made it their 5th straight win by downing the carrier boys 9 to 7. Vaughan and Cromer teamed up to lead the hitting attack with two hits each.

Greece - USS *Columbus* vs. USS *Des Moines* - Score 14 to 2

The *Columbus*, while anchored in Greece, met with the *Des Moines* and for the 3rd straight time they beat the "134 boys" by a score of 14 to 2. "Pop" Warner, going all the way for the *Columbus*, won his 8th straight game. Albunio, stealing the show for the *Columbus* with four hits and three stolen bases. Beattie and Vaughan turned in beautiful plays to keep the *Columbus* out of trouble on several occasions.

Sici1y - USS *Columbus* vs. USS *Arnet* - Score 7 to 3

The *Columbus* softball team in a game played Monday, downed the USS *Arnet*, by a score of 7 to 3. *Columbus* made it six straight, as "Pop" Warner pitched beautiful ball to win his fifth straight. Three fast double-plays by Albunio, Armstrong and Cromer put a stall to the Arnet's threats. Lewis with two hits, along with Beattie and Simmions, lead the *Columbus*.

Sicily - USS *Columbus* vs. USS *English* - Score 0 to 1

The *Columbus* team finally met their waterloo when they encountered the tough DD Sailor's off of the USS *English* 696. Although, Simmons, Second Division, only gave up one hit in a brilliant pitchers battle, the *Columbus* was unable to score off of four hits. Beattie, Executive Division, counted for two hits while Massey and Albunio got one hit each. Their only run came in the last of the fifth. The first man up for the *English* in the fifth bunted and reached first on an error. The next man was hit by a pitch. With a man on first and second and one out, the pitcher came up and looped a single over short and drove in the winning run, and the only run. The *Columbus* team has proven to be a threat against all in their games this cruise under the capable leadership of Ensign Moore and with big John Johnston as the team manager.

Cuba - USS *Columbus* vs. USS *New Jersey* - Score 6 to 7

The strong *New Jersey* softball team downed the powerful *Columbus* team by a score of 7 to 6 in a game which was well-played. Warner going all the way for the *Columbus* only gave up six hits. Johnson lead the hitting with Three hits. The game was high-lighted by a tremendous homer by Russ Massey. The *Columbus* continues to be a hard hitting ball club.

Atlantic Fleet Battleship Cruiser Mediterranean Softball Tournament (BatCruLant Softball)

Three teams are undefeated following first and second round results of the 1953 Battleship Cruiser softball tournament. The USS *Iowa* rousted the USS *Albany* 23 to 0, the USS *Mississippi* shaded the USS *McCahn* 3 to 0, the USS *Columbus* topped the USS *Mississippi* 6 to 2, the USS *Pittsburgh* over the USS *Missouri* 5 to 2 and the USS *Wisconsin* over the USS *Macon* 14 to 12. In the second round games the USS *Newport News* downed the USS *Wisconsin* 9 to 3, the USS *Mississippi* blanked the USS *Albany* 11 to 0 and the USS *Missouri* downed the USS *Macon* 3 to 0. The USS *Columbus* went on to cinch a runner-up spot in this annual Atlantic Fleet Battleship-Cruiser Mediterranean Tournament.

KINCADE WAS HIS NAME AND NOTHING REMAINED THE SAME

BY LOUIS TUCCIARONE

I
When I first came aboard this ship,
I heard no sound of a cracking whip.
The days aboard were bright and colorful
And the smiles on the Gobs were cheerful
I strung along the best I could,
To work on the catapults, not the decks of wood.
I did not care to scrub or curse,
In the heat of the sun, that made it worse.
I worked all through the passing day,
And when I was tired, in my rack I'd lay.
There I would stay as long as I dared too
And cared not, if there was more work to do.
What an easy life this is I said,
As I relaxed more comfortable in my bed.

II
Then one evening a new draft came,
'New men," I said: "to play the game.
Early the next morning, I awoke without grief,
For I knew, those new men would bring relief.
On deck for quarters, a F/C Bos'n was seen.
Plus a second class and two coxswains agleam.
Bos'n Kincade was his name
and nothing ever remained the same.
We listened as he laid down his rules
And to all he addressed reacted like mules.
Then I saw the mighty tides turn,
And soon the deck apes began to learn,
That he was tough a man as could be,
and no one dared to disagree. For Kincade was his name
and nothing remained the same.

III

From early morn, before the sun did rise,
You would see the third on deck, the mighty guys.
How we'd laugh when the ships Bos'n would pipe "Turn to."
Cause we've been working for hours under skies of blue.
One by one the others would rise,
To greet the new day and brightened skies
That was washed clean by the third,
When we scrubbed the skies on a mighty bird.
The fifth and seventh, soon were through,
And he would laugh and mock they're few.
For Kincade was his name
and nothing remained the same.

IV

The ships' bell struck eight throughout the ship.
And the anxious third began to chip.
On the paint work, we began
Then to the decks we scrubbed with sand.
Others would smile as they came our way
To remark about the work we did all day.
The ships bell struck eleven
as the sun climbed toward heaven,
"Knock off work." I heard a gun striker say
But, we'd only laugh, 'cause we earned our pay.
Then you would hear those deck apes course,
The Bos'n grinned, and that made it worse.
For Kincade was his name, and nothing remained the same.

V

When chow was secured at twelve thirty,
We'd go down to eat, with hands always dirty.
At thirteen hundred we finished chow,
and tried to rest, but we'd hear the Bos'n growl.
"On the roof, all you deck hands."
And oh how we prayed for the promised lands.
But there was no time to think or dream,
'Cause he was tough and wanted the decks to gleam.
So back to the sand and scrubbers we'd go,
Working for and aft, to and fro.
Others would sit around and grin,
While the Bos'n heart burned with sin.
He'd cared not, what we'd said or threat,
'Cause when he shouted, the devil would get.
For Kincade was his name,
and nothing remained the same.

VI

Sixteen hundred, the ships' bell rang,
but we continued to work, like a mustang.
"Knock off work, the ships Bos'n would say,
"Shift to the uniform of the day."
"Water barge coming along side."
And inward the boat boom would have to glide.
"One man on the lazy line, one on the after guy."
The Bos'n would shout, and we knew his sign.
"The rest of you men are needed up forwarded,
To bring the boom homeward."
Then in place she would set,
while our foreheads wrung with sweat.
Suddenly from the P.A. system we heard,

"Belay that last call." Was the Boson's word.
We cussed the day that we enlisted,
Cause now all our hands were blistered.
So out went the boat boom once more,
And out went the liberty party going ashore.
For Kincade was his name,
and nothing remained the same.

VI

Seventeen hundred, the ships' bell sang out,
as the second liberty boat turned about.
But the third was still on the job,
From the mighty Bos'n to the lowest Gob.
"You'll work all night." Was his threat?
and we were there when the sun had set.
At eighteen hundred, we thought we were done,
and hoped that soon we would have some fun.
But at nineteen hundred, we still were there,
and then you could hear those seamen swear.
The third liberty party just left the ship,
and we hoped we might give the Bos'n the slip.
But he was there, watching us like a hawk,
He didn't speak, but we could hear him talk.
The first stars began to shine,
As the Bos'n shouted, "Make fast that line."
We cussed and swore under our breath,
That something would happen to cause his death.
But, he was to dammed tough to die,
Cause when he faced hell, the devil would cry.
For Kincade was his name,
and nothing remained the same

VIII

Twenty hundred sang the OLE ships' bell,
And we felt like prisoners in a cell.
"God what kind of a man is he,
Who would bet with the devil, and win all three.
At twenty one hundred, out went the liberty boat.
Soon we all began to give up hope.
Our backs were tired; our hands were numb,
But, he made sure we were there, counting us one by one.
At twenty two hundred, I heard him say,
"Knock off work and secure for the day,"
For Kincade was his name
and nothing remained the same.

IX

Then he called us all together and said,
"I know you all wish that I was dead,
What I do I do for a reason.
It's not for me it's the Captain I'm pleasing,
So grip your teeth and bare your sorrow,
We didn't do much today, but we'll give it hell tomorrow.
We've got the hardest job aboard,
From turret three, to where the planes are stored.
The catapults you can also add,
And a crew for the Gig is to be had.
I know it's no fun to work all night,
But, I like to see the job done right.
So it's up to you to do your job,
And I'll be there with the lowest Gob.

There wasn't much said after that,
We went down below and took off our hat.
Into the showers most of us went,
Cause we knew what the Bos'n meant.
I wonder if the day will ever come'
When a seaman can say, "My work is done."
For his name was Kincade
and nothing ever, remained the same,
Dedicated to the men on the USS Columbus (CA-74).
No hard feelings, Boats.

I'm not sure when Kincade came aboard. He was tough, but one hell of a nice guy.

My cleaning station was the aft rope locker; I loved to cook even then. We had an 18x30 hot plate, a one gallon Jo pot and miscellaneous other cooking supplies.

The Navy supplied the food, while loading, we stored enough canned food for about six months, such as meats, powered milk, powered potatoes, flour, and cans of various vegetables. And, of course, we had a large refrigerator-freezer. I remember one Sunday morning about O-nine hundred, when we were in China. I was cooking a mess of bacon and eggs. (I'm not sure where we got the eggs from, this time.) I looked up at the hatch and saw a pair of blue officers' uniform coming down the ladder. As he descended, I recognized the Captain. Before he was able to speak, I quickly handed him a plate with two eggs, potatoes, four strips of bacon, and toast. I sat him at a small table that we borrowed from the mess hall and placed a cup of coffee next to him. He never said a word. While he was eating, two other seamen came down the ladder, saw him and almost died. He stared speechless for a moment, then said, "Don't just stand there, hand me that bottle of ketchup and have a cup of coffee before it gets cold." Needless to say, every one broke out laughing. When leaving he very sternly said, "I won't tell, if you don't, and I'm sure you won't." We took the hint and nothing was ever said about that morning (until now.)

Shipmates scrub the teak wood deck. Courtesy of Ronald Dolinsky.

The 1949 basketball team. Courtesy of Robert Schaudt.

The Columbus Explorers basketball team. Courtesy of J.R. Williams.

The "K" (King) Division basketball team. Courtesy of Robert Schaudt.

Courtesy of E. Manista

Gitmo, 1952.

"H" Division USS Columbus CA-74. 3rd from left, Back row: Chief Wallace, J. Walter Forest, Porter, LCDR (DC) C.A. Harris, LT (MC) W.C. Sharpe Jr., J.C. Ladenhein LTJG (MC), and J.L. Cogborn HM2.

USS Columbus

Biographies

ROBERT ALESSANDRO, born June 17, 1934 in Tacoma, WA. He attended Washington State University and earned his BA degree in 1957. Alessandro joined the military June 30, 1957 at Seattle, WA with the following assignments: M Div Off, USS *Columbus* (CA-74); Eng Off, USS *Luzon*; Eng Off, USS *Ajax*; XO USN MCIC, Portland, OR. Discharged Jan. 31, 1962 with the rank lieutenant and held the rank of LCDR, USNR, June 30, 1971.

Civilian activity as Sr. Op., branch manager, Solomon Smith Barney. Employed 40 years. Alessandro received several service medals and many community service awards. He and his wife Priscilla have three children: Julie, Camilla and Tom, and two grandchildren, Jared and Jordan.

CARL F. ALTZ, born Nov. 29, 1933 in Utica, MI. He graduated from Utica High School in 1973 after continuing his education. He left school at age 16 to work construction and help support his family. He joined the Navy in 1951 at the tender age of 17.

His first tour he was assigned on the USS *Columbus* (CA-74) on Jan. 1, 1952 and served in the deck-force, 4th Div. and then was transferred to storekeeper, which was a part of ship service. In 1953 he made 3rd class and was again transferred to the USS *New Jersey* in 1954. That fall he was discharged and married his first wife Helen. She was the reason he left the Navy.

Five years later (Nov. 7, 1959) he remarried to Shirley Desotell and remains married to her today. They have two children from her previous marriage: Jack and James; a daughter of their own, Laura Tancy; and adopted daughter, Colleen Rae. Carl has remained working in the carpentry field since 1958.

JOE ARMSTRONG, born Sept. 13, 1947, Boston, MA, where on Nov. 27, 1967 he enlisted in the service. Assignments include RTC Great Lakes; Company Commanders aide, Great Lakes; CS "A" School, Newport, RI; USS *Columbus*, Sept. 28, 1968 to Oct. 26, 1970; and final duty at Naval Facility, Nantucket, MA. He served in the Eastern Mediterranean September to October 1970. He was discharged Aug. 30, 1971 as CS2 and received Meritorious Unit Citation

MELVIN E. BACON, born Feb. 24, 1932, Portland, OR and completed two years college. He joined the service Nov. 10, 1951 in Portland, OR, and served in both Korean and Vietnam conflicts.

He was to first experience USS *Columbus* as she was being outfitted to become a CG at Bremerton, WA and was part of her commissioning crew in 1963. He is a proud plankowner. He once more became a member of her crew beginning in 1968 in Norfolk, VA and made several MED cruises.

Memorable: It was while aboard the *Columbus* that he was fortunate to be captain of the ships bowling team and they won two invitational tournaments in Malta, 1969-70 and 70-71. Also memorable was the holidays of 70-71 when many of their families joined them on the Riviera. It was from the Columbia's deck that he faded into Navy history June 1, 1971, completing his childhood dream of serving his God and country in Uncle Sam's Navy.

Other ships include USS *Iowa, Interdiction, Shelton, Fechteler, Blandy* and *William Wood;* also USN RecSta, San Diego, CA; USN Station Astoria, OR; GCA School, Glynco, GA; USN Astro Grp, Det B.

Awards include the Good Conduct (5), National Defense (2), Korean Service w/3 stars, Korean Campaign, Korean PUC, UN, Navy Occupation (Asia and Europe), Vietnam Service, Vietnam Campaign, Vietnam PUC, Navy Unit Commendation, Meritorious Unit Citation (2) and Korean Gov. War Medal.

He worked for the US Postal Service 1971-92. His wife, the former Ruth King, passed away in April 1991. He has four children: Eugene, Michael, Mark and Amber Lea (Mrs. Hoagland) and five grandchildren: Cassandra, Jacob and Kyle Hoagland; Haley Reann and Dominque Bacon.

JOHN R. BALADO, born Jan. 11, 1935 in New York City, NY and attended Brooklyn Automotive High School. He joined the Navy April 23, 1952 and was sent to Bainbridge, MD for initial training.

After boot camp he went aboard the USS *Columbus* on Aug. 6, 1952 and was assigned to the 1st Division on Aug. 22, 1952. He then transferred to the S2 Division and attended Cooks & Baker's School in Newport, RI for three months. He returned to the USS *Columbus* and separated from the navy Dec. 8, 1955 in Long Beach, CA as CS3.

He enjoyed all ports of call on two Mediterranean cruises, but most memorable was going through the Panama Canal and crossing the Equator. He retired to Florida in 1995 from the plumbing and heating business.

John and Martha married Feb. 14, 1982. There are nine children, 20 grandchildren and three great-grandchildren (combined).

WAYNE C. BEARD, born Dec. 19, 1929, graduated high school and has some vocational school. On Jan. 2, 1951 he left Minneapolis, MN for boot camp at the Great Lakes. After completing boot training, they went to Norfolk, VA to catch the *Columbus* in the Mediterranean.

Memorable was a tour to Rome for six days and five nights for $66, including hotel room and meals - what a deal. Also memorable was on the way back from the Mediterranean when they ran into a hurricane. His duty at the time was helmsman and he got a job well done.

He was left gun captain in No. 1 turret for GQ besides his cleaning and maintenance station. That was fine duty. The ship won E's on all their batteries whenever they fired for competition.

Civilian employment as head lock and dam operator, St. Paul District Corps of Army Engineers. Married Mary Margaret and have three children: David, Dwayne and Gloria. Grandchildren are Spencer and Cassie Beard and Derrick and Alex Yarwood.

RAYMOND E. BEATTIE, born July 25, 1930 in Cranston, RI and graduated from James T. Lockwood High School, Warwick, RI. He enlisted Nov. 8, 1950 and took basic training at Naval Training Center, Newport, RI. From boot camp to London, England awaiting a flight to Istanbul, Turkey to go aboard the USS *Columbus*. He was assigned to Executive Officer's Of-

fice which maintained enlisted personnel records and advanced through the ranks to E-5, Personnelman 2nd Class (PN2). Played center field on the ship's softball team playing various ships of the Sixth Fleet and civilian teams in the Boston area.

Married Millie Zaborski Dec. 1, 1951 and has two children, Ray Jr. and Carolyn. Grandchildren are Michelle, Kyle, David and Kerri. Millie died Mar. 28, 1995 from cancer. He later married Sara (Sinnott) Butler July 12, 1997.

Received the Navy Good Conduct Medal, National Defense Service Medal and Navy Occupation Medal with European Clasp. Raymond received an Honorable Discharge at Fargo Building, Boston, MA, Sept. 3, 1954.

Retired in 1986 after 35 years civilian service with the Navy Department. His last position was employment director, Naval Submarine Base, New London, Groton, CT. Previously employed at Naval Construction Battalion Center, Davisville, RI and as a Personnel Staffing Specialist at NAS, Quonset Point, RI.

Joined the USS Columbus Veterans Association in 1990 and has served as trustee, executive vice president and co-chairman, Hospitality Committee.

FRANKLIN D. BEERS, born Aug. 22, 1933, Walnutport, PA. He enlisted in the service in 1951 at Allentown, PA and assigned ship armorer with home port at Charleston, MA.

Beers participated in the Korean War. Discharged in 1955 as gunner's mate 2/c, his awards include the Good Conduct, Navy Occupation, National Defense Service Medal and Korean Service Medal. Memorable was crossing Arctic Circle.

He was a truck driver for Trojan Powder Co. Explosives for 30 years and parts manager for Krause Dodge, 15 years. He and his wife Ethel have one daughter Karen and two grandchildren, Andrea and Ashlee.

JOHN F. BENCH, born Aug. 16, 1929, North Syracuse, NY. He graduated from North Syracuse High School in June 1948 and signed up graduation night with Boston Braves Farm Club, Kingston, Ontario of the Border League. He played two years then joined the USN Oct. 2, 1950.

Boot camp was at Newport, RI, then to Brooklyn Navy Yard to USS *Maurice Rose* to Plymouth, England where he boarded USS *Columbus.* Transferred to USS *Worcester* for two months before being discharged July 14, 1954. Awards include the Navy Good Conduct, National Defense Service Medal and Navy Occupation with European Clasp.

John and his wife Carolyn have two children, Robert John and Robyn Ann. Grandchildren are Lisa, Shawn, Courtney, Francesca and Zachary. John joined the USS Columbus Veterans Reunion Association in 1989, Orlando, FL and has served as trustee and chaplain at reunions.

ERIC P. BENEDICT, born Jan. 31, 1943, West Plaines, MO and has a master's degree in safety. He enlisted June 6, 1962 at Kansas City, MO and participated in Vietnam.

Boot camp and FT Class "A" School was at San Diego, CA; Talos Radar School at Mare Island, CA; CG-12 FTM, Seattle, WA. Memorable was EastPac and Med cruises.

Discharged from active duty Dec. 20, 1966 and from reserves, June 5, 1968 as FTM-2 (E-5). Awards include Good Conduct, Armed Forces Expeditionary Medal (Vietnam) and National Defense Medal.

A certified safety professional, he worked for Bendix Aviation Corp. in Kansas City, MO and for Bechtel Jacobs, Oak Ridge, TN. He married a school teacher, Louise Spargo, Oct. 12, 1968 and they have two children, Jennifer and Derick.

DONALD E. BENTON, born May 2, 1940, Warren, OH. He joined the service Jan. 10, 1961 at Warren and served in the USS *Osborn* (DD-846), Bremerton, WA; USS *Malaney* (DD-528); and is a plankowner of USS *Columbus* (CG-12).

His most memorable experience was while aboard the *Columbus* when he was the engineman on the Captain's gig and B.M. Burk was the coxswain. They were giving Capt. Boyd and his family a tour of San Diego

harbor. Richard Boyd was standing on the bow when they hit a wake from another boat and he lost his balance and slipped off the bow, but was holding on to the handrail. They stopped and helped him back on board. Capt. Boyd had a few words with his son, then sent him to the after cabin.

Donald was discharged Jan. 10, 1965 as EN3. He received the Good Conduct Medal.

He and his wife Diana have seven children and 13 grandchildren. Donald is retired from Packard Electric.

PAUL F. BLACK, PN2, born April 24, 1930 in Perkinsville, NY. He graduated from Dansville, NY High School in 1948 and was a draftsman at Foster Wheeler Corp. in Dansville prior to enlisting on Nov. 7, 1950 at Buffalo, NY.

Assigned to Boot Camp Co. 66 at Newport, RI then to the USS *Columbus* in February 1951. He transferred to Reserve Fleet, Sub Group II, Charleston, SC in August 1952 then TAD to Savannah, GA. He was discharged Sept. 1, 1954.

He married Anne VanDerwerken Dec. 19, 1953 in Dansville, NY and they have five children and nine grandchildren. Paul graduated from Rochester Institute of Technology in 1961 and served as village justice, Village of Dansville from 1969-77 and retired as the design-drafting supervisor, Government Systems Division, Eastman Kodak Co. on Nov. 1, 1991.

JOHN J. BOHNERT, born Oct. 28, 1941 in New Rochelle, NY. He graduated from Fitzgerald High School in Warren, MI in 1959, attended the University of Miami, FL for two years, then joined the Navy in August 1961.

After boot camp at Great Lakes, he had TAD with VS-30 Squadron at NAS, Key West, FL; attended Missile Technician "A" School in Dam Neck, VA and Talos Missile School in Mare Island, CA. He served aboard USS *Columbus* (CG-12) from February 1963 to August 1965.

John graduated from San Francisco State and taught elementary school for 27 years. He retired in 1997 and moved to Grass Valley, CA. Genealogy and reading are his main hobbies.

PAUL BOSHKO, born Jan. 4, 1929 in South River, NJ. He graduated from South River HS in 1948 and Middlesex County Vocational School in 1949.

He joined the Navy in 1950 and trained in Newport, RI, then sent to Plymouth, England to board the USS *Columbus.*

After serving two Mediterranean cruises, he was given shore duty in Boston, MA until his discharge in August 1953 with the rank of second class damage control petty officer.

Paul and his wife Eleanor were classmates in high school and married April 11, 1953. They have two daughters, Lydia and Ellen, and two granddaughters. Paul worked for Public Service Electric and Gas Co. for 39 years, first as a lineman and then training coordinator, retiring in 1988.

GEORGE M. BOWDEN, born in Atlanta, Georgia on Dec. 17, 1936 and graduated from Chamblee High School in 1954. He joined the USNR in 1953 and was called to active duty in January 1955 to go aboard the *Columbus* in Boston.

After midshipman cruise to Spain and England, later transited Panama Canal in November 1955 to Long Beach via Callao, Peru. Made Far Eastern Mission cruise (January 1956 - July 1956) when *Columbus* was involved in Parks collision, later drydocking for major repairs in San Francisco.

Discharged in 1957 as Personnel Man 3/c. He attended Georgia State University and graduated from George Washington University in 1967 with a BA degree in psychology. Served in the Federal government in the U.S. Department of Labor's Bureau of Labor Statistics, the U.S. Department of the Navy's Personnel Research Laboratory, and as Personnel Officer for the U.S. Department of Commerce's Social and Economic Statistics Administration, and Bureau of the Census. He retired in 1989.

George married in 1975 to the former Mimi Chovan and they have two sons, Cameron and Todd, and another son, Allen, from a previous marriage. He raced small bore production race cars for 22 years, winning a Regional Championship in the Sports Car Club of America's road racing series. Currently living on Lake Lanier in Gainesville, GA.

ROBLEY "BOB" BOWEN, born Jan. 6, 1927 in Brooklyn, NY. Attended H.S. Music and Art in Manhattan. Joined the Navy in December 1944 and went to boot camp at Sampson NTS, Upstate New York.

Formed Ships Company at Newport, RI and took training cruises on USS *Savannah* and USS *Augusta*; plankowner, commissioning crew, USS *Columbus* June 8, 1945. Served WWII Pacific Theater of Operations.

Awarded Navy Good Conduct Medal, China Service, American Defense, Asiatic and Pacific, Victory Medal and Occupation Forces Japan. Discharged Long Beach Navy Base, California, December 1947.

Robley married Marcia Aug. 28, 1947 and has three children: Robert, Cathy and Carol, and one grandchild Melissa. After 40 years he retired from Southern California Gas Co. as a district supervisor.

GIDEON M. BOYD, born March 19, 1915, Lakewood, New Mexico. He entered the Naval Academy from Adairsville, GA and graduated in 1938. Further Navy education included an ordnance postgraduate course in guided missiles at MIT and the Naval War College at Newport, RI.

Other service ashore has been on the staff of OPTEVFOR at Norfolk, VA, and in the office of the Chief of Naval Operations, Guided Missile Division.

All WWII duty was aboard destroyers in the Pacific including USS *New Mexico, McCall, C.K. Bronson and Baltimore.* Other sea duty has included command of destroyers *Fullam* and *R.E. Kraus,* Destroyer Division 302 and just prior to *Columbus,* the *Observation Island,* the Polaris test ship based at Cape Canaveral, FL.

Capt. Boyd retired from the USN Feb. 1, 1968 and worked for Lockheed, 1968 until retirement in 1976. He and his wife Ruth had two children, Nancy Durham and Richard H. Boyd. Grandchildren include Kristen and Becky Boyd, Aulton Durham and D'Ann Wiley. Capt. Boyd

passed away Aug. 11, 1993.

ROBERT J. "BOB" BREWSTER, graduated in the 1950 class from East Providence High School, East Providence, RI and faced a poor job market, so military life was appealing. His brother Ed graduated one year

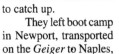

earlier, enlisted in the Navy and was assigned to the "N" Division, USS *Columbus*. He had a nine-month jump on Bob but Bob was determined to catch up.

They left boot camp in Newport, transported on the *Geiger* to Naples, the *Sabine* to Gulf Juan, arriving onboard the *Columbus* in beautiful Villefranche on Christmas Eve.

Separation came four years later in Boston as radarman first class (Ed was second class.) I has no regrets with any cruise they took except it was hot in Cuba.

Bob married a childhood sweetheart in 1954 and they have three daughters and an adopted son. They now have five grandchildren living near by.

He worked at Cape Canaveral for 32 years. Went from RCA, to GE and retired CSR in 1988 establishing a consulting business and patented a Range Safety Space Based GPS Tracking System. Hopefully it will be used in the near future in space and by the FAA on aircraft to increase safety.

Thanks to the officers and men of "K" division.

MARVIN "GENE" BRIDENBAUGH, born April 26, 1929 in Chillicothe, OH. After High School at Southeastern HS, Richmond Dale, OH, he started working for the Norfolk & Western (N&W) Railroad. He

worked about a year, then joined the Navy. Boot training was at Camp Moffett, Great Lakes, July 19, 1948.

After boot training he and his brother (Charles R.) were assigned to USS *Fargo* (CL-106). They were in four years and were together all the time. After 14 months they were transferred to the USS *Missouri* (BB-63). They made one cruise from Norfolk to New York. After they got back they were transferred May 29, 1950 to the USS *Columbus*. On June 12, 1950 at 4:30 p.m., they were on their way to Plymouth, England for a 18 month tour.

Discharged from the Navy July 10, 1952 and went back to N&W Railroad for five months, then worked for Mead Paper Co. and 41 years later retired as a paper machine tender, May 1, 1994.

He married Dorothy J. Detty Feb. 28, 1950, while in the Navy. They have three children: Jeff, Jerry and Julie. Jerry and family live in Tennessee, Jeff and Julie in Chillicothe. There are six grandchildren.

WALTER M. BRODIE, born Oct. 13, 1945 in Charleston, SC. He enlisted in the USNR in 1966 and began active duty at Boilerman "A" School, Great Lakes in March 1968. He was in "B" Division on Columbus from September 1968 until his discharge to the USNR in February 1970.

Walter graduated from Charleston Southern University in 1972 with a BS in economics and from the University of South Carolina with an MBA in 1975. While in school he worked as a licensed power engineer. For three years after getting his MBA, he worked as a marketing representative for the IBM Office Products Division.

In 1979 he began a career in financial services as a stockbroker with Merrill Lynch. In 1993 he began the Brodie Agency in 1993 and is a chartered financial consultant and a chartered life underwriter. The Brodie Agency has customers in Florida, South Carolina, North Carolina and Virginia. In 1974 he married Ann Kennington who is a pharmacist.

DONALD K. "BUZZ" BROWN, born in Berkeley, CA and reared in Placeville, CA. He graduated from Placeville Grammar School in 1947 and from Eldorado County HS in 1951. He joined the Navy in 1951 and graduated from Hospital Corps School, San Diego. He attended many other schools; served at many shore duty stations with the 3rd MarDiv., 3rd Med. Bn., A Co., 3rd Tank Bn., 1st MarDiv; and in many ships.

One of his proudest moments was being selected to put the USS *Columbus* (CG-12) in commission and becoming a plankowner. He is proud to have served his country in the US Navy.

ROBERT T. BROWN, born Nov. 8, 1937 in Pittsburgh, PA and moved to Colorado Springs, CO after WWII. He joined the Navy after high school

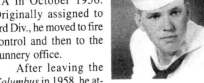

and reported aboard the *Columbus* while in the yards at Hunter's Point, CA in October 1956. Originally assigned to 3rd Div., he moved to fire control and then to the gunnery office.

After leaving the *Columbus* in 1958, he attended Draftsman Class A School and retired in 1979 as chief petty officer. Robert served tours of duty with AmphibBase, San Diego, Fleet Intelligence Center Pacific, Sub Base, New London, Commander Carrier Division Three and Fleet Training Center, San Diego.

While in service, Chief Brown earned advance degrees in teaching, counseling and education administration (Ed.D). His medals include Navy Unit Commendation (2), Meritorious Unit Commendation, Good Conduct (5), National Defense, Allied Expeditionary Medal, Vietnam Service (3), RVN Campaign, Gallantry Cross Armed Forces Vietnam, Civil Action Vietnam, Expert Pistol, Expert Rifle, ROC Honor Medal and ROC Mutual Defense Medal.

Since leaving the service, Robert and his wife Catherine reside in San Clemente, CA, where they both maintain private consulting practices in business and health. They are frequently visited by five children and three grandchildren.

TED BROWN, born June 7, 1920, Highland Park, MI and has BA degree and Tchg. Cred. He joined the military Oct. 16, 1939 at Detroit, MI; served in various ships 1939-41; submarines, 1941-45, 1946-47, 1948-50, OP DEV Force; 1951-57, Training Corps; 1957-59, *Columbus*, 1959-60.

Served during WWII, three war patrols, South Pacific and September 1958 in *Columbus* off Quemoy. Ted was retired from the Navy Oct. 1, 1960. Awards include Good Conduct, three stars, American Defense, Bronze A, American Theater, Pacific Theater, Victory Medal, National Defense.

Memorable experiences and accomplishments include receiving Entertainment Commendation, FSS Key West, contrib. to Op'l Readiness, 1st Flt., 7th Flt., Columbus.

As a civilian he was Boy Scout leader for 45 years; Space System instructor and research engineer, Lockheed, bio Med. Eq. repair, VA Hospital, music teacher and musician (played in halls from Hungary to China and for Pope Paul II in 2000).

His wife Dorothy is deceased. He has five children: Dennis, Michael, Timothy, Patrick and Melinda. Grandchildren are Jeremy, Jeffrey, Kristi, April, Amanda, Brian, Robbie, Jessica, Robbie and Mariana. Also has two great-grandchildren.

LOWELL BRVINS, born Jan. 29, 1930 in Fond du Lac, WI, completed high school and one year college. He joined the Navy Nov. 6, 1950 at the beginning of Korean War and went to boot camp at Great Lakes.

Assigned to USS *Columbus,* Boston, Cuba Naval Yard and Mediterranean Sea. Before being discharged Aug. 31, 1954 as GM3/c, he saw a lot of the world, Mediterranean, Caribbean plus many ports.

Worked 43 years in super market and custodian, six years. Lowell and Marjorie married June 2, 1954 and have three children: Jeffrey, Valerie, Janell; and five grandchildren: Ethan, Erin, Alex, Elizabeth and Tom.

MILTON BUBLINEC, born May 19, 1929 in Johnson City, NY. He graduated from Johnson City High School in 1948 and received an associate

degree in electrical engineering from New York State Institute of Fine Arts and Science in 1950.

Milton joined the Navy Sept. 19, 1950. Received his basic training in Newport, RI, which was newly reactivated for the Korean War. He attended ET "A" School January to September 1951 and Radar Fire Control School in Washington, DC, September 1951. Went aboard USS *Columbus* (CA-74) November 1951 in Boston. He served in T Div.

He was "Honor Man" of Company 17 during basic training. Received National Defense Service Medal, Good Conduct Medal and Navy Occupation Service Medal. Milt was discharged at Boston from the Navy June 29, 1954 as ET-2.

Milt met Reta at IBM, Owego, NY and they married Nov. 3, 1973. He retired from IBM in 1990 after working there 36 years.

DONALD H. BUDKE, born Aug. 28, 1926 and studied architecture at University of Cincinnati. He enlisted in the Navy in June 1944 at age 17

(went with a friend to enlist, also a senior in high school). Donald passed the physical (his friend did not) and left for boot camp on his 18th birthday in August 1944. Attended engineering school in Newport, RI (where the engineering dept. formed for the CA-74). While in Newport, he formed a friendship with E.A. Cook, his wife Leah, and daughter Karen, and after 57 years, that friendship is still in place. They keep in touch by long distance calls between Ohio and Arizona.

Next assignment was Boston NSY for commissioning, shakedown, and sea trials. Sailed to Guantanamo Bay (Cuba), Panama Canal, Hawaii, Shanghai, Tsing Tao (China), Sasabo, Yokohama, Yokosuka and Tokyo (Japan).

Memorable experience was on shore in Tokyo, while walking along the street in front of the Imperial Palace, which was surrounded by a moat on the right, and the DIET building on the left (Gen. MacArthur's HQ), Donald looked up to see a GI approaching him. The Navy may have rejected his friend, but there he was in Army khakis.

From Tokyo, he sailed to Okinawa and onto Long Beach, CA. The last Engine Room Watch (stood in dress blues) was to put the ship in dry dock. Then to the quarterdeck, where he picked up his sea bag and took LCM to the USS *Astoria* (CL-90) anchored in Long Beach Harbor. They were in need of Engine Room Personnel.

He was discharged in 1946 at Great Lakes NTS. His awards include the American Theater, Pacific Theater, China Liberation, Victory Medal and Japanese Occupation. His time in the Navy and aboard ship left him with memories money can't buy. Those were difficult times for our nation. Would I serve my nation and the Navy again, you ask? YES! Tomorrow, if needed.

In 1946 he met Olga and they married in 1949. They have four children and eight grandchildren. Olga died in 1971 and he remarried to Betty in 1975.

In 1956 he formed a family owned construction business, still family owned and run. I still works there in semi-retirement. Presently, he works on ships in a bottle and does wood carvings for a hobby.

ESAU "BURCH" BURCHFIELD JR., born Sept. 6, 1942 in Robbins, TN and graduated from Robbins High School in 1960. Like many young people, he "went north" to find a job in 1961. He joined the Navy Oct. 8, 1961 in Indianapolis, finished boot camp and Firecontrol "A" School at Great Lakes, then to AN SPG 51 Radar School at Dam Neck, VA.

Burch reported aboard CG-12 in January 1963 while she was being converted at Bremerton, WA. He was assigned to T1 Division and made the West Pac cruise in 1964 to Midway, Guam, South China Sea, Philippines and Japan. Transferred to San Diego Nav Station when CG-12 moved to the East Coast in January 1966. He was discharged as FTM2 Jan. 17, 1966.

Esau has taught mathematics and computer science for 30 years at Robbins Elementary School. He is a member of education associations, the USS Columbus Veterans Association and the American Legion. His main hobby is ham radio, to which he was introduced by LT Richard Davis, his Division Officer while aboard *Columbus*.

He married his high school sweetheart, Ruth, in June 1966. They have a daughter Veronica Carson. Veronica and her husband Randy Joe have two sons, Andrew and Aaron.

JACK D. "J.D." BURKETT, born April 1, 1932 in Bristol, VA. Moved to Salisbury, MD in the forties. He worked as a milkman until enlisting in the Navy Oct. 16, 1952.

J.D. served boot in Bainbridge, MD and boarded the USS *Columbus* late January 1953, assigned to 6th Div. While aboard, he participated in the following events: yard period in Boston, shakedown cruise, Gitmo, Caribbean, Mediterranean Cruise, South America. They steamed through Panama Canal, crossed equator, Far East Cruise and had a collision at sea with USS *Floyd B. Parks* (DD) off Philippines March 11, 1956. He played softball on ships' team in 1955 and 1956 and participated in the BatCruLant Tournament, Norfolk, VA in 1955.

He obtained GM3, Gun Captain Mount 34 and was told he was the first to be processed and released to inactive duty directly from the ship; release date was Oct. 15, 1956.

J.D. married his childhood sweetheart, Doris Calcott "Dolly," in 1960. They have two children, Jeffrey and John, and four grandchildren. He operated a small family business almost 40 years as partner, vice-president, president and owner until retirement in 1998.

J.D. joined the USS Columbus Veterans Association in 2001. Hopefully, he will attend his first reunion in 2002.

BENNIE W. BYARGEON, born Nov. 27, 1932 in Bastrop, LA and graduated from Bastrop High School in 1951. He worked at Internation Paper prior to going into the Navy in January 1952.

Boot training was at San Diego followed by three months in Chicago, then to Boston where he boarded the USS *Columbus* July 17, 1952. He worked in the oil shack as oil king until his discharge in November 1955.

Bennie married Carol Cangiamila of Boston on Aug. 14, 1955 and they had one son. A car accident took Carol's life in 1957. In 1959 he married Glenda Willett of Tullos, LA and they have one son and two grandsons. At present he is semi-retired and raising registered Boer meat goats.

ROBERT O. "BOB" CASE, born Feb. 3, 1926 in Portland, OR. He graduated from Grant High in 1943 and got in one year of college before enlisting in 1944. Boot camp was at Great Lakes and Radar schools at Chicago, Monterey and Treasure Island. Bob graduated March 1945 as ETM2/c and assigned as member of USS *Columbus* commissioning crew at Quincy Navy Yard.

Bob was responsible for maintenance of the Aft Secondary Battery Fire Control Radar and participated in pre-commissioning tests and calibrations, shakedown and training exercises at Guantanamo Bay, and Seventh Fleet activities in Asian waters. He disembarked in San Pedro in May 1946 for discharge in Bremerton, WA.

Returned to college in 1946 and married Cynthia Tribou in 1947. He graduated Cum Laude from Yale University in 1949 with a degree in electrical engineering and earned master's degree at Yale the following year.

Bob worked initially in the Physics Department at Oak Ridge National Laboratory. Then, switching to the aerospace industry, worked at North American Aviation, Tamar Electronics, and Ford Aerospace and Communication Corp. Retired in 1987 as vice president of FACC and general manager of the Aeronutronic Division.

Cynthia died in 1993. Bob remarried in 1994 to Jeanne Kirsch and together they have six children and 14 grandchildren.

GEORGE P. CHAN, born May 31, 1934 in Marlboro, MA and graduated from Marlboro High in 1951. He enlisted in the USN July 14, 1951 with recruit training at Bainbridge, MD. He attended Hospital Corpsman School, Bainbridge, MD with duty stations at St. Albans Naval Hospital, St. Albans, Long Island, NY; USS *Columbus* (CA-74) (H) Div., 1952-54; USMCRD, Parris Island, SC. He was discharged in May 1955.

Alumni Boston University; McLean Hospital SON; Massachusetts Memorial Hospital Anesthesia Program. He remained in the Active Naval Reserve until 1963. Highest rate attained was HM1. In 1963 he was commissioned a 2nd LT, USAFR and retired in 1973 with rank of captain.

George married Donna Girouard Sept. 16, 1961 and they have four children: Michael, Brian, Kevin and LeeAnne. Grandsons are Ryan and Peter.

He retired from Anesthesia with 33 years service. He is now a seasonal national park service ranger assigned to Minute Man National Park, Concord, MA.

He has been a member of the USS Columbus Veterans Assoc. since 1991 and is now serving on its Board of Directors.

KYONG WO "JOE" CHEW, born July 8, 1927 Kohala, Hawaii and graduated from Farrington High School. In 1944 he enlisted in the Navy at age 17, discharged as BT2/c, USN in 1949. He re-enlisted to active duty, 1952-54 in the Korean Conflict.

Assignments: (1944) Bishop's Point Pearl Harbor, USS *Cockatoo* Auxiliary Mine Sweeper; (1945-47) USS *Columbus* (CA-74); No. 1 Fire Room B Div., Chief Engineer FOY; (1948-49) Shore duty, NAS Midway Island; (1949) honorable discharge as BT2/c, USN; (1950) Hickam AFB as an aircraft mechanic; (1952) USS *Fire Drake* (AE-14) Korea; (1954) USS *Chemung* (AO-30) Korea;

(1969) Pearl Harbor as a power plant operator. In December 1982 he retired with 36 years of service.

Events that took place during his time of service include the USS *Columbus* participated in sinking 29 captured submarines off the coast of Japan in 1946; USS *Fire Drake* rescued a British Pilot plane in 1952 that crashed in the ocean off the coast of Korea during the Korean Conflict; the *Columbus* was in the China Theatre with the 7th Fleet under Admiral Kits Cruiser Division One; Captain Milton Miles was CO on the *Columbus*. He was a "Mustang" and in later year's became rear admiral.

Kyong Wo received nine ribbons including the Korean Conflict Area. He is a member of the NARFE, VFW, Mason Scottish Rite and Shriner's Aloha Temple. He married Lorraine Hume March 15, 1952 and they have seven daughters and one son: Waonette, Marva Lynn, Crystal, Jowett, Langford, Rayveen, Violyna and Tylee; 15 grandchildren and one great-grandson.

ALAN R. COLEMAN, born July 11, 1928, Detroit, MI. He joined the USN June 20, 1946 in Detroit and trained at Great Lakes. He spent 20 months on the USS *Columbus* as a fireman.

Alan was discharged April 15, 1948. Medals include China – Asian. Memorable was watching S. Goose go up and telling everyone who would listen about smooth flight.

Civilian employment as school custodian. He and his wife Ruth have been married since Feb. 11, 1950 and have one son Glen; granddaughter Wendy; and two great-grandchildren, David and Elizabeth.

ELMER A. COOK, born Jan. 30, 1920, in Hobart, IN and graduated from Hobart High. He married his high school sweetheart Leah Shelby on

March 1, 1941 and after over 60 years of marriage they are still speaking. They have two daughters, Karen and Shelby; one son Roy; three grandsons: Jeff Remaley, Kent and Kevin Bolke; and three great-grandsons.

Elmer joined the US Navy Dec. 29, 1944, with boot camp at Great Lakes and engineering training at Newport, RI. He boarded the USS *Columbus* in Boston, MA, stood number one throtal watch and has good memories of Commander Robins and Chief Papy Sloan. Made the shakedown cruise through Panama Canal, Pearl Harbor, and several China stops on their way to relieve the USS *Missouri* at Yakasaka, Japan. He left the USS *Columbus* there and went aboard the Destroyer *Taylor*, which was part of the escort of the USS *Missouri* to Pearl Harbor. Two days out to sea, they were in the tidal wave Tsunami of 1946. The USS *Missouri* advised all ships to "Make a run for it." The *Missouri* limped into Pearl Harbor with its bow caved in. His destroyer lost an 18 year old overboard and they were unable to look for him, because of the high seas.

Elmer's wife and 3-year-old daughter Karen were on board when USS *Columbus* had Open House while still in Boston, MA. During lunch in the Mess Hall, Karen disappeared; Leah panicked, but Elmer knew she couldn't be very far. He found her on a counter eating frosting with her hands from a gallon container in the bakery. He told the baker it would make her sick, so he gave her 24 ice cream bars to pass out on board.

One night leaving a USO ball, Leah, Karen and Elmer met an admiral and his wife, both attired in formal dress. As Elmer stood rigidly at attention, his daughter said, "Mommy, that lady has on a nightgown just like your." The Admiral laughed and knelt down to talk to her, as Elmer stood full attention.

He worked for US Steel for 35 years, belonged to Hobart Civil Defense for 12 years before retiring to Tucson, AZ. Retired from Sheriff Aux. Volunteer after 18 years of service in Tucson.

He has lost touch with all his mates except for Don Budke. He is the person that informed him of the USS Columbus Veterans Association. and they have kept in touch all these years. Elmer would love to hear from any of the mates he knew "way back then."

FELIX CREPEAU, born Jan. 13, 1925, in St. Paul, MN. He attended the Merchant Marine Academy and served as a deck cadet aboard the Liberty Ship, SS *William Windom*

in 1943 and early 1944. He was aboard the *Windom* in North Atlantic convoys to England and also an Arctic convoy to Murmansk and Molotovsk, Russia.

He joined the US Navy in 1944, attended Quartermaster School in Gulfport, MS, then assigned to the USS *Decker* (DE-47). The *Decker* escorted convoys from the East Coast to the Mediterranean. At Newport, RI, he was assigned to new construction for duty aboard the USS *Columbus* (CA-74). A plankowner, he served on the *Columbus* from commissioning June 8, 1945 until return from the Pacific to San Pedro, CA, April 17, 1946.

Highlight of life aboard the *Columbus* was serving as helmsman at all sea stations, steering the ship during shakedown exercises, through the Panama Canal, entering Pearl Harbor, up the Yangtze and Whangpoo Rivers to Shanghai, China and Tokyo Bay. He attained the rate QM2/c.

He graduated from Macalester College in 1949 and was married to Clenora the same year. They have three children: Kathleen, Diane and Felix H., and four grandchildren.

He retired from teaching, coaching and administrative work in secondary education in 1988.

SHERMAN DEATON, born April 14, 1929. He enlisted July 25, 1946 at Raleigh, NC, followed by Naval Training Center, Bainbridge, MD and naval training, Newport, RI.

He served aboard the USS *Manchester* (CL-83) and USS *Columbus* (CA-74). Discharged in 1953 with the rate GM3/c.

On March 5, 1993 Sherman retired as Supt., C.D. Williams Construction Co. He married Celia Peede Gums and has three stepsons and eight grandchildren.

CHARLES E. DIXON, born March 5, 1936, in Little Rock, AR. He graduated from Lakeside High School of Hot Springs, AR in May 1954. After a year at Henderson State College, he joined the Navy in September 1955 and reported to Great Lakes for basic training.

After boot camp, he was sent to Mare Island for transportation, then flown to Manila, P.I. where he went aboard the USS *Columbus* (CA-74) at Subic Bay.

Charles joined the USS Columbus Veterans Association in 1988 and had not missed a reunion until 2001.

He received a BSBA degree from Henderson State College in 1968 and is now retired from government service as an auditor.

Charles met Mary Ann of Malvern, AR, in 1956. They married on April 11, 1958 and have three sons: Robert, Brian and Douglas, and two grandchildren, Robert and Dylan.

GEORGE P. DODD, RMCM, USN (Ret), born in Neosho, MO. He enlisted in the US Navy at Omaha, NE, on July 18, 1942, received boot training at NTC, Great Lakes, IL; attended RM(A) School at University of Wisconsin and went aboard the USS *Wichita* (CA-45) at Pearl Harbor April 18, 1943.

He participated in the Aleutian and Marshall Islands campaigns; attacks on Truk, Palau, Yap, Wolea, Rota Island, Philippine Sea, Palau, Mindanao, Cebu, Negros, Digos, Leyte, Makan Islands, initial landing and capture of Okinawa Island, bombardment and occupation of Guam, Saipan and Tinian; covering operations incident to landings on Northern New Guinea coast of Hollandia, Wadke and Aitape.

He recovered allied military personnel and assisted in occupation of Nagasaki, Japan; was sent to NOF, Narsarssuak, Greenland; NOB, Argentia, Newfoundland; NAS, Alameda; Naval Communications Station, Guam; USS *Bairoko* (CVE-115) which saw action in the Korean conflict; participated in Operation Castle while aboard the *Bairoko* at the Bikini Atoll in 1954; CBC, Port Hueneme with the SeaBees; Teletype Repair School, NTC, San Diego.

New orders assigned him to the USS *Columbus* (CA-74) for a tour in the Far East, followed by RM-B School at Bainbridge, MD then to Norfolk Navy Shipyard at Portsmouth for further schooling prior to being assigned to the Communication Unit at Argentia, Newfoundland. Three years later he was assigned to the Staff of CINCLANTFLT in Norfolk, VA where he retired after 22 years.

Employed by RCA Service Co in the DC, McDonnell Douglas in St. Louis and as a Real Estate Associate. He married Helen L. Woomer of Xenia, IL, on Sept. 10, 1949. They have two sons, Robin, CDR (Ret), USN and George Jr. There are also six grandchildren: Melissa, Katie, Matthew, Andrew, Miles, James and Phillip.

RONALD P. DOLINSKY, born Oct. 17, 1930 in West Haven, CT and graduated from West Haven High School in 1948, post graduated Boardman Trade School in 1951. Ron enlisted in the Navy, March 20, 1951, New Haven, CT, boot training was at Great Lakes, completed EM School, Jan. 25, 1952 and reported to USS *Columbus* in Boston.

They crossed the Arctic Circle, Sept. 16, 1952 during Operation Mainbrace, entered Mediterranean Sea on Columbus Day 1952, commencing Operation Longstep. Back to the Mediterranean in 1954 for Christmas in Naples and New Year's Eve in Paris, France.

While in Rome, Ron toured the Vatican and had an audience with Pope Pius XII. He was discharged March 10, 1955 as EM2. His awards include the National Service and Good Conduct Medals.

In civilian life he worked in electrical and communication construction. He's presently working as electrical mechanic at General Mitchell International Airport.

Betty Jane and Ron met at a USO Party in 1951 at the Roof Ballroom in Milwaukee and they married May 3, 1952. They have two sons, John and Patrick. Patrick is serving on the *John C. Stennis* (CVN-74) in the Arabian Sea.

Joined the association in 1990 and attended the launch and Commissioning of the SSN-762.

WILLIAM "BILL" DULY, born Sept. 20, 1934. He enlisted in the Navy Nov. 4, 1952 at Fort Wayne, IN and went to boot camp at San Diego. He served aboard the USS *Columbus* from July 1953 to November 1956 during the Korean War.

Memorable experiences include crossing the Equator twice and going through the Panama Canal. He was discharged Nov. 2, 1956 as PO1, EM1. His awards include the Navy Occupation, National Defense and Good Conduct.

Worked for the US Postal Service 37 years, retiring as area manager. Bill and his wife, the former Carol Gross, have two children, William Jr. and James.

ARNOLD H. EGELAND, born March 22, 1933, Brooklyn, NY. After WWII, he moved to Norway for one year at the age of 13. He returned to NYC, attended and graduated from New York High School of Printing. As a senior, he joined the US Naval Reserve. In May 1952, he was activated during the Korean conflict, attended an eight week boot camp at Bainbridge, MD and was assigned to the C.S. Div. on the USS *Columbus*, Boston, MA. He was discharged in March 1954.

Arnold attended Voorhees Technical Institute, NYC on the GI Bill, graduating in 1956 with an associate BS degree in lithography. As an inactive reservist, he attained the rating of 2nd class PO in lithographer, grade E-5.

In 1959 he married Vivian. They have three married daughters, three grandsons and one granddaughter. They reside in Wyckoff, NJ and have been NJ residents since 1963 after leaving Brooklyn, NY. Arnold has been employed in the printing industry in NYC for over 45 years holding positions as production manager, estimator, and sales rep in corporate sales offices of major national printers. He currently is employed by one of New Jersey's largest printing companies as a financial analyst.

All the Egeland's are active skiers and you can find the family on many weekends on the slopes of Vermont or Squaw Valley, CA, where one daughter lives.

RONN WELLER EISS, born Nov. 30, 1931, Buffalo, NY. A resident of Snyder, NY he graduated, Amherst Central in 1949, then worked in radio and TV, repair and installation.

Enlisted in the USN on Friday 13th in 1950, one of 13 men who went to Newport, RI. Served in CA-74, 1950-53, CR-Div. as radio operator and teleman.

Shore duty at Dam-Neck, VA, FADTC, Teleman 3rd Class Petty Officer, until 1954. His ribbons include National Defense, Navy Occupational European Clasp and Good Conduct.

On GI Bill he attended Electronics School (375 hrs.), 1955-59; NGJC, Tigerville, SC, AA degree, 1961; Houghton College, NY, BA degree 1966. He ministered UMC's, one church, one year, and three churches, three years.

He was YMCA Director and Executive Director from 1966-72 and Missionary Western Cherokee Tribe, in Oklahoma, Director of Mission, 1973-76. Went back to College Oklahoma North Eastern State Univ., MEd., psyh. 1978. Did multi-discipline counseling and various positions in Churches and other counseling agencies.

Member of USSCVA 1993 and appointed Chaplain in 1995, and elected 2nd vice president in 1999 and remaining chaplain as well. He is also a member of USSCSA.

He married the prettiest girl in Perry, NY, Donna Lee, on Aug. 16, 1952. Their first born, Marshall Ronn, was baptized by Chaplain Marshall Brenneman at Annapolis in August 1954. Their other son, Jon Weller, is married to Robyn. Grandsons are Jonathan and Curtis.

JAMES E. "GENE" ELLIS JR., born Aug. 16, 1931 in Griffin, GA and graduated from Glenn High School, Birmingham, AL. He started work at *The Birmingham News* in Birmingham, AL while in school as a copy boy in the Editorial Dept. at age 16. Also, worked spare time for the Associated Press as

teletype operator until he enlisted in the Navy Jan. 20, 1951. In San Diego, CA he completed boot camp and Class A School for Telemen.

In August 1951 he reported to US Naval Communication Station (BWKC) 13th Naval District Headquarters, Seattle, WA. In June 1953 he reported aboard USS *Columbus* (CA-74) in Boston, MA. In August 1954 he transferred to USS *Northampton* CLC 1 and later to the USS *Mississippi,* both at Norfolk, VA. Discharged Dec. 8, 1954 at NOB Norfolk, VA as teleman second class.

After his discharge he was employed for 27 years with Alabama By-Products Corp. in Birmingham, the last 13 years as general manager of the Retail Division. Then he was employed by Stoffel Seals Corp. Nyack, NY, as Southeast Regional Sales Manager until retirement in 1997. He splits his time between his homes in Hoover, AL and Destin, FL.

Gene met his wife Bobbi Dawson, a native of Beverly, MA and a WAVE in Seattle, WA in 1952, and they were married there. They have two daughters and one son.

ROBERT "BOB" D. FENNELL, born Boston, MA on Feb. 7, 1932. Enlisted in USMC Feb. 12, 1951 and was discharged May 20, 1960 as a staff sergeant. He enlisted in the USN March 7, 1962, transferred to US Navy Fleet Reserve on April 16, 1973 as PH1 and to the Retired List of the US Navy on May 1, 1981.

Assignments/Locations: (USMC) 1st Marine Division Korea, Inspector-Instructor Staff, 5th Truck Co., Port Newark, NJ, Base Photo Lab, Camp Lejeune, NC. (USN) USS *Columbus* (CG-12) Naval Auxiliary Air Station, Kingsville, TX; Combat Camera Group, Atlantic, NAS, Norfolk, VA.

Wars/Battles: Korea, August 1951-July 1952 and Vietnam August 1964-February 1965 on Yankee Station.

Awards include the Presidential Unit Citation, Meritorious Unit Commendation, USMC Good Conduct (2), USN Good Conduct (2), Armed Forces Expeditionary Medal, National Defense Service Medal (2), Korean Service Medal, Korean Presidential Unit Citation and UN Service Medal.

Civilian activity as motion picture photographer, still photographer and purchasing agent for the Airlie Foundation in Warrenton, VA. from May 1973 until August 1977, then retirement.

He has five children: Stephen, Sheryl, Lisa, William and John and four grandchildren: Molly, Monica, Annie and John Jr. His wife is deceased.

EDWARD PAUL FINE, born Dec. 28, 1923 in Baltimore, MD. He is known to friends and family as Paul, but for official purposes he has always preferred the full name.

He graduated from the University of Maryland in 1943. Paul went off to Great Lakes for his initial boot training, followed by radio and radar training in Gulfport and Chicago.

Then it was off to Pearl Harbor. Prior to service aboard the *Columbus,* Paul was first a tin can sailor, having served as a member of a fighter director team aboard the USS *Eberle* (DD-430) and later the USS *Kearny* (DD-432),

Paul went aboard the USS *Columbus* at Pearl Harbor the day after Christmas in 1945. Two days later, on his birthday, the ship sailed for Okinawa and various ports in China and Japan.

Discharged from the service took place in the middle of June 1946. After his naval service Paul's civilian activities included work in business, as an engineer and as an auditor.

Paul was married to Miriam Goldenberg on June 15, 1948. They have three children, Michael, Adrienne and David, who in turn have produced four grandchildren.

LAWRENCE FINN, born in Toledo, OH, in April 1925. He graduated from Whitmer High School in January 1943 and attended Toledo University for one term before joining the Navy in 1944. After Great Lakes, Larry attended radio tech training at Herzel College Chicago, Gulfport, MS and final training at Navy Pier.

He was sent overseas upon graduation as electronic technician and spent time in Hawaii in the Air Support Control Unit training for the invasion of Japan.

Larry was transferred to duty aboard the USS *Columbus* (CA-74) when it arrived in Hawaii in December 1945 and served as ETM servicing the Sonar and Search & Fire Control radar systems while the ship toured the Pacific to Okinawa, China and Japan.

Following the ship's activity in "Operation Deep Six" off Japan's Sasebo submarine base, the ship returned to San Pedro in April 1946. It was there that Larry left the ship to be transferred to Great Lakes for discharge in June.

Larry married Agnes Wight of Toledo in December 1946 and they reared three children: Cheryl, Laura and Richard. They have seven grandchildren.

After completing mechanical engineering training at Ohio State University and University of Toledo, Larry worked for Owens Illinois and Owens Corning Fiberglas as a process engineer and retired after 39 years in 1989. He continues to sail the calmer waters of inland lakes in the pursuit of game fish using updated electronics.

JOHN J. FLAHERTY, born Sept. 17, 1932 in Boston. He joined the US Navy May 5, 1951 at Boston and served in the USS *Columbus* (CA-74). He was discharged March 20, 1955 and received the Korean Service Medal.

Memorable experience was his visit to Rome and meeting the pope. While aboard the Columbus he became a lithographer.

As a civilian he was court officer and magistrate, Suffolk City, MA. He and his wife Jane have three children: Frederick, Todd and Nicole.

GLENN D. FLINT JR., born July 1, 1948, Lynchburg, VA, and attended Community College. He joined the service Aug. 14, 1968 and served in "A" Division. Memorable experience was back-to-back Mediterranean cruises.

Glenn was discharged May 1, 1971 as E5. His awards include the National Defense Service Medal, Meritorious Unit Commendation and Surface Warfare Medal.

JOSEPH W. FOREST, known to most as Walter, was born Aug. 8, 1928 in Shirley, MA, graduated Ayer High School in June 1946 and joined the US Navy in December 1948. Boot camp and Hospital Corps School was at Great Lakes.

His first duty assignment was at the US Naval Hospital at Annapolis, then to Sick Quarters at Bancroft Hall at the Academy. He

transferred to USS *Columbus* September 1951 to April 1952 and to the USS *Fremont* (APA-44) until his discharge in November 1952. entered U.S. Naval Reserve and was recalled to active duty on the USS *Miller* (DD-535) in October 1961 and discharged May 1962 as Chief Petty Officer.

He entered U.S. Postal Service in September 1962, retiring as Postmaster in 1988. Walter married his high school sweetheart Dec. 25, 1949, and became the father of five beautiful children (one girl, four boys) and seven even more beautiful grandchildren. He is active in the American Legion of which he is a past commander. His hobbies include his ever-growing stamp collection, golf, reading, making puzzles, and his '57 Chevy.

DAVID H. FORTNER, born Sept. 28, 1940 in White County, Cleveland, GA. He went to school 11 years in Cleveland, then joined the US Navy Nov. 25, 1957. He took the GED test and finished high school while in the Navy. Dave was sent to San Diego, CA for his initial training.

After boot camp he was sent to Long Beach and went aboard the USS *Columbus* (CA-74) in January 1958. While there he went on a cruise overseas. After serving about a year, the ship was decommissioned to be converted to a guided missile cruiser.

He transferred to the USS *Piedmont* (AD-17) in San Francisco while it was being repaired in dry dock, then it moved to San Diego. Dave made another cruise overseas and finished his service on the *Piedmont* June 26, 1961. While aboard the *Piedmont* she won the Gold E Battle Efficiency award. His awards include the Good Conduct, Cold War and two overseas medals.

After the service he worked as a welder. He was called as a Baptist minister in March 1968 and has pastored several churches in the area. He is now serving in the White County Color Guard.

Dave met Jenny on a blind date set up by friends in July 1965, and they married Jan. 19, 1968. They have three daughters: Lydia, Lois and Ruthie, and eight grandchildren.

DONALD J. FOSTER, born Aug. 23, 1921, Portland, OR, five minutes before his twin sister Dorothy. He was attending Washington State University when he joined the Navy in 1941. He served as a bridge officer during WWII in the Pacific Theater aboard the LST-707 and was awarded four Battle Stars.

After returning to civilian life, he obtained his medical degree. In 1957 he rejoined the Navy and the USS *Columbus* (CA-74). He served as the only doctor on board until she was decommissioned in Bremerton, WA. He served as a Navy physician until 1961 at Balboa Naval Hospital and Camp Pendleton in San Diego, CA.

His awards include the Asiatic-Pacific Campaign w/4 Bronze Stars, American Campaign, National Defense, Navy Occupation (Japan), WWII Victory Medal, Philippine Liberation w/2 Bronze Stars, Philippine Presidential Unit Citation and Combat Ribbon.

Don joined the USS Columbus Veterans Association and attended his first reunion in Phoenix. He and his wife ruby have three children and five grandchildren.

FRANCIS JOHN FRESENBURG, born July 28, 1926 in St. Louis, MO. After graduation from St. Mary Magdalen Grade School, Frank went to work at Warner-Noll Bake Shop at age 14 until he enlisted in the Navy in 1944.

He went to Great Lakes for basic training and served as a baker aboard the newly commissioned USS *Columbus*. He truly enjoyed working with the other bakers and cooks on the ship. Francis John Fresenburg S1/c was discharged on July 19, 1946.

Frank went back to work at the bakery as the oven man and later became foreman of Warner-Noll bakery operations. This is where he met his wife Gertrude Gier who worked there as a salesgirl and later became an icing girl. They married on May 30, 1953. They opened a bake shop of their own in June 1956 and operated the shop for 23 years.

They have three sons: Brad, Bart and Brian and five grandchildren: Katherine, Kimberly, Michael, Andrew and Nicole. Frank passed away suddenly on Sept. 25, 2001 of a heart attack. He had a full military burial at Jefferson Barracks National Cemetery.

THOMAS A. GARRISON, born on Columbus Day in 1952, Mansfield, OH. He graduated from Malabar High School in 1971 and three days later on June 8, he started basic training at Great Lakes.

After boot camp he was sent to Norfolk, VA, where he spent the next four years stationed aboard the USS *Columbus* (CG-12). He was a member of the 1st Div. and was in charge of ship's sail locker and paint locker. He made two Med cruises the first in 1972 and the second in 1974. He was on the final crew of the *Columbus* when she was decommissioned in 1975 and remained with her as part of a security guard until his discharge June 6, 1975.

After his discharge he returned to Mansfield and was hired by the Penn Central Rail Road which became Conrail and is now part of the CSX Rail Road.

On Valentine's Day 1976, he married his long-time sweetheart Gloria Thrush. They have two children, Tom and Rachel.

L. PAUL GREENE, born July 5, 1930 in Alabama. He graduated from high school in 1947 and from college in 1953. Paul joined the Navy in 1947 at Jacksonville, FL and was sent to boot camp at San Diego, CA.

Other assignments include the USS *Columbus* (CA-74), December 1947 to May 1950 and Naval air Station, Norfolk, VA. Memorable

was being in Rome, Italy, June 3, 1948 and seeing Pope Pius XII. On Nov. 8, 1949 he spoke to King George VI in Portsmouth, England. He was discharged in 1950 as storekeeper third class.

After his discharge he worked for Delta Air Lines for over 40 years. On Valentine's Day in 1950 he met Diane and they married Feb. 11, 1951. They have two children, Paul and Brian, and four grandchildren: Sara, Jeffrey, Christopher and Kaitlin.

JERRY SCOTT GREENFIELD, born Dec. 30, 1928 in Akron, OH, grew up in Hardin, KY and moved to Tampa, FL in 1945. His sports at Plant High School were basketball and swimming. Jerry joined the Navy Aug. 1, 1947 and was sworn in at Jacksonville, FL. He then went to San Diego for boot camp.

He boarded the USS *Columbus* at Long Beach, CA in December 1947 where he was assigned to the Supply Dept., S-1 Division. Jerry served in the USAF from June 1951 to 1953 during the Korean War.

He attended Florida Southern College beginning September 1953. He was a member of the J.V. crew team during his college years. He graduated in June 1955 with a bachelor's degree in science and taught secondary science 1960-90 in the areas of earth science.

Jerry married Joanne in 1991 and has a daughter Jennifer, stepson Gene, four grandchildren and two great-grandchildren. He is very active in civic affairs, cultural arts, Boy Scouts and the Scottish American Military Society. He joined the USS Columbus Veteran's Association in 1990 and served six years on the board of directors, as 1st vice president for the past three years and hosted the 1996 reunion in Orlando, FL.

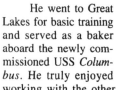

JOHN HOWARD GROSVENOR JR., born Jan. 15, 1948 at the Great Lakes Naval Training Center, IL. John graduated from Kecoughtan High School

in Hampton, VA in June 1966. While in high school, he worked at the Buckroe Beach Amusement Park. He also enlisted in the Navy and went into the Navy Reserves CASH Program. When he went into active duty he was sent to Great Lakes, IL for basic training and Electronics Technician "A "School.

John reported aboard the USS *Columbus*, in Norfolk, Virginia in May 1967 and was aboard until April 1970, leaving as an ET-3. He earned the National Defense Medal and has applied for the Cold War Certificate of Recognition.

After the service he worked for RCA Service Company, the National Aeronautics and Space Administration (NASA), the National Bureau of Standards (NBS) and is presently with the Department of Commerce at the National Institute of Standards and Technology (NIST).

John has served as a director and secretary for the USS Columbus Veterans Association. He started the USS Columbus CG-12 web site which latter also included information on the heavy cruiser CA-74 and the submarine SSN-762.

He is married to Chriss Ann (Jones) and they have four boys: John Howard III, Kenneth Dillon, and twin boys, James Matthew and Mark Richard Grosvenor.

NORMAN R. GUIVENS, born May 6, 1927 in Quincy, MA, birthplace of the CA-74. Entering the Navy in December 1944, Norm attended boot

camp at the Sampson US Naval Training Center. He was assigned to pre-commissioning training in "K" Division. When his North Quincy High School Class of 1945 graduated, Norm was already aboard the CA-74 where he served until April 1946.

Norm joined the post-war Naval Reserve and sailed aboard the USS *Kyne* (DE-744) and the USS *Randolph* (CV-15). Activated in August 1950, he served a year aboard the USS *Libra* (AKA-12) as a radarman second class.

He joined the USS Columbus Veterans Association in 1988, subsequently serving as 2nd vice president, director, auditor, and treasurer. He is a proud recipient of the Hickam Award. Norm is a CPA with degrees in accounting and taxation. After 27 years he retired from the IRS.

In April 1955 he married Lula E. Wager and they have one son, Norman Jr., who served as a lieutenant in the Navy. Norm and Lu sailed aboard the SSN-762 in December 2000. Norm is one of only a few men to have sailed on two US Navy ships named USS *Columbus*.

PHILIP D. HANSON, born Oct. 8, 1938, Phoenix, AZ. He graduated from Santa Ana, CA, High School in 1957 and joined the Navy soon

after at San Diego, CA. Boot camp and FTA School were at San Diego.

Served aboard the USS *Columbus*, Long Beach, CA and Naval Underwater Ordnance Div., Yokosuka, Japan as fire control technician. Discharged June 14, 1961 as seaman first class. He received the Good Conduct.

He married Barbara of Santa Ana, CA on June 19, 1966 and they have two children, Loreen Hanson Faust and Michele Hanson, and two grandchildren, Rebecca and Joshua Faust.

ROBERT J HARDY, born Feb. 19, 1935, in Oakland City, IN. Graduated from Oakland City High School in 1953 and received BS degree from Indiana University in 1957 and MBA from the University of Louisville in 1969. He was licensed as a CPA in Missouri in 1963.

Bob reported to the Navy OCS in Newport, RI in July 1957. Upon graduation, he reported in November as an ensign to the *Columbus* in Long Beach, CA. He was assigned to the OR (radio) division and was entitled to the Armed Forces Expeditionary Medal as a result of a *Columbus* Westpac cruise. Bob rode the *Columbus* to Bremerton for conversion to CG-12. He left the *Columbus* in July 1959 for the staff, Commander First Fleet, where he served until leaving active duty in November 1960.

Bob and Beverly married May 25, 1958. Their children are Tony and Leslie, and grandchildren are Shelby and Coby.

CHARLES J. HARROD, born May 11, 1934, in Albany, NY, and joined the Navy from Pittsfield, MA in 1951. He made boarding *Columbus* in

Boston less than enthusiastic for seeing the world, and with a seven-year apprenticeship from General Electric in his pocket at the time, making the Navy a career was the furthest thing from his mind.

After being one of 23 in the Navy to be advanced to BM3 in 1954 and the ship's orders to the west coast, everything changed. The four years already served started to outweigh the seven years GE was offering. Ironically, *Columbus* provided his first homeport of Boston and delivered him to Long Beach, CA which turned out to be his last for his 20 year career.

He transferred to Mine Forces Pacific in 1956 and served numerous tours off shore and in-country as a "River Rat" in Vietnam from 1960-71. In 1968, with only 59 days as BMC, he was promoted to warrant officer and wrapped up his career as ship's boatswain in Ashtabula AOJ-51.

He turned down OinC of the Boat Test Facility, Bayview, ID and retired only to end up 50 miles from there in the mid-80s.

LELAND R. "RON" HAUGHT, born in Capeheart, WV, Jan. 10, 1927.

He started work at Firestone Rubber Co. at age 16. To help the war effort he joined the Navy in December 1943 and after boot training at Great Lakes and Water Tender School at Quonset, RI, he served in the USS *Augusta* for more training.

Transferred to US Steel Shipyard waiting for USS *Columbus* to be completed. What a relief to get on the *Columbus*. The Augusta's fire rooms were all pressurized - the *Columbus* in just the boilers. They blew a reduction gear in the aft engine room and spent time in the Boston Navy Yard.

After returning from far east tour, he was transferred to USS *Astoria*. He sailed up Columbia River to Astoria, OR, then returned to Long Beach, CA and was discharged.

Ron worked 39 years at Firestone, then retired to Florida. The Navy was a great experience but the most successful part of his life was rearing three children. They are happy and successful in their chosen fields of endeavor. He also has five grandchildren and two greats.

ROBERT S. HAYES, born Aug. 25, 1944, Greenville, TX. Graduated high school and attended Texas Tech for his BA/MBA in Finance.

In October 1967 he joined in the Navy at Newport, RI and served in the USS *Columbus,* Norfolk, as food service officer and ships store officer and at Naval Supply Center, Norfolk, Fuel Dept. He was discharged in March 1971 as LTjg.

Civilian Activity: president, Access Credit Union; president, Texas Share Guaranty Credit Union; member Texas Credit Union Commission; Texas Credit Union League Executive Committee; Optimist Club; Mentor/helped one student to succeed; leadership/Kingswood Methodist Church.

Married Wanda and has two children, Robert Lee and Holly Susan.

THOMAS M. HEALY, born Feb. 28, 1927 in South Boston, MA, the first of nine children. He attended South Boston schools and had to quit

school on his 16th birthday to help support the family as his dad was injured in a fall and unable to work. Thomas went to work in Charleston Navy Yard for one a half years, then joined the Navy in May 1944.

Boot camp and Signal School were at Sampson, NY and amphibious training at Oceanside, CA. At San Diego he boarded the USS *Hulbert* (DD-343), a four stacker, and patrolled the West Coast through Panama Canal to Philly then to Brooklyn, NY; aboard USS *Missouri* for rendezvous with USS *Providence* (CL-82) in Med., 1946-47.

He left the Navy in August 1947 as SM3. His awards include the American Theater and Good Conduct. He was called back in 1950 and served until 1952 when he was discharged with the rate QMS2.

Thomas worked 35 years for New England Telephone Co. and retired Dec. 31, 1983. He married Josephine Jason in 1949 and they have four children: Maureen, Susan, Kathleen and Robert (named after his wife's brother who was killed in the Navy in 1944). Grandchildren are Francis and Dominic O'Donnell; Bryan and Samantha Healy; Jason and Evan Benterou.

LEONARD LARRY HEIMBACH, born June 10, 1936 in Sidney, MT. He graduated from high school, Glendive, MT, in 1954 and was drafted in the Navy Nov. 5, 1955. His initial training was in San Diego, CA.

He flew to Okinawa, boarded the *Columbus* in February 1956 and served in the 7th Fleet in the Pacific doing two tours overseas.

After his discharge Aug. 7, 1957 in San Francisco, he worked at Shell Oil Co. in Baker, MT where he met Arlene. They married April 5, 1959 and have three daughters: Sherri, Cindi and Doreen, and four grandchildren: Dalton, Savannah, Seth and Nicholas. He quit Shell in 1964 and bought a farm in Glendive, MT. Larry and Arlene attended the 2000 reunion in Framingham, MA.

ERNEST R. HELLER, born Jan. 27, 1929, Toledo, OH. He graduated high school and joined the Navy Sept. 15, 1950 in Detroit, MI and assigned to machine shop. He was discharged in June 1954 with the rate MR1/c.

After discharge he was employed as a diemaker. He and his wife Alice have three children: Lisa, Brenda and Joni and four grandchildren: Katelyn, Janell, Todd and Alicia.

GEORGE "HARVEY" HENDRICKS, FT-1, born in 1928, San Mateo, CA, and lived on a farm in the Monterey Bay area in California until Dec. 7, 1941 when his father

went to work as a shipfitter at Marinship building T-2 tankers and they moved to Mill Valley, CA.

He graduated from Tamalpais UHS in 1945, passed the test for Annapolis, but missed the political appointment. He enlisted in 1945 and went to boot camp and FC "A" School in San Diego; "B" School in Washington, DC; then to USS *Columbus* (CA-74) at Mare Island, CA. He went through the Panama Canal and made two cruises to Europe, 1947-51. Next duty was aboard the USS *Norton Sound*. He made chief at Pt. Mugu and went to Portsmouth, RI for OCS, then to USS *Marshall* (DD-676) as ensign.

His career (not in any order): Post Graduate School, Monterey, CA (two tours) *Worcester* (CL-144); *Observation Island* (EAG-154) (two tours) Special Projects Office, Washington, DC (two tours) *Oklahoma City* (CLG-5) (two tours), H&S Co. III Marine Anphip force, Vietnam, Naval Rep to Lockheed Missile and Space Co., Sunnyvale, CA.

His last sea duty was as weapons officer on the *Oklahoma City*. He retired as commander in 1973. Upon retirement he moved to Lake Tahoe. He passed away in 1992.

RALPH HENDRICKS, MR2, born 1929 in Oakland, CA and lived on a farm in Monterey Bay area until Dec. 7, 1941 when his father went to

work at Marinship building T-2 tankers. They moved to Mill Valley, CA and he graduated from Tamalpais UHS in 1947.

Ralph joined the Navy in 1948 and went to boot camp and MR "A" School in San Diego, then shipped to *Albany*

(CA-123). After two reserve cruises to "Gitmo" he transferred to be with his brother, George Harvey. He crossed Atlantic on *Malabar* (AF-37) to *Columbus* at Plymouth, England. He made 1950-51 cruise working in machine shop.

On his return to Boston, he flew home to marry his high school sweetheart, Patricia Dempsey. Ralph was discharged in 1952 at Jacksonville, FL. He went to work at Mare Island Naval Shipyard as inside machinist, heavy tool section. After 15 years he left X-31 and moved to Supply Dept. He retired April 1, 1985.

Ralph and Pat have three beautiful daughters, seven beautiful granddaughters and one great on the way. They keep busy babysitting, traveling in a small RV and he keeps his sanity by sailing on SF Bay in his 32 foot sailboat.

LOWELL D. HILL, born July 23, 1942 in Sacramento, CA, and graduated from San Juan High, Class of 1960. He joined the Navy July 19,

1960 with basic training in San Diego, followed by IC School, then Motion Picture Operator School.

First duty station was USS *Bryce Canyon* (AD-36). After nine months of sitting at the pier in Long Beach a

swap was made for more active sea duty aboard the USS *Ernest G. Small* (DDR-838) While in Hong Kong on a WesPac cruise orders came to join the volunteer crew to commission the USS *Columbus*. After intensive training at San Diego the crew spent three days on a troop train to meet their ship at Bremerton Ship Yard. The E Div. crew was kind enough to take him to the White Swine in Bremerton, WA for his 21st birthday.

The shakedown cruise was the worst ride ever. The ship was making 42 degree rolls and pitching 17 degrees. A signalman, who came from the bridge, said he saw green water going over the pilot house. The life lines on the main deck were either missing or trailing behind the ship when they got back to the pier. After the ship was commissioned she assumed her duty station in San Diego.

While at sea, President Kennedy flow by in his presidential helicopter to inspect the finest ship in the Navy and crew. The ship dipped colors and the crew at quarters gave a right-hand salute. A few months later, while entering San Diego harbor, Scott Teague, IC3, told the crew at quarters the president was shot.

Lowell was assigned to the movie locker, maintaining the projectors, among other jobs. On one job the IC crew worked 36 hours straight pulling the 400 cycle motor-generator sets, below the chain locker, and taking them to the machine shop. They got off for five hours, then back on for 24 straight hours. They weren't allowed time to change into the uniform-of-the-day so they missed dinner. The 1st class didn't put their names in for mid-rats so they missed them, too. That was not a good time for the chief to ask him if he was going to stay with the Navy.

After four years of Navy service he spent 33 years with Pacific Gas and Electric in construction and generation maintenance. Presently enjoying life as a general engineering and building, contractor at beautiful Lake Tahoe with his wife, Janis. They have five children: Steve, Mike, Ken, Matt and Kimberly, and seven grandchildren.

RICHARD S. HUNTER, born on Feb. 25, 1938, in Indianapolis, IN, and after graduation from Culver High School in Culver, IN in 1957, he joined the US Navy.

Richard was sent to Great Lakes for his initial training. After boot camp, he was sent to Pearl City, Hawaii where he was stationed on an inactive service craft for approximately six months. In March 1958, Richard served aboard the USS *Columbus* as an EMFN. He was aboard the *Columbus* until February 1959. During this time, the Columbus was part of the 7th Fleet stationed in the Far East.

In April 1959, Richard was assigned to 18 months of shore duty in San Diego, CA aboard the ARD-26 Dry Dock. Later, he was transferred to the USS *Ashtabula*. It was during this time that he was promoted to EM3. He also served aboard the USS *Delta* (AR-9).

Richard and his high school sweetheart, Royelle, were married in April 1959. Upon his discharge in 1961, they moved to the Los Angeles area where, they still reside. They have three sons and two granddaughters. Richard is retired and enjoys fishing, boating, and driving his 1930 Model A Ford.

ANTHONY JAMES JACOBS, born on Jan. 7, 1927. He quit school in 1942 at the age of 15 to work on a dairy farm. The owner's son Howard

had joined the Navy and Anthony took his place on the farm until 1944 when he also joined the Navy. Three of his brothers went into the service before Anthony, one each in the Army, Air Force and Marines so Anthony took the Navy. Boot camp was at Great Lakes, then onto the USS *Columbus*.

When the *Columbus* was in Tsingtau, China, he met up with his brother James who was in the Marines. They were pulled off Okinawa and sent to China, so he and four of his buddies came aboard for chow and a movie. They could not believe the Navy ate like that. They had to eat out of their helmets. The day Anthony left Tsingtau, China, the Marines left for the United States. Anthony's brother, Wilfred (in Army), was killed Oct. 14, 1944 on Anguar 22 Island, Pacific Ocean.

Alice and Anthony were married Oct. 16, 1954 and have seven children: Anthony, Alan, Dianna, Steven, Theresa, Amy and Carrie, and 20 grandchildren. He started driving truck for Davis Cartage in 1953 and has worked for different driving companies, retiring from Teamsters in 1987 with lifetime membership.

ROBERT JOE "BOB" JANDA, born March 2, 1931, Cleveland, OH. He joined the US Navy Oct. 24, 1950, Cleveland and served in the USS

Columbus during Korean War. He was discharged Aug. 20, 1954 with the rate EM2. His awards include the National Defense Medal, Good Conduct, Navy Occupation and Service Medal (Europe).

Bob first worked at Corey Hospital in maintenance, then at LCE for 32 years as electronic service engineer on nuclear measuring gauges. In 1994 he started his own company, Bob's Hi Tech, and is still working.

He married Katie Jan. 23, 1960 and they have four children: Alan, Bill, Martha, Sue, and 10 grandchildren: Ryan, Aaron, Scott, Ashley, Heather, Katie, Matthew, Elise, Ben and Nicholas.

NEIL E. JENKINS, born April 10, 1930, York County, SC. He entered the US Navy Jan. 30, 1948 and served at the following duty stations: USS

Columbus (CA-74), *Richard E. Kraus* (DD-849), *Everglades* (AD-24), *Rankin* (AKA-103), *Krishna* (ARL-38), *La Salle* (LPD-3), *Grant County* (LST-1174).

He completed 20 years of honorable service at the Fleet Training Center, Mayport, FL on July 15, 1970. His awards include the European Occupation Service Medal, Good Conduct Medal (5th awd.), Armed Forces Expeditionary Medal (Dominican Republic) and the National Defense Service Medal (second award).

After discharge he was a policeman for York County, SC for 25 years.

DONALD V. JOHNSON, born June 12, 1927, Chicago, IL. He enlisted July 22, 1944 and served in the USS LSM(R)-517, USS *Philip* (DDE-498), USS *Rankin* (AKA-103), USS *Pittsburgh* (CA-72), USS *Albany* (CA-123), USS *Columbus* (CA-74), USS *St. Paul* (CA-73) and USS *Pine Island* (AV-12).

He participated in WWII, Korean and Vietnam wars and retired Sept. 1, 1966. His awards and decorations include the European Occupation, Vietnam, WWII Victory, Good Conduct (4), American Theater, Korean Service, China Service and United Nation.

JEFFREY F. JONES, born March 9, 1952, Southampton, NY. He served in the US Navy with basic and Boiler School at Great Lakes, 1970-71, then assigned to #2 fire room. He was discharged in 1974 with the rate BT3.

After discharge he worked as building contractor and carpenter. He and his wife Linda have two children, Megan and Jeffrey Jr. Jeffrey would like to hear from some of his old shipmates.

CLAYTON E. "BUD" KATHAN, born Oct. 18, 1927 in Putney, VT. He graduated from Bratteboro HS in 1945 and enlisted in the Navy at age 17 in December 1945. He was sent to Sampson, NY for boot camp then to Newport, RI.

Bud went aboard the USS *Columbus* when it was commissioned, then to the USS *Wyoming* in Norfolk, VA for Gunner's School, then back to the *Columbus*. Memorable was waling down the dock and seeing his first ship – it was humungous. He had never seen anything so large or as beautiful as the *Columbus*.

In 1949 Bud started his law enforcement career as a police officer, deputy sheriff and court officer. He graduated from the State, FBI and US Marshall schools.

Bud met Doe Currier on her 15th birthday and has been with her ever since. They married June 28, 1947 and have four children: Bonnie, David, Pam and Tommy. David was killed when he was 15 and Bonnie died at age 40. They have three grandsons: Michael, Chris and Ryan and two granddaughters, Jenny and Cory. Bud joined the Columbus Veterans Association in 1993 and has been to all the reunions.

EDWARD K. KENNEDY, S1/c (GM3/c), born June 23, 1928, Sarasota, FL and entered the Navy June 22, 1945. Assignments include USNTC 1945; USS *Indian Island*, 1945; TADCEN, Camp Shoemaker, 1945; USS *Iowa* (BB-61), 1945-47; and USS *Columbus* (CA-74), 1947-48.

He was in the 2nd Div. and a gun sticker; eventually he was a gunner's mate 3/c. Most of the men he served with in the USS *Iowa* also served with him on the *Columbus*, and a lot of them have remained friends and fellow shipmates through the years to date. He was discharged Aug. 24, 1948 and received the WWII Victory Medal.

Married over 53 years to Ramona. They have seven grown and healthy children and too many grandkids and great-grandkids to list.

RUSSELL KILLION, born July 4, 1930, Cambridge, MA. Upon graduation from Boston English High School in 1947 he joined the Navy and attended boot camp at the Great Lakes Naval Training Station. He went aboard the USS *Manchester* in Philadelphia where they took a round trip cruise to the Mediterranean. The next cruise the *Manchester* took was through the

Panama Canal to Long Beach, CA. The *Manchester* was going to the Far East and because he didn't have enough time left in the Navy to complete the cruise, he was transferred to the USS *Toledo*. He was discharged in September 1949 at Long Beach, CA. Awards include Navy Occupation (Europe) and National Defense Service Medal.

He was called back to duty when the Korean War broke out and went aboard the USS *Columbus* in Boston. They stayed in Boston for quite awhile so he was able to commute from home. His 7th Division Petty Officer in Charge was Arthur Christopherson. They met again years later at the Columbus Reunion at Hanscom Field in Bedford, MA.

Russell met his wife, Angelina Marra, on St. Patrick's Day in 1955. They were married the following year and have been together ever since.

They have three great kids: Cathy, Russell and Chris. No grandchildren yet, but maybe someday....

LLOYD L. KINGERY, born April 14, 1935 in Hammond, IN. He graduated from Hammond Technical High School in 1953 and worked at City Water Dept. until he enlisted in the Navy on Nov. 4, 1953.

His initial training was at Great Lakes, then to Boston where he boarded the *Columbus* and was assigned to King Division where he was one of two chart men. From July-October 1954 he attended Radar Class A School in Norfolk then returned to the *Columbus* in Marseilles, France.

The *Columbus* was active in various NATO exercises in the Mediterranean as part of the Sixth Fleet and make Good Will visits in Portugal, Algeria, France, Greece, Turkey, Italy, Spain and Gibraltar. In the summer of 1955 the *Columbus* participated in the first of three annual midshipman-training cruises, visiting ports in England, Spain and gunnery practice at Guantanamo Bay, Cuba. In the fall of 1955 she was reassigned to the Pacific Fleet.

Beginning in November 1955 the *Columbus* participated in joint American-Perusian naval maneuvers. As flagship, Commander Cruiser-Destroyer Force, US Pacific Fleet was on board during this short good-will visit south of the Equator. After completing a six month tour in July 1956 with the Seventh Fleet in the Far Western Pacific, the *Columbus* participated in task force operations and amphibious landing exercises and made good will visits in the Philippines, Hong Kong and several Japanese ports, Buckner Bay, Okinawa and Iwo Jima. The 63,000 mile tour took the ship twice across the 180th Meridian and the Equator.

After completing its second tour of duty in the US Seventh Fleet in the Far Western Pacific, she also served as Flag Ship for the Fleet Commander in Cruiser Division Three. The *Columbus* participated in task force operations and made good will visits after stopping in Pearl Harbor and the islands of Okinawa, Suva, Manus and Guam; ports of Melbourne, Australia; Keelung, Formosa; Hong Kong; Chinhae, Korea; and the Japanese ports of Yokohama, Yokosuka, Kobe, Sasebo and Nagasaki. The 51,074 mile tour took the ship twice across the 180th Meridian and the Equator.

Lloyd, radarmen third class was discharged Oct. 19, 1957. His service medals include the Navy Occupation, National Defense and Good Conduct Medals. Lloyd joined the USS Columbus Veteran's Assoc. and attended his first reunion in 1989.

Lloyd has worked over 43 years in the civil engineering field. He retired April 2000 with 40 years employment with Wight & Co., Downers Grove, IL in an associate position and as project engineer. He married Jean in July 1956 and they have three children: Dan, Debbie and Mark; and 11 grandchildren.

BILLY R. KIRBY, born Nov 1, 1935, Warren County, KY. He enlisted Aug. 17, 1954, Bowling Green, KY and was discharged July 26, 1958 as gunner's mate 3rd class. His awards include the Good Conduct Medal and National Defense Medal. Memorable was being aboard the USS *Columbus* when it collided with the USS *Floyd B. Parks*.

Billy was born in a large family of nine children and wasn't able to attend school as he wanted too. He graduated from high school after he got out of service then went to Barber college and has been in barber business 42 years and still working.

He has been married to Betty for 43 years and they have one son Todd. Billy has been a member of American Legion for 40 years and does a lot of volunteering cooking and other jobs. He also drives the VA van to the VA hospital to carry vets for service.

He is a charter member of the USS Columbus Association, having joined in 1988, and has attended every reunion.

GEORGE T. KITTREDGE, born Nov. 18, 1935, the youngest of four, having two sisters, Mary and Anne, and one brother John. He grew up in Clinton, MA, located just 48 miles west of Boston. Growing up during WWII, he participated in all war effort programs, paper drives with the Boy Scouts, can drives, even loading bomb casing onto boxcars at a local manufacturing plant.

He can remember standing in the butter lines with his two sisters and brother to help his father's restaurant keep in butter. He worked shoveling snow, peddling papers, and just about anything to help out Mom and Dad at home.

He went to and graduated from the local schools, worked at Colonial Press (a book manufacturing plant), as a shipper in a furniture warehouse, and as a gas station attendant at Nugo's. His brother John (five years his senior) joined the Navy in 1951 during the Korean War, and George joined in January of 1953, his senior year in high school, but wasn't called until December. After boot camp in Bainbridge, he joined his brother aboard the *Columbus* while going through overhaul in Charlestown Naval Shipyard in Boston. He was assigned the same division (EX), same compartment. They went down to Cuba on their shakedown cruise and then onto the Mediterranean for a "Goodwill Cruise." Columbus returned to Boston Jan. 28, 1955. Brother John was discharged a few weeks later, and George remained onboard *Columbus*.

The *Columbus* changed home ports from Boston to Long Beach in 1955, they went through the Panama Canal, crossed the Equator, down to Peru than to California. They sailed onto their Far Eastern Mission in January 1956 until July, whereupon he was transferred to COM7THFLEET onboard the USS *Helena* (CA-75). He enjoyed being on the *Columbus* with his brother, the travel experiences he had and serving his country in the Sixth and Seventh Fleets.

MICHAEL J. KLOCZKOWSKI, born Feb. 15, 1931 in Millville, MA and graduated from St. Mary's High School in Milford, MA in June 1950. After high school he worked for six months as a milkman then joined the Navy in December 1950.

After boot camp in Newport, RI, he was sent to Brooklyn, NY Receiving Station then went aboard the troop transport *Maurice Rose* to England. From England he flew to Bizerte, Tunisia where he went aboard the USS *Columbus* on April 5, 1951 and was assigned to able "A" Div. Boat Gang. He served on the *Columbus* until May 1954. At that time he was transferred to the USS *Mount Rushmore* (LSD-14) and served his last six months on this ship. He was discharged in October 1954.

He then went to work for Wyman-Gordon Co., a supplier of aircraft airframe parts, jet engine and nuclear parts. He was trained as an ultrasonic test inspector and worked there for 36 years.

Michael married Laurie Lacroix in 1960 and they have two boys and two girls. Two of them have given them six grandchildren.

CHARLES E. KORNRAUS, born March 12, 1928, River Rouge, MI and graduated River Rouge High School in 1945. He attended the University of Michigan for one year and Lawrence Institute of Technology for one year.

He enlisted March 7, 1946 and went to boot camp at Great Lakes, IL. He served aboard the *General Ernst* (AP-133), LST-834 and USS *Columbus* (CA-74). Discharged Jan. 8, 1948, Pier 91, Seattle and recalled May 29, 1951 for Kwajalein. Discharged again on Oct. 19, 1951.

One night on midwatch, Charles was on the 2nd level and a man dressed in black pants and white shirt came down and sat beside him and they talked for about 30 minutes. After he left, the chief immediately ran up to the 2nd level and inquired as to what he wanted. Charles said we just talked. The chief said "Don't you know who that was?" Charles replied "No." The chief said that was the captain. Another time they were cleaning firesides on the boiler which is a very dirty project. The captain, accompanied by the engineering officer and the chief, peered into the boiler for sometime through the peep hole, then insisted that all three enter the boiler. They immerged all black and sooty and the engineering officer and chief were very unhappy.

His first wife Marjorie is deceased. Children are Kathleen, Richard (USN), Randy (USN), Timothy and Mechelle. There are also six grandchildren. His present wife is Joyce.

Charles worked in several automotive factories and spent about three years in tool and die. In 1964 he went into the plumbing and heating business for himself and in 1971 branched out into industrial and process instrumentation. He retired in 1996 and is now living in Mayhill, NM.

HERBERT W. KROUT, graduated from Doylestown High School in 1942, age 17. In September 1942, he joined the PA National Guard, being a farmer, he had a 4A deferment. In 1944 he enlisted in the US Marines.

After the first and second phase of training, he was sent to Sea School. His assignment was to be aboard USS *Columbus* (CA-74) when she was commissioned in Boston (1945) and be Captain Allen Hobbs 1st orderly.

The ship was sent to Pearl Harbor where she became a flag ship of the North Pacific Fleet. The Admiral's diplomatic duties took them to Okinawa, Sasabo, Japan, Tsingtao, China than to Shanghai. He had the honor of escorting Chaing Kai-Shek, Madame Shek and company aboard ship for diplomatic conferences.

Herbert and his younger brother Ray served together the entire time. He went back to Pennsylvania in 1946 after his discharge in San Pedro, CA. Herbert farmed for 20 years and was an excavating contractor for 20 more years.

He and Sarah have been married for 53 years and have three daughters, seven grandchildren and two great-grandchildren. They winter in Naples, FL for seven months and return to Warrington, PA in the summer.

RAYMOND KROUT, born Oct. 3, 1926, in Warrington, PA and entered the Marine Corps from the Doylestown High School on Dec. 8, 1944, at a recruiting office in Philadelphia, PA. Krout was sent to Parris Island, SC, for boot camp, then to Camp Lejeune, NC, for advanced training where he was selected for Sea School in San Diego, CA.

After training was complete, Krout was shipped to Boston, MA, where he boarded the USS *Columbus* for commissioning. Before being able to reach Cuba for a shakedown, the ship broke down before reaching New York. The *Columbus* eventually reached Cuba, but returned to New York for Navy Day and then to the Pacific through the Panama Canal. The ship returned to Long Beach, CA and he was detached from the *Columbus*.

After leave, Krout reported to the Great Lake for his discharge on Aug. 27, 1946. Awards include Rifle Marksman, American Campaign, WWII Victory Medal, Asiatic-Pacific Campaign Medal, Navy Occupation (Asia) and China Service Medal.

Krout is currently a member of the local American Legion, Marine Corps, VFW and the USS Columbus Veteran Association. He attended his first USS Columbus reunion at Omaha, NE.

Krout met Mary Alice and they married in 1952. They went on to raise six children: Robert, Nancy, Nina, James, Richard, and Rebecca. There are 16 grandchildren, nine great-grandchildren, and more on the way. Civilian employment with Rutherford and McLean (trucking freight).

GEORGE T. LACHANCE, born Nov. 23, 1941, Rochester, NH and christened on Pearl Harbor Day. Graduated from high school in 1960, Portsmouth, NH and enlisted in the service in August 1960, Portsmouth, NH. Following Boot Camp at Great Lakes and Hospital Corps School at San Diego, he was stationed at Naval Hospital, San Diego in 1961.

Sea duty began aboard First Fleet Flagship, USS *Helena*, (CA-75) in 1962, San Diego. Memories include the many people who toured the ship as part of Seattle World's Fair Festivities and hoisting New Hampshire's State Flag at the Fair in 1962.

Transferred to pre-commissioning crew CG-12, 1962, San Diego and rode troop train to Bremerton, WA where an old lumber track took them to within several miles of shipyard. They marched the rest of the way with sea bags over-shoulders. They became plankowners with CG-12's commissioning in November 1962.

Upon deployment to West-Pac in August 1964, *Columbus* (CG-12) became flagship for Cruiser-Destroyer-Flotilla-Eleven, Battle Group. Crew earned Armed Forces Expeditionary Medal for operations in Tonkin Gulf during Vietnam Campaign. He was discharged from Active Duty in August 1965 with the rate HM3. Awards include Navy Good Conduct, National Defense Service and Armed Forces Expeditionary.

George has four daughters: Nicole, Danielle, Stephanie and Antoinette; also, nine grandchildren.

Revisited Guam in 1968 as merchant seaman, delivering jet fuel to our forces. respiratory therapy career started with school, 1973-74, and National Boards, 1975, Towson State, MD.

Memberships include American Association for Respiratory Care, National Board for Respiratory Care, Florida Society for Respiratory Care, life member of VFW, American Legion and USS Columbus Veteran's Association (since 1999).

JAMES CLAYTON LAMBERT, born Jan. 24, 1931 in Premier, WV and lived there until he enlisted in the Navy at the age of 17 on Aug. 27, 1947 at Princeton, WV. He took his bootcamp at Great Lakes, IL and from there was sent to Norfork, VA where he was assigned aboard the USS *Mississippi*. A few months later he was sent aboard the USS *Columbus* where he worked in

the fire rooms; his rank was FA. He stayed aboard until his discharge in 1950.

After getting out he went back to West Virginia, married and had three children: James, Frank and Belinda. He also has eight grandchildren and two great-grandchildren. James left West Virginia and moved to Cleveland, OH where he lived for 22 years and worked at several different places including Ford Motor Company and Dow Chemical.

His first marriage ended in divorce and he moved to Milwaukee, WI in 1972. There he met Carolyn, his wife of 27 years. Jim worked at Boston seating for 10 years before becoming disabled in 1984. In 1997 Jim and Carolyn decided to move to Las Vegas, NV, where they still reside.

ROBERT L. LANE, born Nov. 4, 1953, Zanesville, OH, graduated high school and joined the service June 16, 1972, Pittsburgh, PA.

Assignments: June-August 1972, boot camp at Orlando, FL; August-November 1972, MM "A" School, Great Lakes, IL; November 1972-July 1973, Nuclear Power Training School, Bainbridge, MD; July 1973-January 1974, Nuclear Power Training Unit, Schenectady, NY; January 1974-July 1978, USS *Scamp* (SSN-588), San Diego, CA; July 1978-October 1981, Nuclear Power Training Unit, Ballston Spa, NY; October 1981-November 1984 USS *Dixon* (AS-37), San Diego, CA; November 1984-January 1987, USS *Atlanta* (SSN-712), Norfolk, VA; January 1987-May 1990, NSSF New London, CT; May-September 1990, USS *City of Corpus Christie* (SSN-705), New London, CT; September 1990-April 1992, NSSF New London, CT; April 1992-April 1995, USS *Columbus* (SSN-762), New London, CT and Pearl Harbor, HI; April 1995-June 1998, NSSF New London, CT.

Discharged June 30, 1998 as senior chief. His awards include the Navy Commendation (2 awds.), Good Conduct (6 awds.), Navy Expeditionary and Navy Achievement (6 awds.). Memorable was being part of the USS *Columbus* commissioning crew.

Civilian activity as customer support services supervisor. Robert and his wife Carol have two children, Robert Joseph and Ashley Elizabeth.

RALPH R. LEHDE, born Aug. 3, 1927 in Glen Ullin, ND and moved with the family to Puyallup, WA in October 1942. He graduated from Sumner High School in 1945.

Ralph joined the Navy on Oct. 13, 1945 and took boot training in San Diego and Aviation Fundamental School at Jacksonville NAS. From there he was assigned to Fleet Weather Central at

Kodiak NAS in the spring of 1946. In July 1946 he was assigned to the USS *Iowa* (BB-61) at the Bremerton Naval Shipyard, then assigned to the USS *Columbus* (CA-74) in October 1946 and cruised to China in the spring of 1947.

Ralph was discharged Oct. 11, 1947 at San Pedro, CA with the rank of seaman first class. He was issued the WWII Victory Medal.

He worked for the Dept. of Army as a civilian employee for 33 years and for the Puyallup School District for 11 years. He married Genny Loughlin July 2, 1954. They have two children, Julie and Robert, and one granddaughter, Katie. Ralph and Genny attend church and praise the Lord at Our Savior Lutheran Church in Summit, WA. For a North Dakota kid the Navy and a ship at sea was a real thrill.

LEON LEVY, born May 13, 1926 in Baltimore, MD. He enlisted in the US Navy Nov. 27, 1943 and received basic training at US Naval Training' Station in Sampson, NY. He was assigned Naval Radio Operators School at Bedford, PA in 1944 and graduated with rank of RM3/c.

Sent to Naples, Italy to board USS *Pioneer* (AM-105), mine sweeper) and saw action

in the Mediterranean Sea. The ship participated in the invasion of Southern France and ran convoy duty in the North Atlantic Ocean.

Transferred to fleet Administration Office Radio Station at Charlestown Navy Yard in Boston, MA. In early 1945 he was assigned to original ship's company of USS *Columbus* (CA-74) and participated in shakedown cruise to Guantanamo Bay, Cuba. After which ship proceeded through Panama Canal to Honolulu, Hawaii joining the Pacific Fleet.

He spent time in China and Japan, taking part in deactivating Japanese Fleet, 1945-46. Returned to San Jose, CA in April 1946 and transferred to Bainbridge Naval Training Station for discharge on May 8, 1946. Awards include the European Theatre Ribbon w/star, Pacific Theatre Ribbon, American Theatre Ribbon and the WWII Victory Medal.

Married to Freda for 54 years and has five children and 10 grandchildren. He is a member of Jewish War Veterans Post 167 and a former Commander of JWV Post 192 in Baltimore, MD. Presently CEO Wholesale Footwear Company.

ALVIN S. LEWIS, born on Saint Patrick's Day in 1930, East Chicago, IN and graduated from Washington High School in 1949. He started work-

ing at J.J. Newberry Dime Store at age 13 and worked seven years until he joined the Navy, Jan. 2, 1951. Al was sent to Great Lakes for his initial training.

After boot camp he was sent to Norfolk and went aboard the USS *Salem* for transportation to the USS *Columbus*. He went aboard the Columbus on his 21st birthday in Villefranche, France.

Alvin joined the USS Columbus Veterans Association in 1989, and attended his first reunion in 1991. He served as association secretary from 1994-99 and was elected president in 1999.

He met Renee, of Dorchester, MA, on Columbus Day, 1951 and they married Sept. 6, 1953. They have three children: Lori, Tom and Lance. They also have nine grandchildren and three great-grandchildren.

RICHARD G. L'HOMMEDIEU, born June 24, 1929, Queens, NY. He went to Smithtown High School and joined the US Marine Corps Oct. 15,

1946. Boot Camp was at Parris Island. After graduation he was assigned to Camp Lejeune Combat Engineers, then to 2nd Amphibian Truck Co. In 1947 he was transferred to sea school in Norfolk VA, after which he was assigned guard duty at the ammunition depot in Portsmouth, VA while waiting for a ship.

In October 1948 he was assigned to the USS *Columbus* (CA-74) where his duties included being a driver for Captain Wills in port, a gunner on the 20mm's and other duties of a Marine at sea. When the ship arrived in New York in December 1949 he was transferred to Brooklyn Navy yard for discharge where he joined the inactive reserves. In June 1950 he returned to active duty at Camp Lejeune to the 2nd Amphibian Truck Co. On Nov. 21, 1951 he returned to his home as inactive reserves and was officially discharged in March 1953 with the rank of corporal.

After his discharge he worked for Grumman Air Craft for about one year, then went to work for the Long Island Rail Road. He met his wife, Dolores, in his hometown of Smithtown, NY and they married Feb. 7, 1953. They have three children: Richard Jr., Joyce and Russ, nine grandchildren and one great-grandchild. Richard retired after 30 years of service as a locomotive engineer for the LIRR.

In the year 2000 he was the Marine of the year, Mercury Detachment of the Marine Corps League. In the year 2002 he was made Commandant of the Mercury Detachment.

IRWIN MONROE LINDQUIST, born Sept. 1, 1922 in Iowa City, IA. He joined the service Sept. 10, 1941 at Great Lakes, followed by Treasure

Island Receiving Station, Mare Island, San Francisco.

Assignments: USS *Concord*, 1941-44; precommission of *Columbus* March 1945; shakedown cruise of *Columbus*, October 1945; Navy Day in New York, Oct.

22, 1945; USS DMS *Jeffers,* Norfolk, VA, February 1946. In March 1946 he was sent to the US Naval Hospital, Portsmouth, VA where he received a medical discharge in August 1946 because of rheumatic fever.

He married Barbara in April 1945 and they had three children: Randal Garfield Lindquist, Bonnie Osmer, and Cindy Leduc. Irwin passed away Feb. 19, 1998. There are four grandchildren: Jonthan Irwin and Theron Wendell Peck III, and Aimee Kaye and Laura Beth Leduc.

BOB LOWREY, born March 10, 1944, Spring Garden, CA. Graduated high school and joined the service in March 1960, Sacramento, CA. Memorable was being on the commissioning crew of *Columbus* (CG-12). He was discharged in August 1968.

As a civilian he was a logger and worked in construction. He married Janell Crosby in May 1984 and has three children by previous marriage: Daree, Bud and Ashley, and three grandchildren: Christina, Jessica and Marchelle.

WILLIAM R. LUCAS, born Oct. 30, 1929 in Nashville, TN. He was sworn in as a midshipman in the Navy Officer Training Program at Duke

University, Durham, NC in September 1948. Made training cruises on USS *Missouri* (BB-63) and USS *Shannon* (DM-25) and also trained at NAS, Pensacola, FL and the Navy Amphibious Base at Little Creek, VA. One assignment on the USS *Missouri* was to polish the plaque that marked the spot where four years earlier Japan had surrendered, ending WWII.

Commissioned an Ensign, USN in June 1952, he was assigned to USS *Columbus* (CA-74), going aboard in Boston, MA. Assignments included Assistant Navigator, CS Division Officer and CR Division Officer. The *Columbus* participated in NATO exercises and was Sixth Fleet flagship; Bill was assigned to Sixth Fleet staff for three months.

He transferred to CINCLANTFLT staff in Norfolk in June 1954 and served as Communications Watch Officer until discharged in June 1955. He transferred to Navy Reserves as lieutenant in 1955.

William worked for IBM Corporation until retirement. He married Nancy Vail in 1958 and they have three children: Bill Jr., Jennifer and Matthew, and three grandchildren: Steven, Nathaniel and Joshua.

CHARLES E. MACLAY, born March 25, 1926 in Edgemont, MD, and completed 12 years education at Smithsburg, MD, High School. He en-

listed in the USNR, V6 program on Feb. 2, 1944 at Hagerstown, MD.

Assignments: Boot camp and Radioman School at USNTC Bainbridge, MD; troop train to West Coast and troopship, USS *Gen. A.P. Mann* (AP-115) to Ulithi

Atoll; March 1945, USS *Arided* (AK-73) in time for Okinawa battle; decommissioned *Arided* in December 1945 and assigned to Commandant 14th Naval District Communications.

In 1946 he was assigned temporary duty onboard an aircraft carrier to handle communications during the Bikini atomic bomb test. Transferred in 1948 to Commander Naval Forces Far East in Tokyo, Japan; February 1952 transferred to Naval Supply Depot, Mechanicsburg, PA where he met and married his wife, Jobyna Marie Stoops on Dec. 6, 1953. In August 1954 he transferred to USS *Columbus* (CA-74) and in October 1955 was transferred to Naval Station Argentia, Newfoundland. In January 1958, he was sent to Naval Station Norfolk, VA until February 1962. In March 1962 he transferred to Utility Squadron 8 at Roosevelt Roads, PR until March 1965, then back to Norfolk, VA and a tour of duty with Commander Operational Test and Development Force until March 1969. From there to

USS *Orion* (AS-18) until May 7, 1970 when he retired at Norfolk, VA with 26 years as YNCS.

Medals include the Asiatic-Pacific Service Medal w/Battle Star, Good Conduct Medal (7 awards), National Defense Service Medal (two awards), WWII Victory Medal, Asiatic Occupation Medal with "A" Clasp, American Defense Service Medal, UN Service Medal and Korean Service Medal.

After retirement he was employed at Commonwealth National Bank, Harrisburg, PA and served in various positions and retired on Oct. 30, 1988 as vice president Facilities Management of Mellon Bank, NA. Since retirement he has volunteered an average of 1000 hours a year at the Cumberland County Historical Society.

Charles and Jobyna have two sons, Charles Jr. and William, and four grandchildren: Kiersten, Lindsey, William and Shane.

G. DAVID MAGIN, born Sept. 24, 1927 in New York City. At an early age he did various tasks at his Papa's grocery store and other employment all through school years.

He joined the US Navy Oct 17, 1945, receiving "boot" training at Camp Perry, VA. Served onboard USS *Wisconsin* (BB-64); USS *Houston* (CL-81); and ComCruDiv 12, USS *Huntington* (CL-107).

While on-board USS *Houston*, we conducted a refueling exercise with USS *Huntington* at sea. Suddenly, both ships came too close and collided. After emergency alarms ceased, the first announcement over the P.A. system was, "Will the Navigation Yeoman report to the Captain's Sea Cabin." He was a seaman apprentice recording comments from the Captain for the Ship's Log.

As a yeoman, he was transferred to Flag Allowance, ComBatCruLant, Norfolk, VA and subsequently reported to USS *Columbus* (CA-74) in September 1948. He completed Class "B" schooling 1949-50, returning to *Columbus* as a court reporter. As the Captain's telephone talker during GQ, Magin recall's relaying Captain Will's order, "Main Battery Fire At Will." They would always grin at each other when that was said. The Captain would also duck his head as well. The *Columbus* received orders to proceed to Korea, but bless the Lord, they were cancelled upon arrival at the Suez Canal. The ship was armed to the teeth ready for battle, if needed.

London, England was his next assignment, and there, he met and married his Navy wife, Marie, in November 1951. She was a Canadian citizen. Magin was then ordered to Naples, Italy. They enjoyed visiting Isle of Capri, Blue Grotto, Sorrento, and the volcano, Mount Vesuvious. Their first child was born at Afragola, Italy.

MSTS at New York was his next station. Fighter Squadron VF-84, homeport, Oceana, VA, including squadron assignments to Gtmo; aircraft carriers, USS *Saratoga, Forrestal* and *Lake Champlain* followed.

While on-board Saratoga at Norfolk, VA, he shopped at the Base Commissary one day. Many items were purchased and left in his vehicle. Family was residing at Lansdale Gardens, three miles from Norfolk, and the food was intended to be brought home that afternoon. About 15 minutes after returning to his ship, security was expeditiously set, *Saratoga* getting underway immediately. This sailor returned to Port six weeks later.

Shelburne, Nova Scotia, Canada was his next assignment. After reporting to the Submarine Base, Groton, CT, Magin completed 20 years service with the US Navy and retired as a yeoman first class. He was the only surface sailor (warrior) on the submarine staff.

Awards include Navy Good Conduct Medal w/5 Bronze Stars, American Campaign Medal, WWII Victory Medal, Navy Occupation Medal (Europe) and National Defense Service Medal.

As a civilian, he was employed at Electric Boat Division, Groton, CT for 28 years. Elected, he served his community for several years. Currently, a Director, USS Columbus Veteran's Association, and volunteers at an Elementary School (3rd Grade).

Magin and Marie had six children. She died in September 1986 after an extended illness. He married Penny, his sweetheart, on St. Valentine's Day 1988. Penny died as a result of cancer in February 1999. David Magin feels incredibly lucky, having served his Country and with both ladies in his life. Penny had two children.

ED MANISTA, born June 30, 1930, Cleveland, OH. He attended Fenn College and joined the USNR Oct. 15, 1947, Cleveland. Active duty Feb.

25, 1952, Bainbridge, MD; Med Cruise, 1952-53; Artic Circle, September 1952; Operation Mainbrace. Duty as supply officer and operated CA-74 Ships Store.

Discharged Sept. 10, 1953 with the rate SK2, USNR. Awards include the Navy Occupation Medal w/European Clasp and National Defense Service Medal.

Civilian activity as executive VP, Corp Director, Sr. management, manufacturing engineer, private investor and builder. He and his wife Ruth have two sons, Douglas and Bryant, and three grandchildren: Stephanie, Stacey and Chad.

EUGENE J. MARTELLO, born Sept. 29, 1943, in Brownsville, PA, reared in Fontana, CA and attended Fontana High School. He joined the

Naval Reserve in San Bernardino, CA, Sept. 29, 1960 with boot camp in San Diego as a (TWT). With cruises aboard the USS *Marsh* (DE-699) and USS *Merrick* (AKA-97). By the time of high school graduation (mid-term) he had attained the grade of SN, switched to the Regular Navy and attended Radarman Class (A) School at Treasure Island, CA.

On completion of school, Sept. 28, 1962, he was designated RDSN and assigned to *Herbert J. Thomas* (DDR-833) home ported out of Long Beach, CA. In June 1963 the *Thomas* went to WESPAC and Eugene went to Naval Station San Diego for the Precom Unit USS *Halsey* (DLG-23) commissioned on July 20, 1963 at Hunters Point Shipyard in San Francisco, CA. On Jan. 16, 1964 Eugene was promoted to RD3.

In January 1965 the *Halsey* left for WESPAC and the Gulf of Tonkin, while on station in the Gulf the *Halsey* was (on point) sometimes as close as 15 miles to North Vietnam rescuing down pilots.

Returned to the States in August 1965 and volunteered for the USS *Columbus* (CG-12) which was changing homeports to Norfolk, VA. They traversed the Panama Canal from south to north on Jan. 22, 1966 and stopped at Guantanamo Bay, Cuba where Eugene on Feb. 10, 1966 re-enlisted for six more years. The *Columbus* left Norfolk for the Med in September 1966. While in Ismeir, Turkey, Eugene departed the *Columbus* for FAAWTC Damneck, VA for three-year tour as an instructor in the NTDS system. While at FAAWTC Eugene was promoted to RD2 on April 16, 1966.

In August 1969 Eugene transferred to the USS *Enterprise* (CVN-65) which was being overhauled in Newport News, VA. Eugene was sent back to FAAWTC for Air Intercept Controllers School and was promoted to RD1 on Feb. 16, 1970. In February 1971 the Big "E" went south across the Equator and into the realm of King Neptune, continued south around Cape Horn and on to Alameda, CA, her new home port.

In June 1971 the Big "E" departed Alameda, CA for WESPAC and the Gulf of Tonkin and a little side trip to the Indian Ocean. On Jan. 12, 1972 Eugene hitched a ride (high lined) to the *Mauna Kea* (AE-22) to Subic Bay, Philippines and back to Long Beach, CA. for separation on Feb. 9, 1972. Awards and medals include Armed Forces Expeditionary Medal (Vietnam), National Defense Service Medal, Vietnam Service Medal and Republic of Vietnam Campaign Medal w/Device.

Memorable Experiences: On the "Tall Lady" 01 & OE divisions were berthed on the third deck behind the chain locker. On one cruise to the Caribbean they were to transfer something to the *Yarnall* (DD-541). Over the 1MC came the word to "Standby to receive the *Yarnell* along side." Just then a loud noise was heard and the compartment shook, they all thought the *Yarnell* had rammed them. Everybody scrambled for the weather deck to find that the Captain had ordered the Talos "pretty birds" loaded on the front launcher and one of the birds just kept going and was laid out on the fo'c's'le. Deck Div. lashed it down till they returned to port. Sure scared the hell out of everybody below decks.

Currently married to Lori Lee, he has three children: Lorraine, Mathew and Erin, and four grandchildren: Jessica, James, Joseph and Aaron. Eugene and Lori reside in Tucson, AZ. Eugene works for the AZ Department of Transportation (Highway Construction) and Lori works for the University Medical Center.

JOHN L. MCELROY, born Jan. 10, 1934, Hobart, OK, has BA degree. Entered the service in September 1952, Long Beach, CA and was discharged Sept. 10, 1959 with the rate GM3.

Memorable was getting to meet King Neptune – what a two day ordeal – and since is a card caring- bonafide shellback. Also memorable was Mother's Day in 1957 visiting Melbourne, Australia to participate in the celebration of the Battle of the Coral Sea. In the 1950s before the freeway system, servicemen could hitchhike. He really enjoyed this mode of travel from ship to home and had some real enjoyable experiences and met a lot of real nice people.

John and his wife Marie have two children Cynthia Affolder and Jon Lyn McElroy and one grandchild Christopher R. Harrison. John is active in the Masonic Lodge.

FRANK H. MCFADDEN, born Nov. 20, 1925 in Oxford, MS, graduated from high school in 1943 and immediately entered college. He entered active duty March 1, 1944, in the V-12 Unit at Illinois School of Technology in Chicago; July 1944, transferred to NROTC Unit, Notre Dame University; commissioned Ensign USNR (later commissioned Ensign USN) in October 1945.

He was assigned to the USS *North Carolina,* in the Atlantic Fleet and joined the *Columbus* in Long Beach, CA in April 1946 and served on it primarily as 4th and 5th division officer and deck watch officer until July 1949, when he resigned from the Navy.

He completed his degree at the University of Mississippi and entered Yale Law School in the fall of 1950. In March 1951, he voluntarily re-entered active duty and joined the USS *Wisconsin* in Norfolk, VA for duty in the Atlantic and Korea. From the *Wisconsin* he transferred to the NROTC unit at the University of Mississippi as an assistant professor of naval science.

Released from active duty in September 1953 with the rank of lieutenant, and re-entered Yale Law School, graduating in 1955. He practiced law in New York for 3+ years, then moved to Birmingham, AL to practice law until 1969 when appointed a US District Judge for the Northern District of Alabama in Birmingham. He resigned from the Federal Bench in 1982 and became general counsel and a senior executive for an old client in Montgomery, AL. Retired from that position and is now practicing law with a firm in Montgomery, AL.

Married Jane Nabers on Sept. 30, 1960 and has three children: Frank Hampton Jr., Angus Nabers and Jane Porter, and two grandchildren, Frank Hampton III and Kendrick.

THEODORE R. MCGIVERON, born Jan. 27, 1927 in Middletown, CT. In the summer of 1944, at age 17, he drove Railway Express trucks full time. Still at age 17, he left Woodrow Wilson HS in his senior year to join the Navy on Oct. 7, 1944 at New Haven, CT. Basic training was at Sampson, NY, then to Newport, RI for further training on light cruisers, *Sivanne* and *Diluth*, cruising in the North Atlantic.

In June 1945 he was sent to and went aboard the USS *Columbus* (CA-74). He served in the Fire Control Div., reaching the rank of S1/c and qualified rangefinder operator. His battle station was in an 8-inch gun turret. His medals were American Theater, Asiatic-Pacific, Victory and Occupation (Japan). He left the ship at San Pedro, CA and was discharged a week later at Lido Beach, Long Island, NY on July 7, 1946.

Ted went back to high school, then on to tech school and to Central Connecticut College. For a number of years he worked as an electrician at HELCO generating plant, Prat & Whitney, East Hartford, CT and union construction jobs throughout the state. In 1956 he became a voc-tech teacher at Wilcox Tech HS in Meriden, CT teaching the electrical trade and theory along with basic electronics for 22 years. He then taught adult education at Whiting Forensic Institute for five years.

An ardent outdoorsman, at 33 he took up scuba and skin diving and joined a spear fishing club, becoming a competition diver. Soon after that he joined the Meridan Ski Club and the Meriden Power Squadron. At age 75 he still skis in the winter and skin dives in the summer with woodworking as a hobby.

He has three children by his first marriage: Linda, Bonnie and Donnie and two grandchildren, Eric and Andrew. He is now enjoying a second marriage with his lovely wife of 34 years. Eric and his son Robert (age 24) enjoy the same sports.

JOHN J. MCNALLY, born Nov. 8, 1955 in Philadelphia, PA and graduated from Cardinal Dougherty HS. He enlisted in the Navy July 12, 1973 and was sent to Great Lakes, IL for basic training. He attended Operations Specialists "A" School in Great Lakes, then was ordered to USS *Columbus* in January 1974.

His interest in firefighting began at the two damage control and firefighting schools in Little Creek, VA and Mayport, FL. He will always be grateful for the instruction and education he received there as they were the impetus for his career as a Philadelphia firefighter.

John and his wife Jeanie, also from Philadelphia, were married in 1979 and have four children: Stephen, Meghan, John and Michael, and two grandchildren.

WILLIAM J. MELLISH, born Feb. 26, 1922 west of the Allegheny River in Bradys Bend Township, Armstrong County, PA, and graduated from East Brady High School in June 1940. On Sept. 16, 1942 while attending Grove City College (PA), he enlisted in the USNR as an apprentice seaman. In June 1943 the Navy placed him in the V-12 program at Brown University.

In November 1944 he transferred to the 22nd class of Midshipmen at Columbia University. Upon commissioning as a line officer, ENS, March 8, 1945, he was assigned to and became a plankowner of USS *Columbus* (CA-74) upon its commissioning. He was assigned as an engineering officer to the electrical division (E Div.). Following a shakedown cruise in Guantanamo Bay, Cuba, the *Columbus* returned briefly to New York, Boston and Guantanamo before sailing to the Orient.

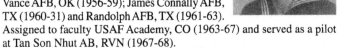

Following ports of call at Panama City, Pearl Harbor and Okinawa, Columbus spent January and part of February 1946 in Tsingtao, China. They went up the Yangtze River to Shanghai for the last half of February. Following calls at Yokosuka and Sasebo, the ship returned to San Pedro, CA April 1, 1946.

Upon release from active duty in September 1946, he returned to Brown University and graduated in June 1947 with BS degree in engineering. As a Ready Reservist he was recalled for Korean duty aboard USS *Missouri* (BB-63) for the years 1951-52. In 1955 he changed his designator from line to civil engineering Corps (5105) to match his USNR service more appropriately with his civilian occupation as a highway construction engineer with the state of California.

As a selected Reservist from July 1965 to July 1968 he was CO of Reserve Mobile Construction Bn. 28. He volunteered to return for a third two-year tour of active duty as head of the Seabee Reserve Program for the 12th Naval District located at Treasure Island, San Francisco, CA.

His campaign and service medals include China Service, American Campaign, Asiatic-Pacific Campaign, WWII Victory, American Occupation Service, National Defense Service, Korean Service w/3 Bronze Stars, Armed Forces Reserve, Naval Reserve, Korean Presidential Unit Citation, UN Service and Navy Rifle Markmanship. CDR Mellish retired from the USNR in July 1971 after 29 years of honorable service.

He retired from state highway construction in September 1987 after 40 years. He is a life member of the Naval Reserve Association, Naval Order of the US, the Association of Naval Aviation and the Navy League. He will always be outranked by his wife, CAPT Lucille Weeks Mellish, NC, USNR (Ret). Family consists of son Markham and his wife Roslyn and their children, Alan and Allison.

RAWLEY L. MILSTEAD, born July 29, 1946 in Stanton, VA and has BA degree in social work from Christopher Newport University. He enlisted in the Navy March 5, 1969, Lynchburg, VA and was discharged June 6, 1971 with the rate RMSN.

Homeport was Norfolk, VA. He graduated Navy Class A Radioman School, Bainbridge, MO and made two MED cruises. He was fleet radioman, CR Div. and participated in the conflict off coast of Lebanon, Israel, Syriad Jordan. Promoted to RM2 (E5), USNR. His awards include the National Defense Medal and Meritorious Unit Commendation Medal.

Civilian occupation as postal clerk. He and his wife, the former Marlene Wiles, have no children.

TONY MOLINAR, born Nov. 16, 1930, Hatch, NM. After high school he joined the Navy April 1, 1948, Albuquerque, NM and was discharged in April 1952 as EN3, Fargo Building, Boston, MA.

Tony served aboard the USS *Sierra* (AD-18), 7th Fleet and USS *Columbus* (CA-74), 6th Fleet. His awards include the Good Conduct, Navy Occupation (Asia) and China Service.

Self-employed 20 years Chevron dealer, Los Angeles, CA and 20 years at York Corp.

RICHARD MOLLICA, born in 1930 in Altoona, PA, the 5th of six children. He graduated from Altoona High School in 1948. Dick enlisted that summer and was sent to Great Lakes NTS for boot camp and Electrician Mates' School.

He was then sent to Norfolk to report aboard the USS *Willard Keith* (DD-775) where he served for the next 11 months.

He was then transferred to the USS *Columbus* (CA-74) in Boston in January 1950. He participated in "The Med Cruise" sailing almost 67,000 miles over a period of 15 months, 23 days, from June 12, 1950 to Oct. 5, 1951. He received his discharge in Boston on Aug. 26, 1952.

Dick met his wife Joanne, of Kendallville, IN, on July 4, 1953 while attending Tri-State College in Angola, IN. They were married June 10, 1955 after his graduation, where he received a BS degree in electrical engineering. They have two children, Tom of Knoxville, TN, and Lisa of Fort Wayne, IN. Grandchildren are Kristin, Dustin and Sydney.

Dick retired as a supervising engineer from Indiana Michigan Power Company (now AEP) in February 1995 after almost 40 years of service.

DR. ROLAND D. MOWER, born Dec. 25, 1928, Mt. Pleasant, UT. He enlisted in US Navy April 2, 1945 and completed boot camp at San Diego, CA. He served on USS *Pensacola* (1945-1946), USS *Columbus* (1946-1948) and USS *Missouri* (1948). Discharged at Norfolk, VA Dec. 17, 1948 as quartermaster.

Graduated University of Utah in June 1955 and entered USAF in September 1955 destined for flight training. Graduated pilot training in October 1956 and Assigned as instructor pilot, Vance AFB, OK (1956-59); James Connally AFB, TX (1960-31) and Randolph AFB, TX (1961-63). Assigned to faculty USAF Academy, CO (1963-67) and served as a pilot at Tan Son Nhut AB, RVN (1967-68).

Memorable experiences include Atomic Bomb Test "A" and "B" and surrender of northern Japan.

Returned to University of Kansas to pursue PhD (1969-71). Following graduation in 1971, he was assigned ASD, Wright-Patterson AFB, OH. Subsequently, assigned Avionics Laboratory, WPAFB, OH. Retired from USAF Sep. 2, 1974.

Joined the faculty University of North Dakota, Grand Forks, ND September 1974 and retired from UND in June 1988. He joined the faculty of Embry-Riddle Aeronautical University, Prescott, AZ July 1988, retiring July 1993. Purchased a ranch near Fairview, UT in June 1994.

Married Nona Iva Lee Hall of Waycross, GA, Dec. 23, 1948 and they have five children: Carol, Connie, Christi, Roland and Richard; also, 16 grandchildren and eight great-grandchildren.

JOHN G. MAY, born Nov. 7, 1929, Washington, DC and attended G.W. University and Northeastern University for his BSIT degree in electrical engineering.

He joined the service in May 1947 at Washington, DC; served aboard the USS *Columbus*, 1949-51, electronics comm. maint.; NSS Radio, Washington, 1951-53; and was discharged in June 1953 as ET1.

Worked two years for Navy Department and 35 years for Raytheon. He and May have been married for 50 years and have three daughters: Carol, Donna and Lori, and four grandchildren: Holly, Natalie, Mikaela and Nicholas.

STANLEY DURL MULLINS, born Oct. 31, 1930 in Edison, TN and attended Sullivan HS in Kingsport, TN. He signed up in the Navy in March 1948 in Huntington, WV.

Stanley pulled his boot camp training in Great Lakes, IL.

At Norfolk, VA he went on board the USS *Mississippi* for two months then to the USS *Columbus* where he finished out his service time. He was discharged March 19, 1952. His awards include the European Occupational Medal. He enjoyed his travels aboard the *Columbus*, especially France.

After his discharge, Stanley began his career as an electrician and retired at Holston Defense Corp. He married Margie May Carver 49-1/2 years ago and they reside in Piney Flats, TN. They have three children:

James, Larry and Sandra Mullins Adams. Grandchildren are Josh, Dustin, Matthew, Justin, Travis and Heather Mullins and Chris Adams.

ANDREW F. MURELLO, attended boot camps at Great Lakes, IL, in 1949 and was sent to the USS *Columbus* where he worked in the 7th

Division until transferred to the King Division. He went to RD School in the states, made 3rd classes and became supervisor of a watch section on a three-section rotation. Discharged in 1952 and went back to school for electronics.

He joined the Navy Reserves as an ET and made chief then senior chief and served in DE/DD's in the 1970s and 80s out of Brooklyn, NY. He was transferred to a maintenance repair unit in Brooklyn and became Command Career Counselor. Retired on his 60th birthday in 1992. Has received Certificate of Appreciation, the Europe Occupation Medal and the Navy Achievement Medal.

He married Doris in 1958 and has three children, 10 grandchildren and 14 great-grandchildren. Retired after 28 years at RCA, GE and Harris Corp in 1991. He was ordained a Deacon in the Roman Catholic faith in 1980 and has been working with people in the community of St. Mary's in Rockledge, FL. He attended first reunion in 1994 in Scottsdale, AZ.

DANIEL J. MUSSEHL, born May 6, 1948, St. Paul, MN. He enlisted in the Navy in June 1965 with assignments at US Naval Mine Defense Lab, Panama City, FL; USS *Northampton*; and USS *Columbus* (CG-12). He made three MED cruises before being discharged July 1969 as E3.

After discharge he started his career as toolmaker. He has two children, Kenneth Wayne and Dean Anthony; also, one grandchild, Katrina.

VICTOR P. NASTAR, born March 10, 1924, Boston, MA. After high school he enlisted in the Navy July 16, 1942 at Boston. Assignments include USS *Davis* (395), USS *Gatling* (DD-671), USS *Amsterdam* (CL-101), USS *Iowa* and USS *Columbus* (CA-74).

He participated in WWII action from Marshalls to Iwo Jima, back to the States for overhaul, then to Tokyo Bay for Japanese surrender. Memorable was rescue of over 300 survivors of *Princeton* and rescuing five Japanese prisoners.

Discharged in July 1948 as MoMM2/c. His awards include the American Theater, European-African, Good Conduct, Asiatic-Pacific w/9 stars, Philippine Liberation w/2 stars and WWII Victory Medal.

After discharge he started as an oil in a power plant and retired as chief engineer. Married 55 years and still going strong. They have three children: Linda, William and Edward, six grandchildren: Victor, William, Christopher, Michael, Beth, Rebecca and Timothy; and two great-grandchildren, Joshoa and Timothy.

HOWARD A. NESPER, born Aug. 2, 1926, Wheeling, WV and attended Colgate University for his BA degree. He joined the Navy July 28, 1944 at Wheeling, WV with boot camp at Naval Training Center, Sampson, NY and Fire Control School at Fort Lauderdale, FL.

Discharged June 10, 1946 as FC3/c. His awards include the Pacific Theater Ribbon, American Theater Ribbon and WWII Victory Medal. He is a plankowner of USS *Columbus* (CA-74).

After discharge he worked for The Sherwin-Williams Co. and retired as sales manager.

JAMES NORTH, born Feb. 16, 1927 in San Pedro, CA. He left high school in 1944 and joined the Navy February 24 in Richmond, VA. Boot Camp was at Great Lakes Naval Training Station.

He was shipped to California and went to the South Pacific in April 1944. From New Guinea he was transferred to the USS *Grasp* (ARS-24)

and saw action in the Philippines and Okinawa. After the war he was sent home for leave and was assigned to the USS *Pensacola* (CA-24) and took that great ship to Bikini Atoll for the A Bomb test. After witnessing this, he didn't want to see another war. Upon returning home, he was assigned to the USS *Columbus* in September 1946 and was a yeoman for the executive officer, CDR Hagberg.

He left the Navy in February 1948, before the *Columbus* left for England. He married Gloria, the girl he met after the war was over, and they have been married 53 years. They have three children, eight grandchildren and one great-granddaughter. James has been retired since 1989 and enjoying every minute of it.

FREDERICK J. OCZKOWSKI, born July 1, 1932 on a farm in Chelmsford, MA. After high school he enlisted in the US Navy on Aug. 2, 1949 and served aboard

USS PCE-851, USS *Johnny Hutchins* (DE-360) and USS *Columbus* (CA-74).

Discharged June 16, 1953 from USN Receiving Station, Boston and served in the Naval Reserve from 1953 to June 1956. He enlisted in the US Coast Guard Reserve in June 1956 and served on extended and inactive duty to June 1985. He retired with the rank of commander.

He served with the Metropolitan Police, Washington, DC from July 1954 to November 1956; with the US Secret Service (White House Police) November 1956-September 1957; transferred to US Marshals Service in September 1957 and served on various assignments and locations in the US and territories to June 1985. He retired with the rank of Chief Deputy US Marshal.

He sailed for 2-1/2 years with wife Diane, CAPT, USAR (Ret) on their 43 foot motor yacht *"Allegiance"* between New England, Caribbean, Key West and Gulf of Mexico. He and Diane reside in Naples, FL (winter) and Bartlett, NH (summer). They have four children.

Fred became general manager for Dalis Lines and captain of M/V Dalis, certified for 125 passengers.

THEODORE M. "TED" OLENDER, born Nov. 11, 1930 in Syracuse, NY. At age 16, Ted began working for the *Syracuse Herald Journal* as a

newspaper copy boy, then later employed by the *Associated Press* as a wirephoto operator until his enlistment in Marine Corps on Oct. 12, 1948.

Ted completed boot camp at Parris Island, SC and was temporarily stationed at Camp Lejeune, NC. He attended Sea School at Portsmouth, VA and was then assigned to the aircraft carrier *Kearsarge* until its departure for Bremerton, WA for conversion to jet aircraft.

In 1950 Ted was transferred to the *Columbus* prior to its departure for the Mediterranean on June 12, 1950. In May 1951 the *Columbus* Marines provided security for the new NATO headquarters in Naples, Italy. Ted was discharged Aug. 29, 1952.

He moved to California from New York in 1953 where he met his wife Marilyn, who had also recently moved from New York, and they were married in 1954. Ted worked in mechanical engineering in the aerospace industry. He and his wife then worked in real estate sales and development from which they recently retired. They have two sons, five grandchildren and six great-grandchildren.

JAMES W. "JIM" O'NEILL, born Jan. 17, 1931 at home on Troy St., Toledo, OH. He earned a BS degree in industrial safety and health from

The Detroit Institute of Technology, while rearing a family. He enlisted in the Navy, March 1, 1948 at Toledo and was discharged as boilerman third class, Feb. 27, 1952, while USS *Columbus* was in dry dock at Boston.

After boot camp, he was assigned temporary additional duty in USS *Mississippi* while waiting for *Columbus* to return to Norfolk from midshipman cruises to the Mediterranean. He served in *Columbus* July 1948-February 1952 in the engineering dept., B Division. He worked in #2 Fire Room a few weeks and in #4 FR until March 1950 at which time he was invited to be an Oil King.

Additional duties during this time: Landing Force (BARman) with the Marine Detachment, Prize Crew involved in two prize ship exercises while at sea, shore patrol in various ports and Radiological Defense Team.

He received Navy Occupation Service Medal, Europe and Good Conduct Medal. Notified of BT2 rating two weeks following discharge.

Married Ginny Ravary Aug. 22, 1953 and together enjoyed rearing four wonderful children: Deb, Ken, Den and Dave. They now enjoy seven granddaughters and one grandson. Family gatherings are of utmost importance throughout the years.

Ginny and Jim like retirement because they can do what pleases them: enjoy family and friends, taking trips driving all over the country, hunting with sons (Jim only) and attending the annual reunion of the USS Columbus Vets Association wherever it may be held.

GERALD OTT, born June 6, 1931 and graduated from Brandon HS May 30, 1949. He enlisted in the Navy Jan. 2, 1951 with boot camp at Great Lakes, IL, then to Norfolk for assignment to USS *Salem* for transport to Ville France and the USS *Columbus*.

He was reassigned to Radio School in Norfolk and was flown there from Italy for four months schooling. He then returned to *Columbus*. He was discharged Nov. 4, 1954 as RM3.

He met Ruth while in high school and they were married June 6, 1953. They have seven children: Susan, Cindy, Lisa, Cheryl, Tammy, Tracy and Mike and nine grandchildren. Gerald spent 23 years farming, then had a farm machinery business for the next 20 years. He is now retired and lives in Rosendale, WI.

JERRY J. PALMER, born Aug. 25, 1925 in San Mateo, CA. He enlisted March 13, 1943 for V1/V12 program at San Mateo JC and University of

Texas. After NTS San Diego boot camp and Quartermaster School, he served in USS *Beckham* (APA) at Iwo Jima, Okinawa, Korea, China and decommissioning at Norfolk.

After short tour ashore as draft runner, he transferred to USS *Maury* (AGS) at Truk Atoll for duty in hydrographic survey and sounding work until December 1947.

Attached Flag Allowance COMBATCRUPAC aboard USS *Helena* (CA) and USS *St. Paul* (CA) before transferring as QM1 to USS *Columbus* (CA) at Bremerton NSY in January 1949 and sailing for Norfolk.

Between voyages, he married Jeanne Pumphrey in Washington, DC on July 31, 1948 before shipping out to Plymouth, England; Jeanne sailing on SS *America*.

Upon return to US, he transferred via RECSTAs Brooklyn and Yerba Buena Island to USS *Arequipa* (AF) for duty in the Philippines until ordered ashore for tour at Signal Tower, Yerba Buena Island. Upon making QMC in 1952, he transferred to USS *Lofberg* (DD) for a four year tour during Korean War. Went aboard USS *Los Angeles* (CA) in early 1956 and left mid-year for OCS Newport.

Commissioned ENS USN in August 1956 and attended Communication School. He joined USS *Columbus* (CA), serving as Crypto and Radio Officer. Tour terminated upon transfer to Staff COMCRUDIV FIVE in cruisers Los Angeles, Rochester, Bremerton and Worchester.

Shore duty at Naval Ordinance Test Station, Long Beach as Sea Range Operations Officer, including a tour as OIC San Clemente Island. Back to sea as XO and CO (Acting) of USS *Pledge* (MSO), moving to operations officer in USS Turner Joy (DD), thence to Deputy District Communications Officer 14ND in Hawaii and completing sea duty as XO USS Henderson (DD) closing out Vietnam War.

He made twilight tour to the Pentagon in early 1970. Elected to go on the retired list as CDR May 1, 1973 and, after civilian pursuits, fully retired in September 1990. He and his wife of 54 years have one daughter Marci, two grandchildren and two great-grandchildren.

PAUL T. PAYNE, born Nov. 16, 1952, McCaysville, GA. Attended University of Tennessee at Chattanooga for his BS degree in environmental science in geology/geography, 1978. He enlisted June 19, 1970, Fort Lauderdale, FL and went to boot camp at Orlando, FL.

Assignments include Basic Enlisted Submarine School, New London, CT; USS *Sea Devil* (SSN-664), Norfolk, VA, 1970-71; USS *Cutlass* (SS-478), Norfolk, VA/Key West, FL, 1971-72; US Naval Underwater Swimmer's School, Key West, FL, 1972; USS *Columbus* (CG- 12), Norfolk, VA, 1972-74. He served as leading seaman and ship's diver aboard submarines and as postal clerk asst. and postal clerk aboard USS *Columbus*.

Awards include Armed Forces Defense Medal, Meritorious Unit Citation and Navy Expeditionary Medal.

Memorable: Christmas in Barcelona (1972); beautiful nights in the Caribbean; and getting in a helo to take the Newport News her mail upon returning to Norfolk after her turret blew up and finding out a minute before lift-off that there was something wrong with the engine.

He's employed as senior energy services technician, Comm. & Indus. with the Tennessee Valley Authority (1978-present). Married Loretta Jane Collins in June 1973, divorced in 1974, no children. Remarried in May 1983 to Brenda Russell Payne and has children, Daniel Travis and Emily Kathryn.

RAYMOND ELDON PAYNE, born July 8, 1929 in Baltimore, MD. He joined the Navy Jan. 9, 1948 and after boot camp attended Electricians Mates School. Promoted to EMFN and later to EM3, and honorably discharged Jan. 8, 1952

Boarded the USS *Columbus* (CA-74) in August 1948. Did time at Mess cooking in the Chiefs Quarters, Boat Engineering, changed countless batteries in Liberty Launches, stood many hours at watch in the firerooms at the switchboards. Accompanied CICNELM on two cruises in the Med with Plymouth, England our "Home Port" and a trip to GITMO.

Ray met his wife Jeanette one month prior to going to boot camp. They married Oct. 27, 1951 and celebrated their 50th Anniversary in 2001. They have one son, Brian, a college graduate and a computer expert with the Social Security Administration in Baltimore, MD.

Ray retired Jan. 1, 1993 from Lockheed Martin after 20 years service of which 13 years were in management in the Quality Assurance Department.

LOUIS A. PELLINO, born Aug. 17, 1932 in Glens Falls, NY. He enlisted in the Navy April 2, 1952 and trained in Great Lakes. After boot camp he was sent to Boston aboard the USS *Columbus* (CA-74) and stayed until 1956.

He made two cruises to the Mediterranean, transferred to the USS *Salem* (139) and made a cruise back to the Med and England. He made third class petty officer Boatswain Mate Gunner in 1955 and was discharged in 1956. His medals include Navy Good Conduct Medal, Navy Occupation Service Medal with EC and National Defense Service.

Married Ann in 1957 and has three children: Mike, Lou Jr. and Jon. His wife Ann passed away in 1971. He married Joyce in 1973 and they had two children, Mark and Robin. Grandchildren are Joel, Justin, Jenna, Sam, Mathew, Nick and Angela.

He worked 31-1/2 years in a chemical plant in Glen Falls, NY, retired at age 55, then worked as manager and bartender for seven years. He's past Exalted Ruler, Elks Lodge (1986-87) and past commander of VFW (1991-92) and presently active as Jr. Vice Commander and Color Guard, VFW 2475

JOHN J. PFAFF, born in New York City on Nov. 23, 1933. Moved to Cincinnati, OH in 1937 during the greatest flood in Ohio Valley history.

Through four years high school (Mariemont 1951) he worked as a "soda-jerk" in Frisch's Restaurants, alongside of Dave Frisch and his wife when they only had five restaurants.

Joined the Navy Oct. 27, 1952 and was sent to boot camp in Bainbridge, MD, then to Electrician's Mate School in Washington DC (Montgomery Jr. College - a co-ed college that was half civilians and half sailors!). He went aboard USS *Columbus* June 1, 1953 and was discharged directly off the ship on Oct. 26, 1956.

Spent the next 31 years in the Cincinnati Fire Division rising to the rank of assistant fire chief. He retired Jan. 1, 1989.

Married the love of his life, Janet, in June 1959. They have two wonderful children, Jennifer and Jason, and so far, two grandchildren.

They now spends half their time in their condo on the beach in Ft. Myers Beach, FL and the other half in their condo in the Cincinnati area.

WILLIAM E. POLCSA, born Sept. 14, 1926, New York, NY. After high school he joined the Navy Aug. 2, 1949 at New York. Boot camp with Co. 267 was at USNTC, Great Lakes, IL.

He reported aboard the *Columbus* (CA-74), Plymouth, England and served 2-1/2 years. Also served 1-1/2 years aboard the USS *Wadleigh* (DD-689). Discharged July 27, 1953 as radarman 3/c. Awards include the Good Conduct, Navy Occupation (Europe) and National Defense.

Married Louise E. McManus on Feb. 24, 1952 in Cambridge, MA and reared a wonderful family of five children: William, Charles, Nancy, Peggy and Juliet. Grandchildren are Gregory, Michael, Joey, Stephan and William.

JOE POPIEL, born April 29, 1945 in Philadelphia, PA and has BS degree in electronics. He enlisted Aug. 1, 1968 in Philadelphia, PA and after one and half years of Electronics and Radar School he was assigned at Norfolk with the 6th Fleet; on board CG-12 from March 1970 to July 1974; assigned aft Talos T-5 Div. then T-7 Div.

Memories: His first time at sea there was a crisis in the mid-east (September 1970) and they headed out at about 30 knots. A day or two out they lost all power for about half an hour. It was a helpless feeling drifting around till power was restored. Another time as they headed into Athens, battle stations were sounded as they entered the harbor. It turned out that a WWII mine was found floating in the harbor. Once while lifting weights with some shipmates between the aft talos radars and having a Soviet destroyer pull up alongside them, wanting to play "chicken" with them.

Discharged July 1, 1974 with the rate E-5 (FTM2). Awards include the Good Conduct, National Defense Service Medal and Meritorious Unit Commendation.

KENNETH R. POTVIN, born June 11, 1925 in Minneapolis, MN and graduated Vocational High in 1943. He enlisted in the US Navy Jan 11, 1943 with boot training at Farragut, ID; assigned Armed Guard Center, Pacific. First ship was SS *Matsonia*, April 1943, a converted luxury liner to troop ship and first leave was in November 1943.

Served in the following ships: December 1943-July 44, MV Cape Florida; August 1944-October 1945, USS LST 896; October 1945-June 1946, USS *Boston* (CA-69); August 1951- November 1952, USS *Burdo* (APD-133); December 1955-March 1957, USS *Monssen* (DD-798); July 1962-October 1965, USS *Columbus* (CG-12); October 1968-September 1969, USS *Albany* (CG-10).

As chief missile technician he was assigned to USS *Columbus* (CG-12) in July 1962 as part of PRECOM Crew. Transferred October 1965 to White Sands Missile Range, New Mexico. Transferred as senior chief firecontrol technician to Computer School at Mare Island for digital computer systems and assignment to Boston Navy Yard, October 1968, USS *Albany* (CG-10) for PRECOM detail. Transferred September 1969 to White Sands Missile Range for transfer to the Fleet Reserve on Oct. 10, 1969. Completed 30 years in the Navy and retired in July 1975. After Navy retirement he specialized in employee group benefits for almost 30 years.

Met his first wife Jacqueline in Pittsburgh while PRECOM crew for USS LST-896 and they married in March 1946 in San Francisco. They divorced upon return from WestPac in February 1965. He met a Russian gal named Monique at the CPO Club at White Sands Missile Range in December 1965 and they married in Juarez, Mexico in September 1967. Divorced in August 1977. Married one more time to a Mexican gal named Beatrice in January 1979. They divorced in January 1986. He is still single and plans to stay that way.

He joined the USS Columbus Association Aug. 1, 1992, launching the Submarine SSN 762.

CHARLES R. PRIBYL, born Aug. 8, 1936 in Exeter, NE. Completed high school and attended two years at the University of Arizona. He joined the Navy in September 1954, Lincoln, NE.

Assignments include USS *William Mitchell,* NCSO Portland; NAVCOMSTA Kodiak; USS *Columbus*, September 1956-July 1958 with duty as postal clerk.

Memorable was celebration of battle of Coral Sea, Melbourne, Australia in 1957.

He worked 31 years at California State University Northridge and retired in 1991.

While serving in *Columbus* he married Betty L. Chmiell in May 1958 and they have three children: Laurel Keller, Scot Pribyl and Wendy McEachen. Grandchildren are Steven, Daniel and Jonathan Keller; Kaitlan, Marrissa and Melanie McEachen; and Danielle Pribyl.

JAMES A. RABIDEAU, born March 7, 1938, Detroit, MI. Completed high school and joined the Navy June 30, 1955 in Detroit, MI. He served in the USS Columbus as radio operator.

Some of the places he was at include Adak, Long Beach, Japan and Australia. He was discharged March 2, 1959 as RM2. His awards include two Good Conduct Medals and Armed Forces Expeditionary Medal for Taiwan Straits.

Civilian employment as computer programmer. He married Barbara Rentchler in 1958 and they reared five children: Julie, Frank, Bill, Elizabeth and Jennifer. Grandchildren are Megan, Mindy, Mitchell, Jesse, Jacob, Jared, Christopher, Cara, Ashley, Cage, Cara and step-grandchildren Garret and Austin.

James attended the 2nd reunion at Orlando, FL in 1989. He passed away in 1993.

CHARLES J. RAGAIN, born March 15, 1929, Highland Park, MI. He graduated from Detroit Bible College in 1957 and Eastern Michigan University in 1966 and has BA and BS degrees in education.

He joined the Navy April 1, 1946 with boot camp at Great Lakes. He went aboard the Columbus in San Francisco headed for China, then back to Bremerton, WA. Discharged in February 1948. Remained in Reserves and was called back in September 1950. He went aboard USS AJAX and was in Japan until discharged as MM in June 1952.

Currently a retired school teacher, but still does substituting. He married Audrey on Feb. 11, 1950 and they reared five children: Jane, Charles II, Robert, Philip and Patricia. They also have 15 grandchildren and one great-grandson.

SETH THOMAS "TOM" RANNEY, born Oct. 26, 1924, Little Rock, AR and graduated from North Little Rock High School in 1942. He volunteered for the US Navy and left July 17th for Boot Camp in San Diego at age 17. First assignment was Norman OK, in 1944 and Alameda, at Livermore in 1945.

A civilian for two years, in 1947 he re-enlisted and joined the USS *Columbus* at Long Beach. The Admiral's Flag ship cruised the Scandinavian area, Mediterranean and British Isles. On March 22, 1949 he met Netta Watson in Plymouth, England, getting engaged in November. Back in the Med, Tom re-enlisted for six years in order to get leave and they married Oct. 24, 1950 in Plymouth.

Assignments include Orange, TX, 1951 and where their first two; 1953, *Olmstead* (APA-188); 1954, *San Marcos* (LSD-25) at Little Creek,

VA; 1956 London, England, where their third child was born; 1960 Kansas City Recruiting Station for two years; his last ship was *Decatur* (DD-936) where he made Chief. He retired Jan. 8, 1964 with 21 years served and returned to Overland Park, KS.

In 1969 their last child was born. They have been blessed with six grandsons and six granddaughters.

ANTHONY V. RENTAUSKAS, born Aug. 5, 1927. After completing high school he entered the Navy Oct. 6, 1944 at age 17. Received training at Great Lakes Center, IL then sent to the USS *Columbus* (CA-74) and was proud to be a plankowner. He spent all his term aboard the *Columbus* and left the Navy July 24, 1946 with the rank S2/c.

He returned home to GI School and married his childhood sweetheart, Marge, and was happily married for 47 years. He was the proud dad of daughter Tonette and granddad of three: Paul, Kristen and Allison. He passed away Jan. 7, 1994 so never got to see his great-granddaughter Abigail. He is greatly loved and missed.

HOLLIS EUGENE ROBERTSON, Navy, born in Peoria, IL on March 4, 1933, He enlisted in the Navy in 1951 and entered the US Naval Academy a year later. He graduated in June 1956 and was commissioned ensign. In 1964 he received a BS degree in mechanical engineering from the Naval Postgraduate School in Monterey, CA. He is a proven ship's engineering subspecialist and co-author of the Naval Engineer's Guide published by the Naval Institute in 1972.

CAPT Robertson has served ashore as an instructor of engineering at the Naval Academy, as Officer in Charge, Fleet Introduction Team TWO, SPRUANCE (DD-963) Class destroyers, as senior member of the CINCLANTFLT Propulsion Examining Board and as Assistant Chief of Staff for Surface Warfare, Operational Test and Evaluation Force, Norfolk, VA.

He has served at sea in USS *Francis M. Robinson* (DE-220), USS *Franklin D. Roosevelt* (CVA-42), USS *Catamount* (LSD-17), USS *Wainwright* (CG-28) and has commanded USS *Charles S. Sperry* (DD-697), USS *Rich* (DD-820) and USS *Biddle* (CG-34).

From November 1965 to August 1967 then Lieutenant Commander Robertson served as Chief Engineer, USS *Columbus* (CG-12). He retired in 1985 with 34 years of continuous naval service and currently resides in Virginia Beach, VA.

Capt. Robertson is married to the former Mary Catherine Debelius of Baltimore, MD. They have five daughters: Cathy, Helen, Barbara, Susan and Beth, and one son Harry. They also have 10 grandchildren.

EDWARD LEE ROBINSON, born May 25, 1930 in California and completed 10 years school. He entered the Navy Aug. 5, 1947, Stockton, CA and served numerous positions in the 5th Division.

He was discharged Aug. 26, 1956 as GM2. His awards include the European Occupation, Korean Medal and others. To serve his country was his greatest accomplishment and the most memorable of his life.

Edward went into heavy equipment for approximately 37 years then went into Mac Tools for 12 years. He married Nell Elsa Robinson and has one daughter Lee Ann, three grandchildren and nine great-grandchildren.

MARION J. ROMANIO, born Dec. 22, 1928, Los Angeles, CA. After high school he entered the Navy July 6, 1946 at Los Angeles, CA.

Assignments include boot camp and Cook and Baker's School, San Diego, CA; USS *Iowa* (BB-61); USS *Columbus* (CA-74); USS *Albany* (CA-123); shore duty, Astoria, OR; USS *Kiswakee* (AOG-9); Submarine School, USS *Remora* (SSA-87); recruiting duty, Coos Bay, OR; USS *Blue Gill* (SS-242), USS *John Adams* (SSBN-620), USS *Hunley* (AS-31).

Discharged in January 1968, his awards include six Good Conduct Medals, National Service Medal (2nd awd.) and China Service Medal. Accomplishments include his 22 year career in the USN; USS *Columbus* Good Will Ambassador, all ports MED, Sea, fore runner while NATO was established and Flagship for ADM R.L. Connley.

He was foreman at a bakery for four years, supervisor 14 years for food processing plant and retired in 1986. Now plays golf, fish and relaxes. Married in 1952, divorced in 1981 and has two sons, Nick and Rick. He is now married to Shirey Lyon. Grandchildren are Adam, Jesse, Jessica, Clair and Brittany.

DONALD ROSE, born May 20, 1931 and completed high school. He entered the service in October 1950, Duluth, MN. Assignments include Norfolk Receiving Station and participating in Korean War. Discharged in August 1954 with the rank PNSN.

Civilian employment as retail manager at F.W. Woolworth Co. He married Patricia Simon on Aug. 13, 1955; she passed away April 4, 2001. He has four children: Michael, Lee Ann, Teri, Mary Beth and eight grandchildren: John Michael, Catherine, Mary Beth Kipta; Stephanie, Patti, Jamie Rose; April and Ashley Nicholson.

DONALD H. ROTHE, born Sept. 12, 1934 in Patchogue, Long Island, NY. He graduated from Patchogue High School in 1953. Enlisted in New  York City and sent to boot camp at Bainbridge, MD, Jan. 21, 1954. After boots he went to Radar School, Norfolk, VA.

Went aboard the USS *Macon* in July 1954 in Norfolk for Med cruise; transferred to USS *Columbus* in Boston, Fall of 1955 for deployment to West Coast via Panama Canal. Crossed Equator twice while aboard *Columbus* bound to Lima, Peru and Melbourne, Australia. He was aboard the *Columbus* when it collided with USS *Parks*.

Civilian employment as firefighter and USPS letter carrier. He married Shirley in September 1960 after his discharge in Long Beach, CA on Nov. 17, 1957. Shirley passed away June 12, 2000. He has three children and three grandchildren and resides at Patchogue, NY.

GERALD L. ROWE, born July 12, 1930, in St. Paul, MN, and went to the University of Minnesota and Electronics School before joining the  Navy on Jan. 2, 1951. After recruit training at Great Lakes Naval Training Center, he went aboard the USS *Salem* for transportation to the Mediterranean.

Gerald came aboard the USS *Columbus* March 17, 1951 while in Villefranche, France. Assigned to the T Division, he was soon sent back to Great Lakes to Electronics School. While there he married his high school sweetheart, Patricia Andreas. He rejoined the ship in Boston in 1952, and after a shakedown cruise to Guantanamo Bay, Cuba, he went again to the Mediterranean.

Gerald left the Columbus at Barcelona, Spain for Point Mugu, CA. Later assigned to the USS *Mississippi* in Norfolk, VA, he achieved the rank of First Class Petty Officer, ET1, before leaving the Navy in December 1955. He went back to college under the GI Bill, and after receiving his electrical engineering degree in 1958, he returned to California to pursue his engineering career and worked on several Navy and aerospace projects until retiring in 1990. Now living in Canoga Park, CA, he has two children, and five grand children.

KENNETH E. ROWLISON, born Feb. 28, 1938 in Stroh, IN and attended Salem Center HS in Indiana. Ken played baseball and basketball. He enlisted in the Navy on April 30, 1956. After boot camp in Great Lakes Naval Station he was assigned to the USS *Columbus* and met the ship in Long Beach, CA, July 1956. Ken also played basketball for the ships team while on board.

On Oct. 30, 1957 Ken married Cynthia Sizemore and they have two children, Tim and Karla, and two grandchildren, Taylor and Tanner.

Ken served on board three years, then helped put the ship out of commission in Bremerton, WA in May 1959. Ken was discharged March 2, 1960 in San Diego, CA with the rate SK3. He received the Good Conduct Medal.

He worked for International Harvester Co. in Fort Wayne, IN until retiring in 1996. He spends his summers in Kendallville, IN, golfing, fishing and with his family. Winters are in Bradenton, FL, golfing, shuffling, and enjoying the warm weather.

DONALD C. SAMHAT, born Nov. 30, 1927 in Detroit, MI. Don graduated from Clarenceville High School in June 1945 and enlisted in the Navy on July 5th. He was sworn in on August 6th, the day the Atomic Bomb was dropped on Hiroshima.

After boot camp at Great Lakes Training Center, he was sent to Long Beach, CA and boarded the battleship USS *Iowa.* He served in the Occupation Force at Tokyo Bay.

After his discharge in 1946, he went into the grocery business with his brother. He married in 1950 and was called back into the Navy. During the Korean War in March 1952, he went aboard the USS *Columbus* and served 22 months. His rank was third class petty officer.

Don and his wife Charley have celebrated 52 years together and they have two children, Linda and Steven, and five grandchildren.

MICHAEL JOHN SAMUEL SANGSTER, born March 12, 1965, Las Vegas, NV. Attended Notre Dame for BS in electric engineering and Western University for MBA degree. He entered the service May 16, 1987.

Assignments include XO, SSN-762, ComSubRon One Ops Off, navigator, USS *Santa Fe* (SSN-763), instructor NROTC unit the Citadel, division officer, USS *Blue Fish* (SSN-675).

Awards include Meritorious Service Medal, three Navy Commendation Medals and two Navy Achievement Medal. Memorable was VIP cruise to Maui in 2000 with USS Columbus veterans.

Sam is married to Denise who is an attorney.

ROBERT C. SCHAUDT, born Aug. 14, 1927 in Oregon City, OR and graduated from Beaverton HS in 1945. He enlisted in the Navy in July 1945 and went to San Diego, CA for boot camp, then Radar School at Point Loma, CA.

He went aboard the USS *Iowa* in January 1946 and was anchored at Yokosuka, Japan until March 1946; transferred to the USS *Columbus* and from 1946-49 they were

at various locations in China, Japan and Europe. Bob played basketball on the ships team, also, for King Division. He made radarman first class in May 1949.

Bob met Norma in London, England in 1948 and they were married there in November 1949. They have two daughters, Nancy and Robin, five grandchildren and one great-grandson.

ROBERT CHARLES SCHRAMM, born July 22, 1922 in Cleveland, OH and graduated from Shore HS in Euclid, OH in 1940. He worked as

an AT&T lineman, coil winder for electric submarine motors and machinist for aircraft bearings prior to joining the Navy.

He was sworn in the regular Navy for six years in September 1942, went on a five day leave prior to attending boot camp and Machinist Mate School at Great Lakes. He graduated from Machinist Mate School as MM2 on February 27, 1943, was promoted to MM1 in June 1944 and to chief in December 1952.

Robert spent onshore duty in Brazil from March 17, 1943 to January 1945. He was stationed at the Navy repair base in San Diego when WWII ended.

Reported aboard USS *Columbus* (CA-74) in May 1948 and was detached in January 1950 to attend Guided Missile School at Point Mugu, CA. During the Korean Conflict he was aboard the USS *Philippine Sea* (CV-47) from October 1950 to September 1952.

He retired March 16, 1962 and was piped over the side of USS *Topeka* (CLG-8). His medals include the European, American and Pacific Theater of Operation, Middle Eastern Campaign, China Service, United Nations, Navy Unit Commendation and Good Conduct (5th awd.)

As a civilian he worked for the Navy at the Missile Evaluation Center at Corona, CA, from March 1962 to April 1982. He graduated from Chapman University in 1972 and spent the next 10 plus years with a Navy contractor at Corona, retiring in December 1992.

He married his first wife Penny on March 6, 1953 and was widowed in June 1995. He remarried June 5, 1999 to Wanda – no children in either in marriage.

WILLIAM C. SHASHAGUAY, born Oct. 1, 1936, Holland, MI and graduated from Albuquerque HS in 1954. He enlisted in August 1954, Albuquerque, NM and had recruit training at San Diego.

Assignments include USS *Wainwright* (CVL-49), USS *Hornet* (CVA-12), USS *Porterfield* (DD-682) and USS *Columbus* (CG-12). Memorable was Radar B School, Air Intercept Controller and Gulf of Tonkin (1964).

Discharged in February 1966 as first class petty officer. His awards include two Good Conduct and two American Expeditionary medals.

After his discharge he was a furniture builder, woodworker, and retired from local power company. Married 43 years to Judy, a retired nurse, and they have four children: Kim, Steve, Kelly and Mark. Grandchildren are Sam, Noah, Kyle, Madison, Ryan (a submarine sailor stationed at Groton), Katie, Nick, Caitlin and Will.

JAMES V. SHERRILL, born Aug. 17, 1927, Morgantown, NC and attended Jr. College. He enlisted Feb. 7, 1945, Raleigh, NC and was a pointer for 40mm guns, Fox Division. He served on the USS *Columbus* (CA-74) from June 1945 to June 1946. During WWII he had occupation duty in China and Japan.

James was discharged July 26, 1946 as S1/c and retired from the Army Reserve as lieutenant colonel, having served in the 11th and 12th Special Forces. His awards include the Army Meritorious Medal, Army Commendation Medal, Army Reserve Achievement Medal, Parachute Badge, Army Reserve Medal, American Campaign Medal, Asiatic-Pacific Campaign Medal, China Service Medal, WWII Victory Medal, and Occupation Medal (Asia).

Retired from the Veterans Administration – Hospital Administration. He married Lillian Rogers on July 2, 1952 in Fayettville, NC, and they have one daughter Mary Sue Zarrabzadeh and two grandchildren, Cameron and Marissa Zarrabzadeh.

ALEX SHIMANSKY, born Sept. 18, 1930, Brooklyn, NY and left high school in 1947. He entered the Navy June 28, 1951 at New York City with the following assignments: Great Lakes, USS *Salem*, and in October 1951 was assigned to the USS *Columbus* with the 2nd Div.

Alex was discharged May 27, 1955 with the rate BM3. He had numerous memorable experiences with the crew of the 2nd Div.

He finished high school and after discharge worked for American Airlines. He retired in 1992 after 37 years. Married to Lynn since March 17, 1956 and has three children: Louise, Alex and Peter and six grandchildren: Christopher, Michael, Tyler, Connor, Dillon and Skylar.

PETER R. SIMMONS, born Sept. 19, 1933, Philadelphia, PA. After service Electrical School, Fitchburg State College for management. He joined

the Navy Sept. 18, 1951, Philadelphia and was sent to Great Lakes for boot camp. From there to USS *Columbus* (CA-74). He was released in September 1955 as FN.

He was in the 6th Fleet and played softball for the ship; his position was pitcher. His awards include the National Defense Service Medal and Navy Occupation Service Medal with European Clasp.

Active in Masonic Bodies where he served as Master of his Masonic Lodge (twice) Master of the district (once), District Grand Marshall, 1st Lieutenant Commander Legion of Honor, a part of the Shriner's; also, active in Boy Scouts, Little League and even Girl Scouts.

He worked for Raytheon Co. over 35 years. Peter met Judi in February 1955 in Dorchester, after writing to her for two months. They married on Oct. 29, 1955 and have four children: Karen, Linda, Robert and Kenneth. Grandchildren are Danny, Beth, Kelly, Robin, Shaun, Kristina, Jolene and Gabre. Great-grandchildren are Anthony Robert and Emily Rachelle. Judi worked after all the children left as an LPN.

Pete passed away on Nov. 3, 2001.

ROGER A. SIMMONS, born Jan. 23, 1933, in Marion, OH. After WWII the family relocated to McAllen, TX; Tucson, AZ and finally Houston, TX.

Roger graduated from Stephen F. Austin HS and University of Houston in 1957. He entered OCS, Newport, RI and received orders to USS Columbus (CA-41). Roger was 5th Division Gunnery Officer, general quarters station was Sky 2 Mk-37 Director Officer, and made two Far Eastern Cruises with *Columbus*. He reported to Gunnery Officer, LCDR W.G. Grace. His JO was ENS John Wellenhofer; both Columbus Veterans Assoc. members and now deceased.

Columbus participated in the Taiwan Straits and Quemoy shows of force. Roger was transferred to USS *Midway* (CVA-41) on decommissioning of *Columbus* for conversion to CG-12. Upon discharge in 1960, he remained in the Naval Reserve for 25 years serving as executive officers of three surface divisions followed by a command assignment. (He rose through the ranks to captain.) His last assignment was as a Navy Department Duty Captain, Pentagon.

His civilian employment was in the defense industry.

Roger met Joy Callaway in Long Beach, CA and they were married May 15, 1959. They have two children, Stacey and Mitchell, and four grandchildren: Sloane, Eric, Evan and John. Roger and Joy are retired and reside in Vienna, VA.

WILLIAM E. SMITH, born Jan. 19, 1928, Grand Rapids, MI and completed high school. He entered the service in October 1945 and served in the USS *Salt Lake City* and USS *Columbus*.

Memorable was Atom Bomb test and visiting China and Japan. He was discharged in October 1947 as fireman first class.

After discharge he was a truck driver. He and his wife Eleanore have three children: Greg, Gary and Gordy, and five grandchildren.

HALLIE J. SNIDER, born Aug. 10, 1926, Superior, NE, and completed 8th grade. He entered the service April 11, 1944, Sterling, CO and trained at USNTS Farragut, ID.

Vessels and stations served include USS *Princeton* (CVL-23), USS *Columbus* (CA-74), USS *Sitkoh Bay* (TCUE-86), USNRS Washington DC, worked at Pentagon for three days sorting papers and USS Naval Hospital, Oakland, CA.

Locations include Pagon, Rota, Guam, Tinian, Palaus, Mindanao, Leyte Gulf. Memorable was being a survivor of the *Princeton* when it sunk on Oct. 24, 1944 and going through the Panama Canal.

Discharged Feb. 7, 1952. His awards include the Philippine Liberation with one star, Asiatic-Pacific with two stars, American Area and WWII Victory.

Hallie and Joan were married April 25, 2002 and have two children, Ricky Lee and Susan Kae. Grandchildren are Courtney, Brittany, Kellee, Samantha and Scott.

RAYMOND C. SOARES, born July 17, 1933 in the small town of West Warwick, RI. His family never moved from this area and he ended up back there. While attending high school he worked at the J.J. Newberry Co. and W.T. Grant. Graduation was from the West Warwick High School in June of 1951.

His father and he had conflicting plans for his future, so he signed up for the Navy in August of 1951. Boot camp training was in Great Lakes, IL after which he was assigned to the USS *Columbus* (CA-74) at Charlestown Shipyard, Boston bound for GITMO. Four seasick years of his life were spent between Boston and the Mediterranean. But, he made some great friends in the service, Malcom Warrender and Paul Neumann to name a few. He was assigned to Fox Division under Mr. Sherman and made rank of FT3.

While in the Navy he married Sandra Jordon from Rhode Island in 1954. That marriage produced five children: Kevin, Mark, Curtis, Kelley

and Wendy. He now has 11 grandchildren. Unfortunately, Sandra passed away in 1993.

He was discharged in August 1955 from the Fargo Bldg. in South Boston. When he returned home he worked as a maintenance technician at various companies until retirement in 1999.

Today he reside with his life partner, Jackie, and spends his time gardening, traveling and fishing. Life is GREAT!

JOHN W. SPROUT, born on May 6 1925 in Hightstown, NJ and graduated from the Peddie School in 1942. After a year at Bucknell University he joined Navy V-12 unit at Yale. Midshipman School was at Notre Dame and Communications School at Harvard.

Assigned to *Columbus* pre-commissioning detail in Newport, RI, in March 1945. Eventually he became radio officer and CR DIV officer in 1946. All sea duty was on the *Columbus* at Boston, Guantanamo, Hawaii, Tsingtao, Shanghai, Sasebo etc. Released to inactive duty July 31, 1946 in the States.

After discharge he was a teacher of mathematics at Bucknell, Rutgers, Douglass, Highland Park, NJ, High School and the Peddie School. He retired from Peddie in 1991, but it still Faculty Marshall. He married Carol Van Alen on July 15, 1950 and they have two sons, John Jr. and Ronald, and two grandchildren, Nicholas and Elizabeth. He has been active in Jaycees, Lions, Masons, church and education.

MICHAEL J. STECHISHIN, born June 2, 1932, Detroit, MI, and graduated in 1950 from Wilber Wright HS. He entered the service in September 1951, Detroit and went to boot camp at Great Lakes.

Assigned to *Columbus* (CA-74), sea duty aft eng. rm; Philadelphia Navy Yard, security, Sub Group 11, Atlantic Res. Fleet. While on board the Columbus he took part in Operations Mainbrace, Long Step and Short Step.

Memorable was his first Columbus reunion in 1999 and meeting old shipmates after 46 years.

After his discharge in September 1955 with the rate MM3, he became a film and video producer, convention manager and business show manager for IBM Corp for 36 years, working in New York City and Atlanta, GA.

He met his wife Yvonne in Atlanta in 1976 and they married in 1979. They have a combined family of six: Michael, Marc, John, Kerry, Kristina and Vicki. Grandchildren are Michael, Casey, Rebecca, Samantha and Jessie. They moved to Kentucky to boat, golf and enjoy a slower life style.

ERIC P. SUNSTROM, born Dec. 4, 1930, Mobile, AL and moved with his family to Marinette, WI in 1936. He entered the service at Marinette on Jan. 24, 1951 with boot camp at Great Lakes, IL, followed by more training at Philadelphia Navy Yard and USS *Columbus*. Home base was Boston, MA.

He made two cruises to Atlantic and Mediterranean and four cruises to Caribbean. Discharged Dec. 17, 1954 as second class petty officer. His awards include the Good Conduct, European Occupation, NATO Operations (one with NATO Forces) and North Atlantic.

After discharge, he attended college to become a vocational teacher and counselor at Milwaukee Area Tech College (34 years). He has BS degree in vocational education and MS in educational administration.

Married Hazel in 1953 who passed away in 1967; married Dorothy in 1969 and divorced in 1984; married Ingeborg in 1989, a very special and talented lady. He has eight children: Mary Nolin; Steven, Mark, Kurt and Sue Sunstrom; Sharon Gilardi, Lisa Ramirez and Kathryn DeBroux. Grandchildren are Lucas and Megan Nolin; Scott, Steven and Shannon Sunstrom; Michael Ramirez and George DeBroux.

Eric is presently involved with a group of veterans from different services and they are near completing the arrangements to bring the *Des Moines* (CA-134) to Milwaukee from the Philadelphia Navy Yard. It will be placed in the inner harbor and established as a war memorial, class rooms and tourist attraction.

EUGENE N. SZOLGA, born April 7, 1934, St. Louis, MO and has a degree in banking and finance. He entered the service June 1, 1952, St. Louis, MO.

Vessels and stations include USS *Calvert* (APA-32), USS *Bexar* (APA-237), USS *Agerholm* (DD-826), USS *Columbus* (CG-12), ComSup Flot 1, San Diego, CA, USS *Alamo* (LSD-33), USS *Peidmount* (AD-17). Shore duty at North Island, 1962-64 and with the PacResFlt, 1968-70.

Discharged June 15, 1972 with the rank EM2. His awards include the American Defense, National Defense, UN, Humanitarian Medal for passage to freedom, Good Conduct, Vietnam Defense and Korean Syngman Rhee Presidential Unit Citation.

Memorable was 1953 and they were the first troop ship to return vets to USA after Korean War; 1954, taking 6,000 refuges from North Vietnam to Sagon; 1954, taking part in largest amph. ops since WWII; going to top of Mt. Suribachi on island of Iwo Jima.

He's retired from Bank of America, 18-1/2 years as special auditor. He and his wife Beverly have two sons, Keith (chief master sergeant) and Kevin (fuels jets for AA Lines, LAX). Grandchildren are Nathan, Jerad and Robert Nick.

W. BRUCE TALIAFERRO, born 1944 in Baltimore, MD. He joined the USS *Columbus* in 1965 as a fire control technician on the Tartar system and left her in 1968. Probably his most vivid memory is of the sinking of the Greek ferry Heraklion in December of 1966 and their subsequent search for survivors, but none were found.

After leaving the Navy in 1969, he completed his graduate degree in education and is currently a high school vice principal. He lives in western Maryland with his wife, Vicki.

WARREN D. TAYLOR, born Oct. 5, 1932, Lynn, MA and has 12 plus years of education. He entered the service April 25, 1951, Lynn, MA and was discharged April 24, 1956 as EM2.

Assignments were at Great Lakes, Electrical "A" School and USS *Columbus* (CA-74). Memorable was stripped and rewound 24 HP motor.

As a civilian he was an electrical construction foreman and worked 40 years for the same company. Warren and his wife Nancy have three children: Tracy, David and Deborah. Grandchildren are Chelsea, Bradon, Hadley, Alexandra and Alex.

DOUGLAS TINDAL, born July 16, 1945, and raised in small Iowa towns. He graduated from the University of Iowa in 1967, married Bonnie Miller, and began Law School. In 1968 the local Draft Board told Tindal he was losing his student deferment, and had better join a military service or he would be drafted into the Army.

Tindal, thinking that it would be interesting to see the ocean and possibly travel to foreign ports, enlisted in the Navy, and graduated from Boot Camp in San Diego December 1968. After finishing A-School he asked on his "dream sheet" for any small ship in

the Pacific. As the Navy was prone to do, it assigned Tindal to a large ship, the USS *Columbus*, then in dry-dock in Portsmouth, VA.

Seeing *Columbus* for the first time, supported in dry-dock on blocks, Tindal thought he would be in for some tough times and he was right. But after three Mediterranean Cruises, there were also some fantastic times, and the opportunity to meet dozens of fine people on the ship. After leaving *Columbus* (as an E-5 interior communications electrician) and the Navy in 1972, Tindal finished law school and has practiced law since 1974.

ROBERT N. TOMLIN, born Jan. 25, 1939 in Harmony, Iredell County, NC. He left school in the 11th Grade, June 13, 1956, to join the Navy.

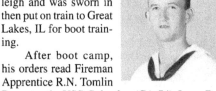

Along with 200 other young men from North Carolina, he went to Raleigh and was sworn in then put on train to Great Lakes, IL for boot training.

After boot camp, his orders read Fireman Apprentice R.N. Tomlin Report to the USS *Columbus* (CA-74), Long Beach, CA. He was assigned to the "A" Division. While on board *Columbus* he made two Far East cruises, was member of the Decommissioning Crew at Bremerton, WA, June 1959.

He got his GED on board *Columbus*, and four Good Conducts, National Defense Service Medal, Armed Forces Expeditionary Medal (4 awards), Navy Achievement Medal, and the US Republic of China Mutual Defense Commemorative Badge.

He served on USS *Scanner* (AGR-5), USS *Long Beach* (CG(N)9) plankowner, USS *Pawcatuck* (AO-108), three tours in USS *Amphion* (AR-13), USS *Yosemite* (AD-19) and USS *W.S. Sims* (DE-1059).

He is member of the commissioning crew of the Naval Training Center, Orlando, FL. Robert retired in 1977 as senior chief machinist mate, NAS (Master Jet Base) Cecil Field, FL.

He has three children: Lisa, Dayna and Wesley; two granddaughters and one grandson. He keeps busy with his plumbing contracting business.

LOUIS M. TUCCIARONE, born 1927 in Vineland, NJ, one of nine children. In 1931 his family moved to Brooklyn, NY, and again in 1938 to Bethpage, Long Island, NY, where two more girls were born, making it five girls and six boys.

In June 1944, at age 17, he joined the Navy and pushed boots at Sampson, NY. Four of his brothers were also in the service. He served aboard the USS *Oklahoma City* from Nov. 17, 1944, part of the Third Fleet.

Re-enlisted on Nov. 17, 1945 while in Hiro Wan, Japan, and served aboard USS *Prinz Eugen* (IX 300). After she was destroyed, he was assigned to the USS *Columbus* from Sept. 6, 1946 to Sept. 27. 1947. He remained a Sl/c and received the Asiatic-Pacific Medal w/2 stars, American Area, Victory and Good Conduct Medals.

Married Jennie in 1951 and had three children: daughter Jennifer and sons, Louis and Perry. He worked at Grumman in Long Island, NY, for 32 years. His wife, Jennie, died in May 1979, and he remarried Janet in August 1980. She has three boys: Robert, Michael and Thomas. They have a total of 14 grandchildren and two great-grandchildren.

He retired in 1982 and lives with his wife in Cocoa, FL, where he is an avid writer.

JAMES GUYER WARNER SR., born Feb. 3, 1928, in Kansas, IL and graduated in May 1946 from high school in Marshall, IL. He joined the Navy in 1948 and served two enlistment's with duty in the European Theater aboard the USS *Columbus* and attached to the S-2 Division from 1951-54.

Jim pitched for the USS *Columbus's* fast pitch softball team the "Discoverers" and the Malden City Softball Leagues "Flamingo Club" in Boston. Newspapers depicted him as a quiet baby-faced mid-western sailor, who at the age of 26, carried the deceiving nickname "Pop." Jim pitched the *Columbus* to runner-up spot in the Atlantic Fleet Battleship-Cruiser tourney defeat-

ing the USS *Mississippi* and USS *Pittsburgh*. Jim pitched with a "swiftness and accuracy that had players holding their heads in wonder." Jim won 18 straight games, pitched two no-hitters, one of which was a perfect game. "A feat which would not soon be duplicated" and earned him a most valuable player award.

Jim married the former Yolanda Stornauilo of East Boston and on April 22, 1954, became the father of James Guyer Warner Jr. Jim joined the USS Columbus Veterans Association in 1997, attending his first reunion in 1998 in Norfolk with his current wife, Eileen.

JAMES EDGAR WARRINGTON, born Jan. 14, 1943 and died Dec. 27, 1999. James, known as Jim to his friends and shipmates, was born in Cedar Rapids, IA and graduated from Ankeny High School in Ankeny, IA. Jim was in the Naval Reserves from 1960 until June 1962. During this time Jim was on board the USS *Famington* PCE 894 for basic seamanship training.

Jim enlisted in active duty June 21, 1962 in Des Moines, IA and went to Great Lakes for basic training. He then went to Electronics School in Mare Island Naval Shipyard, CA. Jim, along with several others, reported aboard *Columbus* and armed with tremendous amounts of knowledge were ready to go to work. However, the *Columbus* was at sea so they were assigned to a barracks, given a paint brush and told to commence work. After just finishing Electronics School this didn't seem to be what they had been trained to do, but they painted daily until the *Columbus* returned to port. They then reported aboard and he was assigned to T-5 Division. He was aboard *Columbus* until December 1966 and left in Athens, Greece.

He was discharged Jan. 5, 1967 from the Brooklyn Navy Yard with the rank FTM2. Jim received the Navy Good Conduct Medal, Armed Forces Expeditionary Medal, National Defense Service Medal and the Cold War Certificate of Recognition. He was a member of the Horse Plains, Montana Veterans of Foreign Wars.

He worked for RCA and the Chicago and Northwestern Railroad. Jim served as a Director of the USS Columbus Veterans Association.

Jim was married to Kathryn Michelle (Parmenter) Warrington. Kathy, at the time of this writing, lives in Montana where they had built a lovely home. They had no children.

ROBERT D. WELK, born March 19, 1925, Brooklyn, NY and has BS in business administration. He entered the service July 28, 1943 in Hartford, CT.

Assignments include USS *San Jacinto*, V-3 Div. and USS *Columbus*, K Div. during WWII. He was discharged April 25, 1946 with the rank RdM3/c. His awards include the Pacific Theater and WWII Victory.

After discharge he worked in Industrial Engineering Dept., Pratt & Whitney Aircraft Div. United Technologies. He married Mary Ellen Monroe on Oct. 13, 1951 and they have three children: Elizabeth, Robert and Margaret, and one grandchild, Matthew McClure.

RICHARD L. WESTFALL, born June 4, 1936 in Charleston, WV and started working for Glass Dairy at age 9. He graduated from Poca High School in 1955 and has some college and other classes. He joined the Navy June 2, 1955 and went to boot camp at Bainbridge, MD, and MM/A School at Great Lakes, IL.

Assignments include USS *Pandemous* (ARL-18), Charleston, SC, 1956; USS Canberra (CAG-2) Philadelphia, PA, Naval Ship Yard for recommissioning preparations, 1956-58; Presidential Cruise Dwight D. Eisenhour, March 14-24, 1957.

He became a Shellback June 26, 1957; Blue Nose Sept. 21, 1957; European Cruise 1957-58; USS *Columbus*, 1958-59; flew from Naples, Italy to Long Beach, CA; Asian Cruise; patrolled the Taiwan Straights daytime as a Cruise and as a aircraft carrier at night with no liberty or leave for anyone during this time. Many of the crew had a hard time handling it. Richard's brother, William Westfall was a chief radioman aboard and Richard was in turbo generators. The *Columbus* was transferred to Bremerton, WA where they prepared it for the Mothball Fleet.

Richard was discharged at Treasure Island, CA as MM2, E-5 on May 19, 1959. He went to Dunbar, WV and worked for many different companies, but retired as department head of construction for Bethlehem Steel on Aug. 17, 1996.

He met Judith Queen on Feb. 16, 1960 and they married Oct. 8, 1960. They had one daughter, Tamara, born Oct. 26, 1962, and one grandson, Rodney E. Frank III born April 5, 2001. After 40 years and 8 months with a beautiful and wonderful lady, he lost Judy on June 15, 2001 to Lymphoma cancer.

W.O. "BILL" WHITESIDE, born May 5, 1930, Abilene, TX. He joined the USN Jan. 19, 1948 and served in USS *Neches* (A)-47); USS *Repose* (AH-16); USS *Bushnell* (AS-15); USS *Norfolk* (DL-1); USS *Boxer* (CVS-21/LPH-4); USS *Columbus* (CG-12) and USS *Iwo Jima* (LPH-2).

Stations were NTC San Diego; 124th NCB Adak, AK; Retraining Command, Norfolk, VA; Commissary Stores in Philadelphia, PA and Portsmouth, VA; Navy Recruiting Branch Station, Austin, TX. He participated in Inchon Invasion (1950) and later evacuation's. He returned to CONUS in December 1951.

Transferred to Fleet Reserve in May 1974 and placed on retired list in September 1977 with rating of chief petty officer. He received six Good Conduct Medals, Korean PUC w/cluster, Korean Service Medal w/6 stars, two National Defense Medals, Occupation Medal, China Service Medal and UN Medal.

Memorable experiences included 15 years as a Navy deep sea diver; participation in an eye witnessing detonation of 31 Atomic and four hydrogen bombs in 1958.

Bill and his wife Edna have five children: Sandra, Marie (deceased), Billy, James and Darlene. They also have 15 grandchildren and 16 great-grandchildren. He worked as a policeman, auto mechanic and real estate agent before final retirement in 1986.

LEONARD C. WILCOX, born April 6, 1929 in Pittsfield, MA. After high school he enlisted in the USN in Framingham, MA and took his physical in post office building in Boston. He left by train for Chicago and up to Great Lakes NTS.

After graduating in July 1948, he was assigned to USS *Dayton* (CL-105) in Boston and went to CIC Team Training School at the Fargo Bldg. Shortly after that, the *Dayton* was scheduled for decommissioning in Boston and he was transferred to the USS *Fargo* (CL-106). They operated out of Boston and Newport, RI until they left for the MED on Feb. 28, 1949, the weather was cloudy and cool with some rain.

On the way across they got word from the USS *Columbus* that they needed about 50 men, so Leonard put in his transfer (smartest thing he ever did) and if some of you remember it was Friday, March 11, 1949 and the weather was clear and warm, and the water very calm. Both ships, *Fargo* and *Columbus*, lay adrift close by. They went back aft on the *Fargo*, down a cargo net into a motor whale boat and over to the *Columbus*, then up the cargo net on the fantail, down to the mess hall and was assigned to King Div. where he remained until his discharge in Boston at the Fargo Bldg. in May 1952. His rank was radarman third class. Awards include the Good Conduct and European Occupation medals.

The USS *Columbus* (CA-74) is the best ship in the Navy.

Leonard and his wife Evelyn have two children, Mark and Chris, and one grandchild, Patrick.

JERRY R. WILLIAMS (WISHNOVITZ), born Oct. 8, 1937, Pittsburgh, PA. He joined the USN in 1954 and went to boot camp at Bainbridge, MD.

Assignments include USS *Macon* (CA-72), Norfolk, VA, Med. Cruise; transferred to *Columbus* in October 1955 and made one West Pack cruise in 1956; USS *Helena* (CA-75), 1957; and USS *Frontier* (AD-32), 1958.

Memorable was surviving the fiasco at the Boston Hotel and Panama Canal; the Shellbacks during the Equator crossing to Lima Peru; being a member of the basketball team that played and won the game against the National Team of the Philippines in Zamboanga.

Tragedy struck on March 11, 1956 in the South China Sea, when during night maneuvers the "BUS" struck and sheared over 50 feet of the bow off the USS *Floyd B. Parks*. Like most of the crew, Jerry was sleeping topside and awoke as the bow section floated past. At times one can still hear the screams from the Chiefs quarters, trapped on the bow.

Jerry received an honorable discharge in October 1958. The *Columbus* was a good ship and he earned his GED and rate while serving on it.

He married Sharon Lee Shephard in 1962 and they have one son Marc and two beautiful twin grandsons, Alan and Eric.

DAVID J. YEATON, born Sept. 12, 1946, and grew up in Shrewsbury, MA. He graduated from Shrewsbury High School and joined the Navy in

May 1966. Boot camp was at Great Lakes, IL. He reported to Norfolk Naval Base and was assigned to mess duty while awaiting the *Columbus* to return from a North Atlantic cruise.

Reported aboard and assigned to the deck department, Division 2, where he spent the next six months. He was assigned as the first lieutenant's yeoman where he spent the next three years

and had the good fortune to work for LTs Strickland, McNelly, Walters and McDaniel. It was a rewarding experience and set the ground work for a career in business.

Separated from active duty in March 1970 and went on to college under the GI Bill and eventually obtained a master's degree in finance.

He married the former Kathleen Navin on Aug. 26, 1972 and they have two children, John and Katie. He took an early retirement in January 1999 and now consults on a part-time basis.

EUGENE F. ZERNIA, born March 16, 1928 in Milwaukee, WI. He finished high school and some college courses. Eugene entered the service on March 17, 1945. As-

signments/Locations include Philippine Island NSD 3149, Atomic Bomb, Bikini Atoll, USS *Columbus*, China Tour, Panama Canal and New York.

Memorable was taking the USS *Pennsylvania* (BB-38) to Bikini Atol Atom Bomb Test. He was discharged March 2, 1949 with the rate metalsmith third class. Awards include the Good Conduct, Navy Occupation, China Service, Victory Medal, Asiatic-Pacific, Philippine Liberation and American Theater.

He was a sales rep. for Roto Dyne for 25 years. Married to Esther Mae since Nov. 26, 1949 and the father of seven children: Shari, David, Mark, Andrew, Karlew, Elaine and Jerry. There are 19 grandchildren and six great-grandchildren.

In Memoriam

The USS Columbus Veterans Association wishes to honor their members who have passed away.

As of September 2002

Adamski, Robert F.

Anderson, Paul B.

Austin, John

Barker, James O.

Barnstien, Robert F.

Barrett, Joseph

Barth, Fred J.

Behar, Jacob D.

Behl, John H.

Bell, Robert J.

Bennett, Donald C.

Bennett, Elwood L.

Bernardy, Mark H.

Best, Cyril

Bigelow, John F.

Bird, Richard

Blair, Charles J.

Bloecker, Robert J.

Bogue, MM1, Douglas E.

Bonin, Dr. Louis J.

Bowdren, William J.

Bowers, Jr., Freeman Ray

Boyd, Capt.Gideon M.

Bratt, Albert B.

Brothers, William Patrick

Butler, Allan

Cady, Capt. John P.

Campbell, Capt. Gordon

Cecere, Thomas G.

Champagne, Donald S.

Chase, John R.

Churchey, Warren S.

Clark, Donald A.

Clark, Sterling M.

Cleveland, Keith

Coffey, Leland E.

Coleman, Alan R.

Connolly, Richard L.

Cook, Edgar W.

Cozzola, James

Craig, Dwight M.

Curran, James A.

Darr, Donald D.

Dauphineas, D. J.

Davenport, William K.

Delparo, Richard J.

Dennstaedt, William C.

Dilley, Donald

Dillon, Joe M.

DiVincenzo, Emilio R.

Doxey, Robert C.

DuBois, John R.

Duhon, Thomas

Edwards, Charles R.

Edwards, William H.

Ege, Louis S.

Ely, Fred

Emery, Roy

Farrell, Edward V.

Farr SHCS, Manford

Felsinger, Charles R.

Flanigan, Gregory A.

Flott, Kenneth E.

Flowers, Jr., Roney Elton

Force, D. R.

Ford, GM1, Fred H.

Fox, Thomas L.

Fresenburg, Frank

Futak, Francis G.

Galligan, Jr., David F.

Gardner, William W.

George, James E.

Gephart, R. James

Ghise, Nicholas

Gibbons, John A.

Gish, Jesse Lee

Goldman, Louis

Goode, Billy R.

Grace, William C.

Graham, Lincoln

Grant, J. Donald L.

Gross, Sydney

Gydosh, Joseph R.

Haas, Joseph A.

Hagberg, Oscar E.

Halse, Donald J.

Hamlin, Robert

Hammitt, Kenneth L.

Harding, Floyd Sam

Harris, Clyde

Heep, Richard J.

Heller, David H.

Hendricks, Carl W.

Hendricks, Gordon Harvey

Herra, Walter

Hewitt, Curtis

Hickam, Gene E.

Hicks, H.H.

Hideg, John

Hildreth, Sidney G.

Hill, Dale E.

Hobbs, Allen

Holmes, Chester K.

Holmes, Richard (Dick)

Hook, Jr., Laurel D.

Houlihan, John C.

Howe, Maurice H.

Huey, Donald B.

Hundley, Fred H.

Hunnicutt, Tommy J.

Hunt, Harry E.

Imhoff, William J.

Johnson, Fred

Johnson, Ralph C

Jones, Benjamin

Jones, Glennus

Joslin, Royal K

Kelly, James T

Kittle, DeWitt S.

Knowles, Francis

Kulow, Ralph L.

Landry, Thomas E.

Lane, Richard D.

Leblanc, Ruffin Joseph,

Lee, Stuart A.

Lindquist, Irwin M.

Lord, Richard E.

Martin, Walter

Mayfield, Jr., Harry S.

McDaniel, Billy R.

McGill, Walter S.

McIntosh, Charles

McLean, Jr., Ephraim R.

Meek, Richard R.

Merta, Kenneth

Miles, Milton E.

Miller, Robert

Minard, Robert U.

Mitzelman, Irwin

Moore, Walter E.

Moran, Charles J.

Moss, Robert F.

Mullarky, Robert D.

Mumford, L. K.

Munroe, Robert

Murphy, Marvin S.

Myler, James V.

Neighbors, Dorsey

Nestlerode, Jr., George E.

Newrohr, Robert H.

O'Brien, Gerald D.

Olson, Kenneth E.

Ortiz, Pablo Paul

Page, S. Everett

Parent, Dana

Parsons, Jack E.

Pasquale, Carl M.

Pauley, Hubert E.

Perkins, Raymond F.

Pedersen, Paul M.

Peterson, Capt Robert A.

Pippin, Roscoe L.

Pisculli, Mike

Powell, James D.

Rabideau, James A.

Reed, Frank P. (Pappy)

Renney, Jack L.

Rentauskas, Anthony V.

Reynolds, R. Adm (ret), Luther K.

Richardson, John L.

Riha, Robert L.

Riley, James W.

Robbins, Bill F.

Robinson, Herschel E.

Robinson, Robert Henry

Roper, Joseph C.

Ruef, Nicholas

Ruland, Dale

Ryan, Vincent J.

Sanger, Robert H.

Schumann, Clarence John

Scott, Burton D.

Seay, RADM, George C.

Sedivy, Anton J.

Seifert, Leroy

Sell, Curtis W.

Senibaldi, Alexander A.

Shepard, Floyd L.

Signore, Frank J.

Silver, Morton E.

Simmons, Peter R.

Smythe, Gary

Snyder, William

Spaulding, Robert E.

Startiowski, Frank

Stecher, Louis J.

Steele, Billy R.

Steinbrunn, William

Stombaugh, MMC, Robert F.

Strathdee, John F.

Sullivan, Jr., James D.

Surina, Jr., John

Sweeney, Robert J.

Thomas, John Harvey

Timmerman, FN, Donald R.

Tirrell, Thomas E.

Townsend, Richard W.

Tracey, Lawrence V. Dick

Tucker, Claude T.

Uehling, Gordon A.

Volkman, Gordon

Voorhees, Robert R.

Walters, John J.

Walton, Nelson C.

Wappelhorst, Gene

Warder, RADM Frederick

Warner, James Butterball

Warriner, Cdr Victor

Warrington, James

Watkins, William T.

Weger, Charles R.

Weldon, James

Wellenhoffer, Jr., John L.

Wellings, Joseph H.

Wickham, Lawrence V.M.

Wiley, James

Will, John M

Williams, Dallas K.

Williams, Joseph D.

Wilson, Perry M.

Wilson, Richard (Dick)

Wise, Donald A.

Wyatt, Ira O'Neal

Wyatt, William

Yaccino, Michael W.

Zagorski, Theodore S.

USS Columbus Veterans Association Membership Roster

Abbott, Harry D.
Abercrombie, Daniel W.
Ackland, Earl
Adams, Earnest Q.
Adams, John L.
Adams, Phillip
Addison, Stanley J.
Adell, CDR Allan A.
Ahrens, James M.
Aiton, Donald J.
Ajemian, Andre V.
Albunio, Pasquale
Alderman, Luis (Ed)
Alessandro, Robert D.
Allard, (wint)Robert R.
Allard, Robert R.
Allen, Benjamin G.
Alls, Willie H. Jr.
Altz II, Carl F.
Anderson, Gary W.
Anderson, James H.
Anderson, Mrs. Virginia
Anderson, Richard W.
Anderson, Robert A
Anderson, Stewart F.
Antrim, Stanley R.
Araujo, Jr., Frank
Argento, Salvatore C.
Arias, Gonzalo Z.
Arico, Ernest A.
Armstrong, Joseph A.
Arnett, David W.
Arthur, CAPT William A.
Ashton, Daniel
Atkins, Calvin C.
August, Ed
Austin, Harold V.
Avila, Joe F.
Backus, J. William
Backus, James S.
Bacon, Melvin E.
Bailey, Frank
Baker, Alex
Baker, DeForest
Baker, Harold E.
Baker, James L.
Balado, John R.
Baranski, John E.
Barker, John P.
Barker, Mrs. Thelma
Barnes, Edward F.
Barraclough, Sr., Harry P.
Barth, Mrs. Janet
Barton, Arthur J.
Bartoszek, Stanley G.
Bartsch, Lawrence P.
Basye, Kenneth F.

Battey, Maurice W.
Baudino, Joe
Baur, Ray
Baxter, John F.
Beach, Raymond H.
Beard, George W.
Beard, Wayne C.
Beattie, Raymond E.
Beberniss, Jr., Don R.
Beck, Harry Warren
Becker, Ralph W.
Beecoff, Stanley A.
Beers, Franklin D.
Belfert, Roger D
Belknap, Robert W.
Bell, Mrs. Corinne
Belongie, Robert C.
Benacka, August (Gus)
Bench, Jr., John F.
Benedict, Eric P.
Bennett, C.S., Rev. Peter
Bennett, William T Bill
Benton, Donald E.
Berg, Jerry L.
Berger, Carl E.
Bertoldi, Albert G. (Gary)
Best, Galen H.
Beyer, Charles E.
Biancavilla, Dominick
Bicanich, Thomas P.
Bieber, Kevin F.
Biel, Otto
Binker, Paul A.
Birk, Matt
Bishop, Jr., Benjamin C.
Black, Paul F.
Blair, Mrs. Mary Lee
Blaisdell, S. Arthur
Blanchard, Fred C.
Bland, James F.
Blank, Robert V.
Blum, James R.
Bodenschatz, George
Boggs, William A.
Bohnert, John J
Boos, Donald J.
Boris, Emile
Boshko, Paul
Bourque, Ronald R.
Bowden, George M.
Bowden, Glenn
Bowden, Glenn
Bowdren, Mrs. Maryann
Bowen, George E.
Bowen, Robley (Bob) D.
Bowman, Charles M.
Boyd, Mrs. Ruth

Boyd, Richard H.
Bradley, Arthur L.
Bradley, John W.
Brady, Terence J.
Braid, Herbert C.
Brainer, Eugene M.
Brandon, Gunny (P.E.)
Branham, Charles E.
Bredeck, Terry F.
Bremer, Richard K.
Brennan, James P.
Brentzel, Daniel E.
Breor, CDR Mark R.
Brewster, Edward W.
Brewster, Robert J.
Bridenbaugh, Charles R.
Bridenbaugh, Marvin G.
Bridges, Ted L.
Briggs, Donald E.
Brodie, Walter M.
Broome, Warren W.
Brown, Ballard C.
Brown, C. Joseph
Brown, Dale R.
Brown, Donald K. Buzz
Brown, Harold G.
Brown, James M.
Brown, Ken A.
Brown, Lawrence S.
Brown, Robert T.
Brown, Theodore H.
Brown, William M.
Brubaker, Harold R.
Bruins, Lowell J.
Brunnelle, Oliver P.
Brush, George H.
Bryan, Frederick H.
Bublinec, Milton
Bubniak, Alexander L.
Buckalew, Edmund B
Budke, Donald H.
Buell, James J.
Burchfield, Esau
Burda, Paul G.
Burgess, Danny J.
Burgess, Jay A.
Burkett, Jack
Burn, Richard H.
Burnette, Billy C.
Burton, Sr., Jerry W.
Busche, Charles A.
Bushey, Emile G.
Butler, Edward R.
Butler, Garland O.
Butler, Ramsey G.
Butterfield, John F.
Byargeon, Bennie W.

Byrnes, Jr., Edward J.
Cable, Don R.
Cahaney, John J.
Cain, Jack C.
Calabrese, Michael
Callahan, Joseph W.
Callas, Nick
Callin, Bruce J.
Campbell, Mrs. Addo
Canada, Jimmy D.
Canel, Paul
Canfield, Charles J.
Carames, Armando
Cardwell, Jr., Joseph A.
Carey, James F.
Carlsen, Richard C.
Carlson, Martin L.
Carlton, Robert F.
Carpenter, Harold L.
Carpenter, Reynolds D.
Carr, Richard J.
Carroll, Anthony H.
Carter, Ernest M.
Cartmell, George E.
Casanova, Alonzo A.
Case, Harold R.
Case, Jr., Robert O.
Cashel, Myron E.
Castonguay, Leon H.
Catone, Joseph S.
Chambers, Howard L.
Champagne, Mrs. Joan
Champion, Andrew A.
Chan, George P.
Chandler, John C.
Chandler, John C.
Chapman, James T.
Chew, Kyong Wo Joe
Choiniere, Leo G.
Christofferson, Arthur B.
Christofferson, Edward M.
Cisneros, Sergio A.
Clark, Jay L.
Clark, Richard W.
Clarke, Ted
Clay, Jr., Henry Q.
Clemmer, Danny L.
Coates, Dan
Coffey, Leon E.
Coffey, Mrs. Mary
Cole, William R.
Colella, Evan J.
Coleman, Garland L. (Lanny)
Coleman, Mrs. Ruth
Coletti, Edward J.
Collick, William A.

Collins, Lawrence K
Collins, William L.
Conboy, Richard F.
Concannon, Joseph T.
Concannon, Ronald
Condon, Patrick R.
Constantine, George B.
Constantine, William L.
Conte, Sr., Robert J.
Cook, Elmer A.
Cook, John S.
Cooper, Paul E.
Coppernoll, Richard W.
Coppernoll, William L.
Cosgrove, Henry S.
Cosgrove, James M.
Cox, Robert L.
Cox, Thomas L.
Craig, George A.
Craig, Mrs. Betty
Cratch, Zan
Crater, James L
Creeden, Wayne S.
Crepeau, Jr., Felix J.
Cresswell, John W.
Crinigan, Richard H.
Crochet, Joey C.
Cromwell, Norman L.
Cronauer, Jr., Edward A.
Crosby, Harry J.
Culp, Frederick L.
Cunningham, Jerry L.
Cunningham, Lewis E. Gene
Cunningham, Marvin L.
Cupples, William C.
Curtis, Robert G.
Cvinar, Edward B.
Dailey, Lester H.
Dalrymple, Herbert F.
Daveler, Earl B.
Davidsen, George J.
Davidson, Ronnie (Harley)
Davies, Edward J.
Davis, Joseph H.
Davis, Lloyd C.
Davis, Robert P.
Davis, William H.
Day, Robert E.
Dayberry, John E.
Dayhaw, James E.
Dean, Robert
Deaton, Sherman M.
Dedecko, Charles A.
DeLong, Edgar E.
DeMango, Marino J.
deMarigny, William

Deming, Robert F
Demmons, Sr., John L. Jack
Denice, Jr., J.J.
Denslinger, Paul
Deuter, Paul W.
DeVore, Carroll C.
Dew, Patrick F.
DiGiulio, Peter N.
Diimmel, Terrance L.
Dill, Mylnor A.
DiNova, Vincent A.
Dion, Roland G.
DiPietro, Anthony
Dishong, David L.
Ditmore, Richard R.
Dixon, Charles E.
Dixon, Robert H.
Dodd, George P.
Dodd, Richard E.
Doherty, Patrick E.
Dolinsky, Ronald P.
Dombi, Martin A.
Dominguez, Fred M.
Dorton, William L.
Doss, Cecil H.
Dossie, Thomas J.
Doucette, Forrest H.
Douglas, M.D., Gilbert F.
Downey, Denis-James J.
Drapac, Thomas F.
Driggers, Howard S.
Driver, Darrell E.
Drosos, Donald F.
Dudley, Loren H.
Duffy, Joseph J.
Duke, Glen O.
Duly, William R
Duncan, Otis D.
Dunlavey, Phillip K.
Dupuis, Maurice J.
Dworkin, Robert P.
Dziuk, Gary L.
Edelman, Thomas
Edenfield, Rea L.
Edgar, C. Lawton
Edsall, Larry T.
Edwards, Archie L.
Edwards, Ronald
Egeland, Arnold
Einspruch, Jr., Henry
Eiss, Ronn W.
Ellevold, Ronald J.
Elliott, John C.
Elliott, Kenneth P.
Ellis, Jr., J. Eugene
Ellis, Michael R.
Emert, David
Emert, Denise
Emory, James E.
Emrich, Thomas P.
Erdmann, Dean V.
Ermi, John F.
Estlund, John F.

Eull, Kenneth H.
Evans, Billy C.
Evans, Thomas O.
Fairservis, Richard
Falls, William F.
Fantacone, Peter J.
Fary, Walter L.
Fennell, Robert D.
Fenzel, Frederick A
Field, Irl G.
Filazzola, Anthony R.
Filipsic, William M.
Fine, Edward Paul
Finn, Jr., Paul T.
Finn, Lawrence
Fischer, Tracey A.
Fischetti, Vincent
Fisher, Douglas W.
Flaherty, Jr., John J.
Flaherty, William B.
Flanagan, Mathew J.
Flanigan, Mrs. Barbara
Flaws, James M.
Fleetwood, Fred L.
Fleming, Dick
Fletcher, Boyd W.
Fleury, Paul V.
Flint, Jr, Glenn D.
Flucker, Ronald L.
Flynn, Lanny
Ford, Richard
Forest, J. Walter
Forrest, Charles D.
Fortner, David H.
Fossett, Phillip
Foster, Dr. Donald J.
Foutch, Bobby O.
Fox, Fred I.
Fox, Thomas J.
Frame, Eldon B.
Franckowiak, Jack R.
Franklin, Wayne E.
Frause, Edward F.
Freeh, LaVern A.
Freeman, James A.
French, Robert E.
Fresenburg, Mrs. Gertrude
Fricker, Richard L.
Frisbey, John F.
Fritz, Harold E.
Fulcher, Dick M.
Fulton, Forrest M.
Futak, Mrs. Leah
Galla, John S.
Gambill, Jodie W.
Ganeles, Burton F.
Ganley, Robert G.
Garber, Bernard D.
Garber, Bernard D.
Gardiner, E. Michael
Gardner, William P.
Garrison, Jr., Thomas
Gates, E. Eugene

Gatten, James I.
Geis, Thomas A
Geiss, Thomas G.
Gendreau, Edward C.
Gessel, Charles G.
Gilliland, Wiley O.
Girt, Gerald D.
Glisson, Benjamin F.
Godialis, Anthony N.
Golden, John K.
Goldman, CAPT Roy E.
Gommo, Robert J.
Gonzales, Frank M.
Gonzalez, Lawrence L.
Good, Jr., Fred O.
Gorham, Thomas
Gorley, Walter L.
Gorton, Robert J.
Gosso, Roy C.
Gradel, Gary D.
Graham, Kermit G.
Graham, Thomas
Grant, William P.
Gravelin, Richard
Green, William P.
Greenberg, Kenneth F.
Greene, L. Paul
Greenfield, Jerry S.
Gregg, Donald R.
Gregovich, Fred T.
Grella, Jr., Lawrence J.
Gribble, John R.
Griffin, Sr., Charles A.
Grimm, John R.
Gross, CDR Mike E
Grosvenor, John H.
Grover, Kenneth L.
Groves, Robert A.
Grubb, Harvey A.
Guin, John V

Guivens, Norman R.
Gunn, Jimmie D.
Gurzenski, Joseph L.
Guthland, Robert E.
Halligan, John L.
Halman, Charles R.
Halse, Mrs. Lois
Hamilton, Emmett
Hamilton, Ralph N.
Hankins, Henry
Hansen, Albert S.
Hanson, Francis E. Gene
Hanson, Frank D.
Hanson, Philip D.
Harding, Mrs. Zillah
Hardy, Robert J.
Harrigan, R. Emmet
Harrison, Donald
Harrod, Charles J.
Harvey, Dayton R.
Harvey, Dean L.
Harvey, Larry Z.
Harwood, John W.
Hasson, Sam
Hathaway, George F.
Hathcock, Henry
Haught, Leland R.
Hausman, Mark
Haven, Stanley
Hayes, Robert S.
Healy, Jr., Thomas M.
Heberden, Donald R.
Heberling, R.B. Bob
Hebrew, Kenneth L.
Heep, Mrs. Lorna
Hegarty, Lawrence J.
Heil, Phillip E.
Heimbuch, Larry
Heliin, John E.
Heller, Ernest R.

Helms, Jr., Raymond E.
Henderson, Joseph F.
Hendricks, Ralph C.
Hennum, James H.
Henry, Jr., Ira I.
Herrod, C.E. Hotrod
Hickam, James R.
Hickam, Mrs. Edith
Hickman, Carl G.
Hickox, Robert L.
Hicks, John Gus
Hiebing, John L.
Higgins, Robert C.
Hill, Lowell D.
Hill, Mrs. Mary
Himmelstein, Frederick
Hindal, Marvin O.
Hine, Francis C.
Hinson, Ausie Jr.
Hite, Eugene F.
Hoback, Wilbur R.
Hoeft, Donald E.
Hoffis, Louis G.
Holbrook, Hilliard B.
Hollander, David G
Holmes, W. Richard
Homer, Donald C.
Hope, Allen R.
Horning, Phillip A.
Hosker, George E.
Hough, James D.
Houk, John P.
House, Leland E.
Howard, Fletcher L.
Howard, William D.
Howery, Duane E.
Hruniak, Wallace
Hubbard, Jr., Lawrence
Hubbard, Alan L.
Hudacko, George M.

Ship's reunion in 1992, Columbus, OH. Back row, left to right: Harry Pursell, Publio Zampedro, Commander Smeigh, John Grimm, William Moody, Robert Foutch, and John Heibing. Front row: Donald L. Samhat, Mert Lockwood, and Ike Stewart. Courtesy of D.C. Samhat.

Huffman, William M.
Hughes, James E.
Hughes, Walter T.
Huizenga, Delbert G.
Hunnicutt, Mrs. Ramona
Hunt, Peter D.
Hunter, Richard S.
Hurd, Leiland
Hussell, Robert A.
Hutchins, Floyd F.
Hutchinson, Jon L.
Hutchison, Rollie R.
Hutson, Logan BC
Iannaco, Vincent
Ilas, Robert P.
Ippolito, Jr., Joseph L.
Irle, Charles F.
Ivory, Wendell R.
Jackson III, Hartley E.
Jacobs, Anthony J.
Jalbert, Llewellyn E.
Janda, Robert J.
Janisch, William J.
Jarrett, Elmer R.
Jefferson, William E.
Jelsema, Jon N.
Jenkins, Neil E.
Johanson, Keith F
Johnson, Donald V.
Johnson, Douglas C.
Johnson, Earl Gene
Johnson, Howard (Ed)
Johnson, Mrs. Josephine
Johnson, Raymond W.
Johnson, Robert Wm
Johnson, Tom D.
Johnston, Lester D.
Johnston, William H.
Johnstone, Campbell
Jones, Donald B.
Jones, J. Stephen
Jones, Jeffrey F.
Jones, Mrs. Gladys
Jones, Seburn J.
Jones, Sterling W.
Jones, Sydney V.
Joy, David W
Joyner, Lionel E.
Jump, Roy H.
Kacerski, Stephen A.
Kaczmarek, Walter G.
Kanable, Dale A.
Kander, Gilbert P.
Karanas, John
Kately, Fred
Kathan, Clayton E.
Kauphusman, Edward L.
Kawiecki, Edward G.
Kellar, Charles E.
Kelley, Jr., William C.
Kellum, Jr., William C.
Kelly, Joseph E.
Kelly, Joseph T.

Kendall, Norman J.
Kennedy, Edward K.
Kenny, Elroy J.
Kerns, Alexander
Kerr, Edward E.
Kerr, John W.
Kesseli, Richard V.
Kierych, William J.
Killion, Russell C.
Kimbrough, Andrew G.
Kingery, Lloyd L.
Kings, Walter George
Kingsley, Harry E.
Kinney, George R.
Kinney, Joseph E
Kirby, Billy R.
Kirby, Harvey B.
Kiska, Frank
Kittredge, George T.
Kittredge, John P.
Klingler, Dale R.
Kloczkowski, Michael J.
Knight, Cecil F.
Knisley, Patrick J.
Koch, Charles S.
Kocher, Eugene C.
Koenig, Charles G.
Kohal, Donald D.
Komorowski, Capt.
Raymond
Komraus, Charles E.
Kopitke, Robert L.
Kopsky, Andrew G.
Koshes, Jr., Frank J.
Koski, Neil W.
Kovacs, Julius Jack
Krauthamer, Richard J.
Kriner, Barry
Kronen, Robert J.
Krout, Herbert W.
Krout, Raymond R.
Krueger, Richard L.
Krukin, Capt. Lawrence E.
Kuchinsky, Louis E.
Kuhn, Frank R.
Lachance, George T.
Ladwig, Gerald W.
LaForce, Peter B.
Lagerblade, Keith H.
Lambert, James C.
Lammy, James E
Lamphier, Alan C.
Landhauser, Robert
Landini, Michael J.
Landry, Louis C.
Lane, Edward L.
Lang, Lemond D.
Lang, Robert L.
Lanoue, Frank E.
Lanzendorfer, William J.
Laprise, John W.
Larsick, Paul R.
Larson, Kenneth E.

Four friends, forever, Fred Fox, Paul Greene, John Demmons, and Neil Koski Columbus, OH, September 1992. Courtesy of L.P. Greene.

Larson, Stanley M.
LaVarre, Jerry
Lawrence, John A.
Lawrence, Kenneth H.
Leary, Roy L.
Leary, Timothy R.
Leavitt, Gerald R.
Leazenby, Albert H.
Ledvora, Joseph A.
Leh, John J.
Lehde, Ralph R.
Leiberger, Robert N.
Letherbury, George F.
Lettrich, Kenneth P.
Leuschner, Robert J.
Levy, Leon
Lewis, Alvin S
Lewis, Charles R.
Lewis, Donald E.
Lewis, Ronald V.
Lewis, Sam F.
L'Hommedieu, Richard G.
Lichniak, Richard E.
Lindquist, Mrs. Barbara
Livengood, David W.
Lockwood, Merton L.
Lombardi, Joseph W.
Lombardo, Patsy J.
Long, Orval H.
Lora, Carl L.
Loughrey, Paul R.
Love, Jerry W.
Love, Robert L.
Lowrey, Bob
Lubick, Jr., John S.
Lucas, Charles L.
Lucas, Don E.
Lucas, William R.
Luce, Raymond K.
Lueddecke, Wilbert E.

Luffman, Lee R.
Luizzi, John V.
Lyczkowski, Alfred S.
Mabe, James D.
Mace, Thomas C.
Maclay, Charles E.
Macomber, Edward S.
Magin, G. David
Magiske, Mike
Magnuson, Henry H.
Mahoney, Joseph F.
Mahoney, Robert M.
Mancini, William J.
Manifold, David G.
Manion, Edward A
Manista, 05-10 Edward A.
Manning, Michael D.
Marchick, James B
Marks, Gorden E.
Marshall, Robert L.
Martel, Lucien W.
Martello, Eugene J.
Martin, Henry I.
Martindale, James D.
Martinek, Peter P.
Mashak, Clements L.
Mastro, William F.
Mathews, Charles R.
Matthews, McClellan
Matthews, Ralph D.
Mayo, David K.
Maze, Robert
McAdam, Vincent F.
McAuliffe III, Denis
McBrayer, Gary D.
McCabe, E. Mac
McCain, David A.
McCall, Jr., John W.
McCamey, John E.
McCann, David W.

McCarthy, John J.
McCarty, George F.
McCaskill, L. Blue
McCreary, John L.
McDade, Thomas W.
McDevitt, Edward P.
McDonald, Raymond T.
McDonald, Robert R.
McDonough, James G.
McElroy, John L.
McFadden, Frank H.
McGaffey, Jr., Robert S.
McGinley, Thomas J.
McGiveron, Theodore R.
McGovern, Jr., Neal J.
McGuire, Steven J.
McHugh, Edward L.
McKinley, Donald E.
McLane, Reed H.
McMahon, Kenneth G.
McNabb, Lawrence L.
McNair, Henry S.
McNally, John J.
Means, Johnny C.
Meek, Mrs. Diane
Mellish, William
Melonas, George E.
Meltzer, Neil
Merritt, Robert H.
Meyer, David P.
Meyer, David P.
Meyer, Fred G.
Meyer, H. Frank
Mezzano, Joseph
Michalski, Vaughn L.
Millard, John Jack
Millard, Robert E.
Miller, Francis W.
Miller, Kenneth W.
Miller, Robert F.

Miller, Robert L.
Millikan, Keith E.
Milstead, Rawley L.
Milton, Larry E.
Mirano, Edward A.
Mitchell, John V.
Mitzelman, Mrs. Arlene
Moffitt, Robert C.
Molinar, Tony
Mollica, Richard
Monson, Dennis O.
Moody, William R.
Moon, Hubert A.
Moore, CDR Norman B.
Moore, CDR Norman B.
Moore, Donald P.
Moore, John R.
Moore, Robert C.
Morabito, Daniel M.
Moran, Mrs. Carol
Morgan, John W.
Moritz, Robert L.
Morrissey, William R.
Morrow, James L.
Morton, Thomas L.
Mower, Roland D.
Moy, John G.
Muise, Joseph G.
Mulhern, Robert D.
Mullarky, Mrs. Joyce
Mullenberg, George C.
Mulligan, Philop E.
Mullikin, Jerome L.
Mullins, Leonard M.
Mullins, Stanley
Mulvey, David
Murello, Andrew F.
Murphy, James D.
Murphy, Thomas J.
Murray, William D.
Mussehl, Daniel J.
Myers, Edward F.
Nagel, Richard P.
Nagy, Joseph A.
Naill, Robert E.

Nastar, Victor P.
Nehl, Walden M.
Neidenbach, Thomas A.
Nelson, Dr. E. Russell
Nesbit, William S.
Nesbitt, Tom F.
Nesper, Howard A.
Nester, Ernest
Neumann, Paul R.
Newland, John P.
Newlon, John W.
Newrohr, Mrs. Simone
Nicholas, Gerald
Nicholson, Arthur F.
Nickels, William E.
Niclas, Daniel J.
Nicolas, Joseph R.
Nightingale, William
Nightingale, William A.
Niles, David P.
Nix, Loy V.
Noe, Raymond W.
Noll, Robert G.
Norden, Elmer
Nordseth, Dean A.
North, James
Norton, E. Lynn
Oates, John T.
O'Brien, James F.
Oczkowski, Frederick J.
Oder, Ronald A.
Oglesby, Milton L.
Oldenburg, Herman H.
Olender, Theodore
Olinger, William H.
Oliver, Ray E.
Olsen, Charles E.
Olson, Wallace
Olson, Wallace F.
O'Neal, Mrs. Mary Ann
O'Neill, James W.
Openshaw, Jr., Henry A.
Opfer, Harold E.
Oraboni, Ken J.
O'Rourke, Robert R.

Orras, George
Oswald, Larry R.
Otis, Donald
Ott, Gerald H.
Otten, Werner W.
Ouellette, Maurice R.
Overton, Robert A.
Pabst, Harold Skip
Paiva, James D.
Palmer, Jerry J.
Papajohn, John
Pappas, Chuck
Paratore, Dominic S.
Pardoe, Jr., Donald E.
Parrish, Jr., Mark A.
Patterson, Duane L.
Patterson, Jr., James
Patterson, Sidney Pat
Pavlick, Marvin G.
Payne, Paul T.
Payne, Raymond E.
Pearce, Jr., Charles L.
Pearson, William W.
Pearston, David L.
Peart, Gary
Pedersen, Alton A.
Pedersen, Mrs. Alice
Pellino, Louis A.
Pennebaker, James C.
Penney, Allen F.
Perez, Jr., Jose A.
Perino, Charles L.
Perkins, Daniel J.
Perkins, Robert W.,
Perlatondo, Anthony J.,
Perry, Harry A.,
Persutte, Harry C.,
Peterman, Ronald E.
Peters, John D.
Petersen, Francis E.,
Peterson, Jack
Peterson, Robert A.,
Pewett, Capt. Robert H.
Pfaff, John J.
Phalin, Harry,

Phelps, L. Crayton
Phillips, Floyd W.,
Phinney, Everett L.
Pierce, Robert R.
Pigg, Robert L.,
Pignone, Richard R.
Pilliod, Francis B.,
Piper, Earnest M.
Pippin, Mrs. Louise
Pitts, Norman
Polcsa, William E.
Polk, James G.
Pollard, Arthur W. (Sam)
Polston, Claude R.,
Pomphrey, William,
Ponsock, Eugene C.,
Ponzo, Michael
Popiel, Joseph R.,
Porter, Albert W.
Porter, Nick J.
Porzio, Raymond,
Potvin, Kenneth
Powell, Charles H.,
Powell, Mrs. Opal
Powell, Robert T
Prentiss, Hugh L.
Pribyl, Charles R.
Price, Larry B.
Pullen, James P.
Pursell, Harry J.
Puthe, Kurt A.
Pyles, John L.
Quertermous, Elmer
Quinn, William B
Rabideau, Mrs. Barbara
Rable, Richard A.
Raczka, Bernard
Raczka, Bernard D.
Ragain, Charles J.
Railsback, J.G.
Ranney, Seth (Tom)
Rayfield, Glenn E.
Recek, Lawrence S
Reed, Fred A.
Reed, Jr., H. Vince
Regan, Harry E.
Reichenbach, Robert W.
Reid, Joseph J.
Reid, Louis L.
Rentauskas, Mrs. Margaret
Reuther, George W.
Richard, Joseph
Richardson, Harry L.
Rickard, Norman E.
Riddle, Earl L.
Ridenour, Bary D.
Riffe, Kemper B.
Riley, Mrs. Eileen
Rios, Gregory
Rivers, Philip M.
Robbins, Robert C.
Robertson, Hollis Robbie
Robinson, Alden F.

Robinson, Edward L.
Robinson, John A.
Robinson, John A.
Rodgers, Melvin R.
Rolin, Jr., Leon A.
Rolzinski, Leon J. (Rollin)
Romanio, Marion J.
Root, Donald C.
Rose, Donald M.
Ross, Gene R.
Ross, Richard B.
Ross, Ronnie S.
Rothe, Donald H.
Rounds, Ralph W.
Rouse, Charles H.
Roux, Gerard J.
Roux, Robert J.
Rowden, VADM William H.
Rowe, Gerald L.
Rowlison, Kenneth E
Roy, Cyril E.
Ruberto, Joseph A.
Rubino, Bernard P.
Rudewicz, Alex M.
Ruef, Mrs. Janet
Rulison, Charles A.
Ruohonen, Peter W.
Ruskin, Edgar A.
Rutledge, Peggy
Sackenhiem, John F.
Salesman, Richard L.
Samhat, Donald C.
San Felice, Frank A.
Sanborn, Robert R.
Sanders, William G.
Sangster, Sam
Sare, Victor W.
Sauer, George S.
Savio, Jr., William P.
Sawyer, Frank E
Sawyer, Jr., Beverly H.
Sayers, Charles T.
Sayles, James M.
Scamfer, Robert C.
Schaudt, Robert C.
Schlapkohl, William C.
Schlenk, Harold F.
Schmidt, Wesley W.
Schmitt, Alfred K.
Schmitt, Kenneth L.
Schmitt, Walter H.
Schmitt, Walter H.
Schneider, Nick
Schnupp, John D.
Schrader, Louis H.
Schramm, Robert C.
Schrope, John R.
Schuliar, Edward P.
Schultz, Harry J.
Schwitzer, Arthur B.
Scinta, Roy J.
Scoppetuolo, Edward W.

Ship's mini-reunion in 1993. From left, Marse and Ben Williams, James and Jo Kelly, Paul and Diane Green, Bedford, MA.

Scott, James H.
Scott, Roy T.
Seabury, Clyde W.
Sedlacik, Michael R.
Sekol, Carl T.
Sellers, Clarence D.
Sepe, Dr. Walter W
Sequete, Carl R.
Sever, Darriell R.
Sharper, Donald A.
Shashaguay, William C.
Shea, Eugene C.
Shea, James J.
Shelp, Erwin J.
Shepard, Charles A.
Sherrill, James V.
Sherrill, Junior G.
Shierk, Robert D.
Shimansky, Alex
Shively, Morris Chet
Shogren, Dennis E.
Short, Jr., Stafford A.
Shortell, Paul
Sies, Don Gary
Sigg, CDR Daniel
Simmons, Mrs. Judith
Simmons, Roger A.
Siuta, Jack R.
Skoko, Thomas
Slater, William O.
Slepicka, Lambert C.
Smeigh, Jr., Capt. Carl M.
Smith, A. LeRoy
Smith, Charles W.
Smith, David M.
Smith, Earle
Smith, Milford C.
Smith, Paul K.
Smith, Stephen C.
Smith, William E.
Smoak, Esmond C.
Smyer, Jr., F. Virgil
Snider, Hallie J.
Snyder, Dr. Bernard S.
Snyder, William C.
Snyder, Winfred W.
Soares, Raymond C
Soldi, Jr., John
Sovis, Robert J.
Spalding, David
Spann, Raymond L.
Spears, Derrell K.
Speelman, Charles J.
Spignese, Joseph R.
Spooner, Arthur
Sprake, Robert B.
Sprout, John W.
Squitieri, Joseph P.
St. Clair, Robert E. L.
St. James, Albert S.
Stachowiak, Daniel J.
Stafford, George S.
Stanley, Norman A.

Stanley, Vito
Stapf, Al J.
Stark, Ted
Statham, Larry W.
Stechishin, Michael J.
Steele, Barbara
Steele, Evans B.
Stefanko, Michael
Steffa, Oliver M.
Steinbis, John G.
Steinbrunn, Mrs. Martha
Stensgar, James F.
Stevens, Charles A.
Stevens, Warren
Stewart, Ike
Stewart, John E.
Stiffler, Franklin R.
Stone, Clyde
Stone, Dr. Arthur
Stone, J. C.
Strano, Louis
Strickland, Gordon E.
Strickland, William M.
Stromberg, Marvin J.
Stursa, Rudolph G.
Sudano, Dennis R.
Sullivan, CDR Edward T.
Sullivan, Jr., Mrs. Bernice
Sullivan, Robert J.
Sunstrom, Eric P.
Supry, William F.
Surina, Mrs. Iva
Svoboda, Mildred
Swartz, Steven O.
Swickey, James N.
Swoboda, Robert G.
Sykes, Jr., William E.
Szemly, John
Szolga, Eugene N.
Sztejter, Albert R.
Tabor, Frank A.
Talbot, Edward G.
Taliaferro, W. Bruce
Talley, Jerry D.
Taub, Jack H.
Taylor, Warren D.
Teal, Edward A.
Terry, William H.
Tesar, George E.
Theuring, Charles T.
Thomas, Garnett L.
Thomas, Mrs. June
Thomley, Arthur G. (Bob)
Thomley, Oscar D.
Thompson, Jr, Frank A.
Thompson, Scott M.
Thrasher, Sr. , Thomas E.
Thrombley, Robert J.
Tindal, Douglas L.
Tintle, Robert H.
Tisdale, Webber E.
Tittsworth, Thomas A.
Toler, Sr., Raymond L.

Tolley, John F.
Tomlin, Harry R.
Tomlin, Robert N.
Torcivia, Henry J.
Toups, Clay J.
Townsend, James R.
Townsend, Mrs. Ellen
Trainor, Bernard E.
Trainor, Walter W.
Trella, Frank J.
Triolo, Nicholas
True, William R.
Truini, Joseph J.
Trump, Donald R.
Tucciarone, Louis M.
Tucker, John
Tucker, Robert B.
Turley, Edward R.
Turner, Quintin A.
Turner, William R.
Tutko, Eugene G.
Tynes, James E.
Utt, Alon E.
Valliere, Donald E.
Vander Yacht, Robert K.
Varraso, Nicholas A.
Vekony, Eugene L.
Venezia, James J.
Vestich, Mark A.
Vicknair, Wally J.
Vise, Delbert L.
Volkman, Mrs. DeLaine
Voorhees, Mrs. Joyce
Wacaser, Emery E.
Wachob, James R.
Wade, Robert J.
Wade, Robert J.
Waggoner, Robert L.
Wagner, Jr., Charles P.
Wagner, Kurt J.
Wajda, Richard E.
Walker, Jr., Walter G.
Walker, Jr., Walter G.
Walker, Larry E.
Walker, Paul D.
Wallace, Jr., Donald C.

Walsdorf, Theodore J.
Walters, John W.
Wanek, Al M.
Ward, Patrick J.
Warner, Mrs. Eileen
Warren, CAPT Robert H.
Warren, Charles D.
Warrender, Malcolm
Warrington, Kenneth R.
Warrington, Mrs. Kathy
Wasylyk, Dean
Waters, James P. D.
Waters, Phillip L.
Watkins, Mrs. Dottie
Watson, Gerald E.
Watts, Henry A.
Waymire, Jack R.
Weakley, Irving M.
Weatherwax, Joseph M.
Weaver, Jr., David
Weaver, Fred E.
Weaver, Robert D.
Weddersten, William
(Bud)
Wedel, Henry L.
Wegryniak, Jr., Andrew J.
Weigle, John B.
Weiss, Jr., Conrad
Weldy, Harry G.
Welk, Robert D.
Wellenhofer, Jr., Linda
Wenger, James E.
Wenger, P. Robert
Wertz, Michael A.
Westfall, Richard L.
Westfall, William G.
Whatman, Michael E.
Wheeler, Daniel W.
Whelchel, Lawrence Guy
Whetham, Leslie J.
White, C. Henry
Whitesell, Carl
Whiteside, William O.
Whiting, Dean G.
Wilcox, Leonard L.
Wiles, Robert E.

Will, Jr., John M.
Willburn, Gerald D.
Willcoxon, Clinton D.
Williams, Ben H.
Williams, Donald H.
Williams, Jerry R.
Williams, Jr., John E.
Williams, Kennth W.
Williams, Richard E.
Williamson, Robert O.
Wilson, James
Wilson, James L.
Wilson, Jr., Wayne L.
Wilson, Kurt T.
Wilson, Mrs. Ruth
Wilson, Paul W.
Wimbish, Francis M.
Withrow, Charles F.
Wogan, Gordon E.
Wolf, Glen R.
Wolfe, Norman
Wolford, William F.
Woods, Anthony G.
Woody, Dennis
Wooley, Dwight I.
Woudwyk, Roger D.
Woytko, George S.
Wright, Clyde
Wright, Halford S.
Wright, Jerry S.
Wyatt, Mrs. Sandy
Wylie, Dan P.
Yale, Richard E.
Yates, Julian P.
Yeager, John E.
Yeaton, David J.
Young, Bill D.
Young, Donald E.
Young, Malcolm C.
Zakowsky, Jr., Joseph J.
Zampedro, Publio V.
Zernia, Eugene F.
Ziegenhirt, Jr, Carl A.
Zuk, Frank
Zwieg, Walter H.

Ship's reunion, Charleston, SC, 1993. From left, Tom Ranney, Bob and Norma Schauldt, and Netta Ranney. Courtesy of L.P. Greene.

Printed in the USA
CPSIA information can be obtained
at www.ICGtesting.com
JSHW060055150824
68134JS00032B/2740